Race and Crisis

As the European Union seemingly teetered from a financial crisis to an immigration crisis around 2015 and onwards, discourses of race appeared to congeal in various member states. In some instances, these came with familiarly essentialist constructions; in others these were refracted cautiously through concerns about security, national and cultural integrity, distribution of public resources and employment, and so on. New political alignments surfaced on the back of such concerns, and established organizations changed their agendas accordingly. The border regimes of EU member states became increasingly fraught, both in terms of their everyday operations and in terms of the close attention and vociferous debates they attracted. In most instances, the internal and external borders of the EU hardened, and with increasing frequency the cohesion of the transnational union seemed on the verge of fracturing. Indeed, very real fissures opened up with secessionist moves and referendums. Through each step in this juncture of upheavals, the significance of race has been reiterated in tangential ways and sometimes with unabashed straightforwardness.

This volume explores this juncture around 2015, and the constructions of race and of crisis therein, for specific contexts and from a range of disciplinary perspectives. The introduction gives an overview of the juncture, focusing on the rise of Eurosceptic nationalist political parties and their electoral success. Subsequent chapters are addressed to the management and representation of immigrants crossing the Mediterranean, border regimes in the Czech Republic, the narratives that converged on Brexit, riots in England, antagonistic popular movements in Sweden, racialization in crisis management in Italy, perceptions of migrants in Greece, and how race may be structured in and challenged through classroom pedagogy.

This book was originally published as a special issue of *Ethnic and Racial Studies*.

Suman Gupta is Professor of Literature and Cultural History at the Open University, UK, and has recently co-ordinated the international project *Framing Financial Crisis and Protest: NW and SE Europe*.

Satnam Virdee is Professor of Sociology at the University of Glasgow, UK, and founding Director of the Centre for Research on Racism, Ethnicity and Nationalism.

Ethnic and Racial Studies

Series editors:
Martin Bulmer, *University of Surrey, UK*, and
John Solomos, *University of Warwick, UK*

The journal *Ethnic and Racial Studies* was founded in 1978 by John Stone to provide an international forum for high quality research on race, ethnicity, nationalism and ethnic conflict. At the time the study of race and ethnicity was still a relatively marginal sub-field of sociology, anthropology and political science. In the intervening period the journal has provided a space for the discussion of core theoretical issues, key developments and trends, and for the dissemination of the latest empirical research.

It is now the leading journal in its field and has helped to shape the development of scholarly research agendas. *Ethnic and Racial Studies* attracts submissions from scholars in a diverse range of countries and fields of scholarship, and crosses disciplinary boundaries. It is now available in both printed and electronic form. From 2015 it will publish 15 issues per year, three of which will be dedicated to *Ethnic and Racial Studies Review* offering expert guidance to the latest research through the publication of book reviews, symposia and discussion pieces, including reviews of work in languages other than English.

The *Ethnic and Racial Studies* book series contains a wide range of the journal's special issues. These special issues are an important contribution to the work of the journal, where leading social science academics bring together articles on specific themes and issues that are linked to the broad intellectual concerns of *Ethnic and Racial Studies*. The series editors work closely with the guest editors of the special issues to ensure that they meet the highest quality standards possible. Through publishing these special issues as a series of books, we hope to allow a wider audience of both scholars and students from across the social science disciplines to engage with the work of *Ethnic and Racial Studies*.

Most recent titles in the series include:

Migrant Mothers' Creative Challenges to Racialized Citizenship
Edited by Umut Erel and Tracey Reynolds

Celebrating 40 Years of *Ethnic and Racial Studies*: Classic Papers in Context
Edited by Martin Bulmer and John Solomos

Rethinking Reconciliation and Transitional Justice After Conflict
Edited by James Hughes and Denisa Kostovicova

Migration and Race in Europe
Edited by Martin Bulmer and John Solomos

Why Do We Still Talk About Race?
Edited by Martin Bulmer and John Solomos

Race and Crisis
Edited by Suman Gupta and Satnam Virdee

Race and Crisis

Edited by
Suman Gupta and Satnam Virdee

Routledge
Taylor & Francis Group

LONDON AND NEW YORK

First published 2019
by Routledge
2 Park Square, Milton Park, Abingdon, Oxon, OX14 4RN, UK

and by Routledge
52 Vanderbilt Avenue, New York, NY 10017, USA

First issued in paperback 2020

Routledge is an imprint of the Taylor & Francis Group, an informa business

British Library Cataloguing in Publication Data
A catalogue record for this book is available from the British Library

ISBN 13: 978-0-367-58333-0 (pbk)
ISBN 13: 978-1-138-39370-7 (hbk)

Typeset in Myriad Pro
by RefineCatch Limited, Bungay, Suffolk

Publisher's Note
The publisher accepts responsibility for any inconsistencies that may have
arisen during the conversion of this book from journal articles to book chapters,
namely the possible inclusion of journal terminology.

Disclaimer
Every effort has been made to contact copyright holders for their permission to
reprint material in this book. The publishers would be grateful to hear from any
copyright holder who is not here acknowledged and will undertake to rectify
any errors or omissions in future editions of this book.

Contents

Citation Information

The chapters in this book were originally published in *Ethnic and Racial Studies*, volume 41, issue 10 (August 2018). When citing this material, please use the original page numbering for each article, as follows:

Introduction
European crises: contemporary nationalisms and the language of "race"
Suman Gupta and Satnam Virdee
Ethnic and Racial Studies, volume 41, issue 10 (August 2018),
pp. 1747–1764

Chapter 1
The "migrant crisis" as racial crisis: do Black Lives Matter *in Europe?*
Nicholas De Genova
Ethnic and Racial Studies, volume 41, issue 10 (August 2018),
pp. 1765–1782

Chapter 2
The hieroglyphics of the border: racial stigma in neoliberal Europe
Imogen Tyler
Ethnic and Racial Studies, volume 41, issue 10 (August 2018),
pp. 1783–1801

Chapter 3
Racism, Crisis, Brexit
Satnam Virdee and Brendan McGeever
Ethnic and Racial Studies, volume 41, issue 10 (August 2018),
pp. 1802–1819

Chapter 4
Rioting and the politics of crisis
Karim Murji
Ethnic and Racial Studies, volume 41, issue 10 (August 2018),
pp. 1820–1836

Chapter 5

"Race" and the upsurge of antagonistic popular movements in Sweden
Carl-Ulrik Schierup, Aleksandra Ålund and Anders Neergaard
Ethnic and Racial Studies, volume 41, issue 10 (August 2018),
pp. 1837–1854

Chapter 6

Racialization and counter-racialization in times of crisis: taking migrant struggles in Italy as a critical standpoint on race
Federico Oliveri
Ethnic and Racial Studies, volume 41, issue 10 (August 2018),
pp. 1855–1873

Chapter 7

Migration, crisis, liberalism: the cultural and racial politics of Islamophobia and "radical alterity" in modern Greece
Elisabeth Kirtsoglou and Giorgos Tsimouris
Ethnic and Racial Studies, volume 41, issue 10 (August 2018),
pp. 1874–1892

Chapter 8

Blackboard as separation wall: classrooms, race and the contemporary crisis in Germany
Russell West-Pavlov
Ethnic and Racial Studies, volume 41, issue 10 (August 2018),
pp. 1893–1911

For any permission-related enquiries please visit:
http://www.tandfonline.com/page/help/permissions

Notes on Contributors

Aleksandra Ålund received her education at the University of Belgrade, Yugoslavia, Umeå University and Uppsala University, Sweden. She received her PhD in sociology at Umeå University. She is a Professor at The Institute for Research on Migration, Ethnicity and Society – REMESO – at Linköping University, Sweden. Her research focus is on migration, especially gender, youth, ethnicity, social movements, social exclusion/inclusion, civic activism, identity, and cultural production.

Nicholas De Genova is a scholar of migration, borders, race, citizenship, and labour. In the Fall of 2018, he will commence an appointment as Professor and Chair of the Department of Comparative Cultural Studies at the University of Houston, Texas. He previously held teaching appointments in urban and political geography at King's College London, and in socio-cultural anthropology at Stanford University, Columbia University, and Goldsmiths, University of London.

Suman Gupta is Professor of Literature and Cultural History at the Open University, UK. He has led several international collaborations, including *Framing Financial Crisis and Protest: NW and SE Europe.* His research interests are in contemporary social texts and politics.

Elisabeth Kirtsoglou is an Associate Professor at the Department of Anthropology at Durham University, UK. Her research interests focus on Gender, Politics and Migration in Greece. She has published a monograph on Gender and Identity and since 2006 she has been working on themes like terrorism, cosmopolitanism, globalization, power asymmetries, and the fragility of the social contract. She is currently conducting research on migration and refugee issues, the Greek crisis and South European politics.

Brendan McGeever is a Lecturer in the Sociology of Racialization and Antisemitism at Birkbeck, University of London, UK. His research interests include 'Race' and racism; antisemitism; racialization; the former Soviet Union; Marxism; social theory; historical sociology; and ethnographies of the archive. He has published in the journals *Ethnic and Racial Studies* and *Patterns of Prejudice.*

Karim Murji is Professor of Social Policy and Criminology and belongs to the British Sociological Association International Sociological Association at the University of West London, UK. His research is concerned with culture, ethnicity and racism and these are applied to fields such as race equality, policing, public sociology, and diaspora and identity.

Anders Neergaard is a Professor in the Department of Social and Welfare Studies at Linköping University, Sweden. His research projects include *Beyond Racism: Ethnographies of Anti-racism and Conviviality; Trade unions, Migrant Workers and Extreme Right-wing Support; Counter-Movements of the Precariat?; Civil Societies Organisations and Educational Achievements; Women and Migrants within the Sweden Democrats; Equal Work-Places in a World of Inequality; Informalisation, Labour Migrants, and Irregular Migrants.*

Federico Oliveri is a Research Fellow at the Science for Peace Interdisciplinary Centre, at the University of Pisa, Italy. His research interests include Immigration, nationality, diversity and anti-discrimination theories and policies at European and national level, contemporary theories on citizenship, democracy, human rights, justice, governance, mobility, labour exploitation, crisis, war, and peace.

Carl-Ulrik Schierup holds doctoral degrees in social anthropology and sociology. He has led several research projects and programmes and is currently directing the REMESO research programme on migration, ethnicity and society. His major current focus is on race and class, social movement unionism, new social movements and subaltern struggles for reclaiming the commons under conditions of neoliberal globalization.

Giorgos Tsimouris is a faculty member in the Department of Social Anthropology at Panteion University, Greece. He has published in Greek and English on forced migration, refugee condition, nationalism, intercultural education, and oral history. His research interests include anthropology of migration, refugee studies, minorities, nationalism, maritime anthropology, oral history, critical and intercultural education, globalization, tourism, and performance studies.

Imogen Tyler is a social theorist and sociologist. Her teaching and research is concerned with social inequalities (of multiple kinds), power, injustice, and resistance. A Philip Leverhulme Prize (2015–2018) is supporting her current research project on stigma and power. The major outcomes of this project are: *A Sociological Review* monograph 'The Sociology of Stigma' (2018); a single-authored book 'Stigma Machines' (Zed, 2019); a series of peer-reviewed journal articles; and a collaboration with the graphic artist Charlotte Bailey on a zine of her essay 'From Stigma Power to Black Power'.

Satnam Virdee is Professor of Sociology at the School of Social and Political Sciences at the University of Glasgow, UK. His research interests cover Sociology of Racism and Ethnicity, Sociology of Class and Stratification,

Social Movements and the Sociology of Collective Action, Historical Sociology, and Historical Materialism as theory and method.

Russell West-Pavlov teaches and researches Comparative Global South Cultural and Literary Studies with a focus in the areas of Australia, Africa and the Caribbean. His research interests are the poetics of space and time and their transformation in the contemporary moment. He co-convenes the MA Cultures of the Global South and teaches in the Comparative Literature programme in the German Department at the University of Tübingen, Germany. He is a co-convenor of the Interdisciplinary Centre for Global South Studies at the University of Tübingen, Germany.

Introduction: European crises: contemporary nationalisms and the language of "race"

Suman Gupta and Satnam Virdee

ABSTRACT

The Introduction begins by outlining the general theme of this special issue, "Race and Crisis". It then moves to examine populist right-wing politics from 2015. Of the various ways in which the rise of such politics could be charted in this period, here the "success" of anti-immigrant and anti-E.U. parties in national-level elections is the focus. Success is understood in terms of share of the popular vote at national level, and the appeal of the right-wing parties in question gauged from their manifestos. In particular, manifesto proposals for renegotiating the principles of citizenship are considered, and their implicitly racist underpinnings noted. The final part of the Introduction presents some general observations on coded ways of evoking race and prompting racialization in contemporary political discourse. How the contributions to this special issue deal with that is briefly summarized.

The beginning

This special issue on "Race and Crisis" was initially planned in 2015, in the context of a project on *Framing Financial Crisis and Protest* (2014–2016, funded by the Leverhulme Trust). The idea was to analyse race-centred discourses in Europe amidst the financial crisis from 2007–2008 onwards. In the interim between 2015 and 2017, as this special issue moves toward publication, the thrust of those key words ("race" and "crisis"), and their purchase in political and public discourse, have shifted. By way of introducing this special issue, it is necessary to pause on these shifts – they are reflected in the papers that follow.

The editors and authors had decided to use Stuart Hall's "third position" on ascriptions of race, replacing the broadly realist and the purely linguistic, as an analytical anchor for contributions to this issue:

The third position is that there are probably differences of all sorts in the world, that difference is a kind of anomalous existence out there, a kind of random series of all sorts of things in what you call the world, there's no reason to deny this reality or this diversity. [...] It's only when these differences have been organized within language, within discourse, within systems of meaning, that the differences can be said to acquire meaning and become a factor in human culture and regulate conduct. That is the nature of what I'm calling the discursive concept of race. Not that nothing exists of differences, but that what matters are the systems we use to make sense, to make human societies intelligible. [...] I think these are discursive systems because the interplay between the representation of racial difference, the writing of power, and the production of knowledge, is crucial to the way in which they are generated, and the way in which they function. (1997)

The discursive concept suggests that the enunciation of "race" is always more than simply a matter of talking *about* race. Or, more precisely, in discursive systems and practices the signification of "race" radiates into broad political dispositions and social structures; "race" is an unstable signifier which enables those structures and dispositions to apparently acquire meaning rather than denoting anything firmly in itself. Focusing on the instabilities of signifying "race" – with normative inflections, as synecdoche, as concretization, as simile, through substitution, allusively, ironically, by implication or even by elision, and so on – in specific contexts enables the social and political tendencies and contradictions of those contexts to be put into relief. Other or all significations of difference may, no doubt, serve a similar project – the signification of "race" is at issue here.

However, the discourses that build around enunciations of "race" usually appear with some preconceived and uncritical notion of talking *about* race – that is, *as if* "race" consensually means something and has a firm core. The discursive concept contends that a firm core cannot be articulated because enunciations of "race" offer none; significations of "race" are always contingent and elusive. Nevertheless, for analytical purposes it is unhelpful to not try and articulate *the perception* of this core to a minimum extent, that is, to the extent necessary to activate the discursive concept. As a minimum statement then, talking about race as if it means something involves an assumption of essentialist human categories: "the assumption, consciously or unconsciously held, that people can be divided into a distinct number of discrete 'races' according to physical, biological criteria and that systematic social differences automatically and inevitably follow the same lines of physical differentiation", as Jackson (1989, 132) had usefully put it.[1]

With Hall's discursive concept in mind, the contributions to this special issue were not conceived according to a moral imperative, for advocacy against prejudice and discrimination; the idea was to explore significations of race in contemporary Europe. Prejudice and discrimination usually underpin racializing discourses and therefore cannot but be addressed. But it was clarifying the mechanics of discourses at this historical juncture rather than

2

the general denunciation of prejudice which motivated this project. An anti-racist position is a given for this project; it is the only rational position from which analysis can be undertaken with Hall's third position in mind.

The historical juncture the authors and editors had in mind in 2015 was the financial crisis in Europe from 2007–08 onwards, that is, in the transnational formation of the E.U., within and across member states and neighbouring states. The financial crisis was understood here as follows: it was not simply located within financial institutions and national governance structures, but, rather, appeared as a juncture which crystallises and puts pressure upon various facets of political, economic and cultural life, widely dispersed. These facets of life have naturally obtained for long but, amidst the financial crisis, appeared to become inextricably grounded in a dominant – and oppressive – political and economic rationale. The rationale could variously be apprehended under the rubric of "financialization", "neoliberalism", cost-benefit accounting in "biopolitics", the ethical weight of "sovereign debt" and strategies of "austerity" regimes; and the agencies of the rationale were being tested through numerous modes of resistance (ballot boxes, marches, occupations, riots, strikes, hacktivism and so on). In brief, the financial crisis incorporated and generated a web of crises gripping social life at various levels. Though the financial crisis had been prolifically explored along these lines by 2015, few attempts to examine it directly in relation to race and racism had appeared then. Scholarly publications that did so were focused pri-marily on the U.S.A. (e.g. Dymski 2009; Wyly et al. 2009; Chakravarty and da Silva 2012; Rugh, Albright, and Massey 2015) or specific European countries (for Britain, e.g. Gillborn 2013; Redclift 2014), and very occasionally attempted a global view (Castles 2012). It seemed in 2015 that relatively few studies on race and racism generally across the nation-states of Europe had appeared recently (those included Lentin 2004; Fekete 2009; Taras 2012; Fella and Ruzza 2013), and, in relation to the financial crisis, tended to be refracted through the lens of immigration (as in Livola 2013).

So, within the webs of crises growing around the financial crisis from 2007–2008, the editors and authors proposed a sequence of thematic nodes wherein significations of "race" have played a part:

- Disinvestments and vulnerable populations: the gradual minimization of welfare arrangements and the corresponding production of vulnerable or dispossessed populations – the poverty-stricken, unemployed or precar-iously employed (especially youth), etc.
- Tied in with the above, anxiety about migration: at two principal levels, into the E.U. and across member-states.
- Tied in with both of the above, a surge of neo-nationalisms fracturing always-shaky E.U. integrities (raising the spectre of exits) and also pressing upon the integrity of nation-states (e.g. prodding secessionist moves).

- Activated through all the above, hardening protectionist policies and declaring states of exception: securing boundaries and policing populations in the name of economic necessity and security.

That's where this project stood in 2015; now, this project finds itself on somewhat different ground. In brief, in the interim priorities in the sequence of bullet-pointed thematic nodes above have changed: the first point has now dropped to the bottom, and the second and third points are now squarely and equally at the top, concretizing and pushing the fourth. In other words, in dominant public and political discourse the financial crisis has been superseded by – appears to have become conditional to – an "immigration crisis" and coevally an "E.U. crisis" (of the transnational formation). Intensifying concern from 2015 about how to deal with refugees from conflict-ridden Syria, Libya, Iraq, Yemen, Afghanistan, etc., morphed into a generalized anxiety about immigration and the presence of immigrants, in fact exacerbating long-simmering sensitivities about religious and cultural and "racial" difference. Simultaneously, the E.U. is increasingly held to be an apparatus for supporting immigration and the accommodation of difference, for which neoliberal policies are considered the pathway and of which austerity measures are understood as symptoms. Disaffection has gradually come to be focalized more on immigration and immigrants than on neoliberalism and austerity. A drift towards hardening nation-state boundaries, both physically and conceptually, has followed, so that the fluidity of European contexts contemplated in 2015 seems increasingly anachronistic. Under these circumstances, it is to be expected that articulations of "race" would be more forcefully and explicitly foregrounded in public and political discourse, and in academic discourse, than it seemed to be in early 2015. That indeed is the case. A more evidenced and nuanced, albeit still sketchy, discussion of these interim developments follows.

The interim

The shift in political discourses between 2015 and 2017 can be tracked variously: by examining media coverage of immigrants or refugees, by investigating regime changes for processing immigrants and policing borders (Fekete 2009 persuasively argued that these embed "xeno-racism" in Europe), or by exploring legislation concerning ethnic minorities within political states. By way of a manageable overview of a significant area of Europe, a more schematic path is followed here: considering nation-state-level elections from 2015 onwards, with a focus on the electoral success of nationalist right-wing parties with anti-E.U. stances. Electoral success is understood here in a narrow way, as consisting not so much in finding a place in government (though some have) but in achieving a growing share of the popular vote in state-level elections (proportion of all voters relative to the previous election) where the full range of parties competed. From this point of view, for two-round systems – such as presidential elections in Austria and France – the first round is more indicative than the final. Such electoral success of nationalist parties is considered here as indicating polarization against mainstream or new centrist and leftist parties; this means that the latter have to then either co-opt from what gives nationalist parties popular appeal or make stronger counter-appeals. Since anxiety about immigrants and minorities features significantly and consistently in the proposals of electorally successful nationalist parties, racist attitudes simmer close to the surface of their claims – but seldom explicitly or directly. Here, successful nationalist parties' policies are gauged from their official manifestos; it is assumed that these offer politically legitimate (or legitimized) interventions in a public discourse sphere, and have a direct bearing on their electoral success. Admittedly, this is a simplistic assumption. For each election in each political state, a range of other factors play into the political appeal of a party (such as local activity, record of performance, personalities of leaders, media interventions), and, equally, the popular-vote share as response is complicated by regional variations, controversies, etc. These complexities are prolifically debated around each election event. For a broad comparative view, however, a relationship between official manifesto and share of popular vote at state level may be considered a reasonable assumption.

Given our interest in the language of "race", only some parts of the manifestos in question are registered here. Naturally, attention is given to definitions of nationality, to statements about national solidarity and belonging, and equally to statements on immigrants and minorities which situate them in relation to definitions of nationality. Particular emphasis is laid on proposals for adjusting the legal norms for citizenship. The first principle of citizenship in all European countries and generally in modern political states is that each citizen is equal in the eyes of the law. This principle undergirds all other policies and measures. Its contravention is only contemplated now in a condition of exception or corruption (e.g. conflict situations), or as a temporarily ratified policy (such as, in positive action measures, which are usually designed to effect pragmatic social equalization for discriminated groups to the extent that equality before law becomes meaningful) – almost never *within the norm of the law*. Sought-after adjustments in this legal norm have wide-ranging implications for entire populations; any measure of public support of such proposals is politically and socially significant within the life of a nation state. It is in such proposals that racial preconceptions are most directly if not explicitly encountered.

The 2015 start point and the above delimitations bring the following right-wing parties squarely into focus here: The U.K. Independence Party (UKIP) had the third largest share of voters at 12.7 per cent in the May 2015 general elections, from 3.1 per cent in 2010, but secured only a single seat in parliament; Prawa i Sprawiedliwośći (PiS), or Law and Justice Party of Poland, became the ruling party with an outright majority and the largest share of votes in the October 2015 parliamentary elections, with 37.58 per cent compared to 29.89 per cent in 2011; Schweizerische Volkspartei (SVP) or Swiss People's Party increased its share of votes in the October 2015 federal elections to 29.4 per cent from 26.6 per cent in 2011, having been the largest since 1999; Dansk Folkeparti (DF) or Danish People's Party had the second largest vote share in the December 2015 general elections, 21.6 per cent from 12.9 per cent in 2011, providing parliamentary support to the new government; Partij voor de Vrijheid (PVV) or Party for Freedom in the Netherlands had the second largest vote share in the March 2017 general elections, 13.1 per cent from 10.1 per cent in 2012; Alternative für Deutschland (AfD) or Alternative for Germany is expected to get a higher share of votes [opinion polls put it as 8–12 per cent] in the September 2017 federal elections over its 4.7 per cent in 2013, having won seats in eleven state parliaments in the interim from none at the end of 2013. Among two-round presidential elections where the first round gives a good sense of the popular vote at state level: in April 2016 Norbert Hofer of Freiheitliche Partei Österreichs (FPÖ) got 35.1 per cent of the vote where Alexander von der Bellen (Green) got 21.3 per cent, though the latter won the presidency narrowly in the run-off – in the one-round 2011 election the FPÖ candidate Barbara Rosenkranz got 15.4 per cent as opposed to Heinz Fischer's (SDP) 79.33 per cent; in April 2017 Marine La Pen of Front National (FP) in France secured 21.3 per cent in the first round of the Presidential elections and then 33.9 per cent in the run-off against the eventual winner, Emmanuel Macron. The FN's share of the vote under Marine has almost doubled since 2002 when her father, Jean-Marie, secured 18.2 per cent of the vote when losing to Jacques Chirac in the final round.

The 2015 start date here focuses attention on the effect of the so-called refugee crisis, but it is still somewhat arbitrary. It draws attention away from similar nationalist and electorally successful parties, such as Fidesz in the April 2014 Hungarian parliamentary elections, the regionalist Nieuw-Vlaamse Alliantie (N-VA) or New Flemish Alliance in the May 2014 Belgian general elections, and Moderata or Moderate Party and the Sverigedemokraterna (SD) or Swedish Democrats in the September 2014 Swedish general elections. The dynamics of N-VA's Flemish nationalism is internal to the federal state of Belgium; Moderata and, especially, the nationalist SD, with respectively the second and third largest shares of the popular vote in Sweden, have strong anti-immigration agendas (Schierup, Ålund and Neergaard's paper discusses the Swedish context); and Fidesz has taken a particularly hard line against refugees since 2015. Other state-level elections in this period include the two in Greece in 2015 (January and September), in which the recently formed anti-austerity left-wing Syriza alliance took the upper hand in the popular vote and in government, while the popularity of right-wing Laïkós Sýndesmos or Golden Dawn and Anexartitoi Ellines (ANEL) or Independent Greeks dipped, though the latter joined Syriza in a government-forming coalition (Giorgos and Elisavet address the Greek situation for immigrants below). New anti-austerity and broadly progressive parties, such as Podemos and Citizens (Cs-C), were also, at least initially, electorally successful in Spain's otherwise indecisive general elections in December 2015 and in June 2016. Indecisive also were parliamentary elections in Bulgaria in March 2017, after previous elections in 2014 and 2013, with centre-right GERB (Citizens for European Development of Bulgaria) dominating the popular vote but failing to achieve the majority it had in 2009. Other new parties, with ambiguous agendas about immigration, emerged with notable success in the popular vote in 2013 elections: the Movimento 5 Stelle (M5S) or 5 Star Movement in Italy (racism in the Italian context is discussed in Oliveri's paper), and ANO 2011 in the Czech Republic (the hardline Czech response to refugees in 2015 is explored in Tyler's paper). The 2015 legislative elections in Portugal, and 2016 general elections in Ireland and legislative elections in Romania presented no significant disturbance or sharp polarization in the established political order, though in the latter the new Uniunea Salvați România (USR) or Save Romania Party, with a domestically centered anti-corruption and development agenda, made an impression in the popular vote (with the third largest share). Various referendums are enormously significant here for this period, and fall outside the schematic approach taken: especially, the Greek bailout referendum of July 2015, the Italian constitutional referendum of December 2016, and, particularly momentously, the Brexit referendum of June 2016. The relevance of the Brexit referendum to the theme of this special issue can scarcely be overstated, and two papers – by Virdee and McGeever and by Seed – are devoted to it; Murji's paper is also addressed to the British context, but with regard to the earlier juncture of the 2011 riots.

The concepts of nationality outlined in the manifestos of the electorally successful nationalist and anti-E.U. parties named above – UKIP, PiS, SVP, DF, PVV, AfD, NF, FPÖ – in common with other similar parties named above but not focused on here (Fidesz, Golden Dawn, ANEL, Moderata, SD), have a distinctive thrust. They are designed to stop social fluidities and ambiguities and make the contours of history stand still, to harden and neaten a social order and render it perpetual. In brief, they seek to: make the political boundaries of states firm and impervious; have political states as the final arbiters for all internal matters and dealings with other states and external alignments ("sovereignty"); render the populations within states ethnically homogeneous and self-procreating. The last, wound in with the former two, is where racial ascriptions play their part directly but through careful misdirection. The

careful play of direction through misdirection works with two familiar strategies in manifesto definitions of nationality.

The first is to declare nationality as being forged through a *long* process
of history and evolution whereby a unitary national character has developed, embodied in the authentic present-day citizen, which consists in
an inextricable combination of language, culture, religion, values and inherited legitimacy (usually, bloodlines). Historically validated authenticity and
the unitary character of national citizenship are the keys. Presence over
several generations (the longer the better) also authenticates the citizenship of ethnic minorities to some degree, and permits some tolerable
departure from the unitary national character of citizens. The presentation
of this position is contextually varied in the different manifestos in question, but enables an explicit rejection of "multiculturalism" in all cases –
which is associated with the E.U. establishment. For NF as for UKIP such
time-honoured national belonging is too obvious to need defining, and is
evoked as already shared ground. NF (2017) uses loaded abstractions to
remind the electorate of this shared ground. The consonance of *patriote*,
"patrimoine historique et culturel", "patriotisme économique" works to
that effect, bolstered by historically resonant terms like *laïcité* (generally
but ineffectively translated as "secularism" in English) and the constitutional
verve of *La République* (relatively rarely used as synonymous with nation in
English, and naturally never in Britain). So, the following NF proposal involving a constitutional amendment is quite difficult to convey succinctly in
English and asserts a collectively recognized national principle against the
intersection of "multiculturalism" and "religious community" (i.e. minority
religious community):

> **Promouvoir la laïcité et lutter contre le communautarisme**. *Inscrire dans la Con-
> stitution le principe : " La République ne reconnaît aucune communauté. " Rétablir
> la laïcité partout, l'étendre à l'ensemble de l'espace public et l'inscrire dans le Code
> du travail.* (15)

> [Sort of:] Promote secularism and fight against communitarianism. Insert the fol-
> lowing principle in the Constitution: "The Republic does not recognise any com-
> munity". Restore secularity everywhere, extend it throughout the public sphere
> and inscribe it in the Labour Code. [On all translations, please see the note at the
> end.]

More straightforwardly, UKIP (2015) pins its manifesto slogan, "Believe in
Britain", to a nationalist version of "international history" in quick strokes:
"We led the way in the abolition of the slave trade. Our Industrial Revolution
transformed the world. A plethora of great Britons stream through international history. Our language is the most widely spoken on the planet."
(61). Other nationalist manifestos present the knot of unitary citizenship
and historical authenticity directly. Thus the AfD (2017) manifesto:

Cultures, languages and national identities have developed historically over centuries. For those attached to them these provide indispensable spaces of identification, which are only available within national states having a democratic constitution. Only thus can people's sovereignty be made alive, which is the mother and the heart of democracy. (6)

The only allowance to diversity that AfD makes is with regard to the cultural prerogatives of the federal states [zur Kulturhoheit der Bundesländer], while promising to stop any initiative to do with "politically correct" (using the English phrase) art and culture (43). And similarly, the DF (2009) programme, which has held since, maintains that "only the Judeo-Christian, Western cultural circle has managed to do away with the medieval worldview", and promises to fight "opposition to the old norms and authorities [that] have developed into a rejection of our own cultural background and the moral and ethical norms which Denmark is built upon", and which is leading to "the conflict between our civilization and immigrant civilizations that have not undergone [gennemgået] reformations" (17). And FPÖ's (2011) programme says:

> The language, history and culture of Austria are German. The vast majority of Austrians are part of the German peoples' linguistic and cultural community. The indigenous ethnic groups of the Burgenland Croats, Slovenians, Hungarians, Czechs, Slovaks and the Roma are historical minorities in our country and as such both enrich and are an integral part of Austria and our nation. (5)

A slight precarity in the undeniable acceptance of these minorities of "autochthonous groups of people which have developed through history" (17) by the majority German peoples might be discerned there; they mark a boundary of necessary tolerance. In this vein PiS's (2014) programme is of particular interest since it is characteristic of former Eastern Blok countries before the 2015 "refugee crisis". This was generally more concerned with emigration and population decline than immigration, and preoccupied with underdevelopment as the perpetual effect of a communist past. It declares:

> We do not define the nation in an ethnic sense – not only because we do not accept nationalist superstitions [narodowych przesądów], but also because of our knowledge of Polish history. Polish nationality evolved and matured by bringing together people of different ethnic backgrounds. (9)

At the same time:

> We see our belonging to the Polish nation as a value not just because it was given to us through birth and cultural heritage and is the result of our traditions. Our belonging is also inextricably tied in with Christianity [...]. (9)

So PiS's (2014) programme struck a historically informed anti-nationalist stance to assert quite a restrictive sense of historically affirmed national authenticity, bearing in mind that it put at least "autochthonous groups", such as

Tatar Muslims who have lived there since the fourteenth century, and, of course, Jews since the tenth century, in an invidious position. How receptive the PiS would be to more recent Muslim immigrants and refugees can be inferred from that.

In contrast to such historically authenticated and unitarily characterizable citizens, appear those that are not historically authenticated and threaten the unitary character. There are three consistent motifs here in these nationalist manifestos. First, "criminals" are predominantly "foreign", and "terrorists" are invariably "foreign" and "Islamic", and are imposing upon and corrupting (infiltrating) the authentic citizenry. In all cases, the line between "criminal" and "terrorist" is indistinct ("terrorism" is a particularly heinous subset of "crime"), and that between "foreign" and "Islamic" is blurred ("Islamic" is "foreign" accentuated). So: UKIP (2015) devotes a section to "dealing with foreign criminals" because, "There is significant public concern about the ability of convicted foreign criminals first to gain entry to the UK and subsequently to obtain British citizenship" (55); DP (2009) details how, "Many immigrants from non-Western countries commit violent crimes as well as property crimes at rates that are several times higher than those by the Danes" (9); AfD promises a much firmer line that the present "against the high proportion of violent and drug-related criminal acts performed by foreigners" (21), and has a marked agenda directed towards terrorist organizations and "criminal clans" [*kriminellen Clans*, a term reserved primarily for gangs from Eastern, especially Muslim, countries]; SVP (2015) makes the following smooth inference, "There are 932 break and enters per 100,000 inhabitants each year. That makes Switzerland destination country number one in Europe for gangs and thieves." (43); and so on. Second, the putatively adverse impact of immigration on historical authenticity and unitary culture has become synonymous with the term "Islamization", and explicit measures to deal with the "increased immigration [that] can lead to a devastating Islamization of Europe", as DP (2009) puts it (and dwells upon), are detailed by most – at length in SVP (2015), NF (2017) and AfD (2017). At the level of the formal manifesto, FPÖ (2011) and UKIP (2015) are circumspect in this respect and avoid naming Muslims/Islam. The most emphatically exclusionary is PVV (2017), where half of the one-page manifesto is devoted to the subject and is worth quoting:

> Millions of Dutch citizens have simply had enough of the Islamization of our country. Enough of the mass immigration and asylum, terror, violence and insecurity.

> Here is our plan: instead of financing the entire world and people we don't want here, we'll spend money on ordinary Dutch citizens.

> This is what the PVV will do:

1. De-Islamize the Netherlands

- No Islamic headscarves in public functions

- Prohibition of other Islamic expressions which violate public order

- Preventive detention of radical Muslims

- Denaturalization and expulsion of criminals with a dual nationality

- Jihadists who went to Syria will not be allowed to return to the Netherlands

- Close all mosques and Islamic schools, ban the Koran

This programme made PVV the second largest party in terms of the popular vote in the Netherlands in 2017. The third motif apropos of authentic and unitary citizenry is the most familiar: that the state's existing population is being swamped and overtaken by immigrants by putatively statistical gauges. As UKIP (2015) puts it pithily, "Immigration is not about race; it is about space" (11). More often in these manifestos, there is the fear of Islam and prejudice against Muslims woven into spatial concerns, without denials of a racial quotient. And, perhaps the unusual section on African immigration which occupies a whole section of the AfD (2017) manifesto (Section 5.1, entitled *Die demographischen Probleme Europas und Afrikas*) is more than a little "about race". Much unreferenced statistics is quoted there to assert that: "Europe [now] faces a migration pressure which assumes the proportion of dealing with an invasion of peoples [*der Dimensionen einer Völkerwanderung*]" from Africa. Consequently:

> Given this problematic background it is obvious that migration from Africa to Europe along the anticipated lines can destabilize our continent in a few years. Overall immigration quotas for those who are willing to emigrate would be unethical because they would simultaneously exclude the great majority. Political demands made along these lines are thus pseudohumanitarian and self-destructive. Individual rights of protection and asylum guarantees were created in 1949 for persecuted individuals. They made promises which are impossible to maintain under current conditions of mass global migratory movements.
>
> The aim of the AfD is self-preservation, not the self-destruction of our state and people. The future of Germany and Europe must be secured in the long term. (25)

What this means in policy terms is not spelled out in AfD (2017); it is left to the imagination of the electorate.

The historically authenticated and unitary character of citizenship in these manifestos is articulated in terms which are unproblematic in common parlance now: the "nationality", "ethnicity", "identity" of "indigenous" or "autochthonous" "peoples" or "majorities", wherein "language"–"culture"–"values"–"traditions" are all inextricably fused and sealed by "history", the passage of "centuries", and proximity, in a uniformly salutary way. Similarly, the threat to this authentic citizenry is couched in terms which are unexceptional in everyday and formal usage: "immigrants", "refugees", "foreigners", "Muslims", especially associated with "crime", "terrorism", "violence", "fanaticism", identified by different "languages"–"cultures"–"values"–"traditions", all those also fused and sealed into homogeneous forms from "outside-Europe", "non-European cultures", and embodying "multiculturalism" within Europe. It is evident to electorates reading these manifestos that there are ascriptions of race amidst this binaristic play of terms, but the precise mechanics of ascription are elusive. The terms have race in them, but always in a deniable way; there is a racial quotient, but equally there is more than that in every term. These terms' suggestiveness to essentializing and discriminating gazes (associating social behaviours with physiognomies and anatomies, genes and bloodlines) is countered at the selfsame moment by obviously social constructionist connotations. The logic of essentialist racialization is often implicit and always ambiguous. It comes through in how terms are welded together into inextricable singularities for describing peoples, in the implicit "nativity" within "nationality", in the "father" within "patriot". But these terms are slippery: there's race in there, but not necessarily.

Nevertheless, in such manifestos the essentialist ascriptions of race are also unambiguously tractable in relation to the legal norms for citizenship. Many of these manifestos emphasize the racial quotient of citizenship in legal terms (birth and parentage), and often propose adjusting the legal norms to (re-)harden that racial quotient. So, when FPÖ (2011) states that, "Austria is not a country of immigration. This is why we pursue a family policy centred around births", effectively the racial basis of citizenship is asserted. And when AfD (2017) declares: "We want to withdraw the birthplace principle [Geburtsortsprinzip] (acquisition of German citizenship by birth in Germany, even though neither parent is German), and return to the principle of origin [Abstammungsprinzip] as applied till 2000" (29), that's a bid to retrieve an unambiguously racial basis for citizenship. Almost all the manifestos mentioned above seek to adjust the legal norms of citizenship so as to putatively defend the historically authenticated citizen from the threat of corruption and infiltration by suspect immigrants. On the one hand, this involves introducing legal provisions for withholding citizenship from those who would be entitled to it under the existing regime; on the other hand, it involves adjustments to the legal norms to enable withdrawal of citizenship where that is already acquired or owned. The first could be regarded as a short-term way of using citizenship as a bargaining chip; the first and second together could be considered a long-term programme for purifying the citizenry. It is the second which is worth focusing on: that implies *making it a legal norm to introduce distinctions or gradations within the body of existing citizens in a political state.* Such proposals disturb the legal first principle of the equality of citizens in the eyes of the law; ergo, they suggest that certain existing citizens should be considered more suspect than others by legal definition, and as having different fundamental rights compared to others in law. These proposals rebound into the existing populations of political states to legalize second-class citizenship. Variously, such proposals for making existing citizenship removable apply to persons with dual citizenship, naturalized citizens, and in one case (AfD) "citizens from migrant backgrounds" who may be accused of or suspected of being criminals or terrorists (as observed above, these terms merge into each other). If such proposals become enacted in law, *all* dual citizens, naturalized citizens and "citizens from migrant backgrounds" would become legally different from other citizens. They would become more suspect than other citizens, subject to punishments that are different from those for other citizens committing the same offences – therefore, second-class citizens in law.

The conditions set for such proposed measures underline racial identification of suspect citizenship relative to racial baselines for historically authenticated citizenship (by parentage and birth over generations). That is, the identification of the suspect citizen is laid bare to shared essentialist preconceptions. Thus: DF (2009)

> wishes for naturalization legislation to be designed in such a way that Danish citizenship can be revoked by a judgment if the person in question commits a serious crime, or has been part of or has participated in terrorist acts in Denmark or abroad (32);

UKIP (2015) "take the view that British citizens who choose to fight alongside terrorist organisations effectively abdicate their rights to citizenship" (13); PVV (2017) has a succinct promise in its programme to "de-Islamicize" the Netherlands by the "Denaturalization and expulsion of criminals with a dual nationality". With regard to suspect citizens, AfD (2017) proposes measures grounded on its bid to return to a racial basis for citizenship:

> The naturalization of criminals should be controlled by: 1. Stopping the acquisition of German nationality by mere birth in Germany, since, among other things, members of criminal clans automatically become German citizens thereby; […].

> Finally, the expatriation of criminal citizens with a migration background should be made possible when: 1. There is evidence of serious criminality within ten years after successful naturalization; 2. In case of participation in terrorist organizations (e.g., IS); 3. If they are affiliated to criminal clans, even if that means expatriation so that they become stateless. (21)

Similarly, there are the NF (2017) campaign promises, which effectively remove the threats of immigrants procreating or migrant miscegenation:

26 Reducing legal migration to an annual balance of 10,000. Ending automaticity of family consolidation and reconciliation, as well as the automatic acquisition of French nationality by marriage. Remove the suction pumps from immigration.

27 Delete the right of the soil: the acquisition of French nationality will be possible only by filiation or naturalization, the conditions for which will become more stringent. Deletion of dual extra-European citizenship. (6)

SVP (2011) is clearest in suggesting that all naturalized citizenship is suspect:

Problems "naturalised": Due to the mass naturalisations of the past few years, many people who received the Swiss passport have not been integrated. A not insignificant number of new Swiss do not understand any of the country's national languages, do not accept the local customs and, shortly after their naturalisation, commit a criminal offence. Statistically though, these people are then counted as Swiss. As a result, many problems with foreigners were simply "naturalised". (32)

The schematic approach taken here to focus on electorally successful nationalist parties and their manifestos might give the impression that such concepts of citizenship are entertained, and measures proposed, only by that category of parties. It is possible that parties which are otherwise liberally inclusive or even socialist might also uncritically accept and promote similar measures, especially under the pressure of political polarization. Readers of this special issue can determine for themselves what share of the electorate of any contemporary European nation-state might subscribe to such notions irrespective of the parties they vote for.

The language of "race"

Denials of reference to race in the manifestos cited above usually appear with the suggestion that such reference is the province of irrational liberal moralism ("political correctness"). Thus, UKIP's (2015) manifesto observes dismissively that "even our prime ministers have labelled good, decent people 'closet racists' and 'bigots'", before announcing that "Immigration is not about race; it is about space"; and AfD's (2017) manifesto states that it "is opposed to any defamation of rational religious criticism as 'Islamophobia' or 'racism'. We urge everyone to replace such polemics by intellectual discourse". As observed above, such circumspection about referring directly to race opens space for implicit insertions of race, thereby rendered all the more subliminally persistent; the terms used have a racial quotient while connoting more than race or also something other than race. Under these circumstances, engaging with race and racism seriously seems narrow-minded – especially when those perceived as belonging to racialized minorities do so. For the latter, contemplating race, however analytically, seems a self-fulfilling compliance with their own racialization.

This kind of language, which is and yet is not quite about race, has naturally exercised researchers investigating racialization and racism. On the one hand, they have felt at times that a new "post-racial" or "colour-blind" political discourse has emerged (which often focalizes "class"); on the other hand, they have simultaneously suspected that "post-racial" and "colour-blind" claims are often mendacious, seeking to evade, perpetuate or even exacerbate existing racism; and, underpinning both hands, they have then felt that their own language – their academic discourse itself – needs to be rejuvenated to be equal to analysing such slippery articulations of race. Negotiating with academic discourse itself amidst putatively "post-racial" discourses has been a fraught matter at times. For instance, amongst race researchers in the USA, Barrack Obama's victory in the 2008 Presidential elections appeared to put the academic language for analysing race into question. Thus, Wise (2010) had to assert soon after that "Race continues to matter" (20) and analyse Obama's own colour-blind pronouncements to explain why. Leonardo (2012) observed that "Race scholars carry on as usual, but we do so with an increasing sense of doubt and doom about the very nature of our topic" (126), and offered a precise statement of the sticking point: "Race does not disappear because we alter conceptualizing each other as post- or non-racial *if we act on the world in a racial way and with racial consequences*" (136, emphasis in original). In introducing an edited volume on the "post-racial" era, Ivery and Bassett (2015) came up with the programmatic demand for "new models of 'talking about race' – or similarly, a *new language of race*", especially to "vigorously interrogate the ascendance of class (i.e. class theories) as a new dominant rationale in explaining racial inequalities" (3, emphasis in original). Other similar observations may be cited, but the point is evident: at least until 2014 or 2015, it seemed that a putatively "post-racial" or "colour-blind" political discourse has emerged which might be suspect, and which necessitated self-reflection within academic discourse. Such self-reflectiveness complicated and deferred analysis of the ambiguous language of race out there in the political sphere ("post-racial"/"colour-blind" discourse), suggesting some degree of sceptical complicity between scholarly and political references to "race". López's (2014) *Dog Whistle Politics* presented a relatively rare attempt to pin down the evasive language of race in American politics, tracing it from Civil Liberties movements to Obama's presidency, without turning self-reflectively upon academic discourse itself. The succinct generalizations he offered of "coded racial appeals" are worth noting here, since, though centred on the U.S.A., they effectively describe the discursive context wherein the European nationalist manifestos outlined above make their appeal:

> The new racial politics presents itself as steadfastly opposed to racism and ever ready to condemn those who publicly use racial profanity. *We fiercely oppose racism and stand prepared to repudiate anyone who uses the n-word.* Meanwhile,

though, the new racial discourse keeps up a steady drumbeat of subliminal racial grievances and appeals to color-coded solidarity. *But let's be honest: some groups commit more crimes and use more welfare, other groups are mainly unskilled and illiterate illegals, and some religions inspire violence and don't value life.* (3–4, emphasis in original)

That these messages are coded, López argues, is an acknowledgement that many do not sympathise with their racial content; their coding also underlines that they contradict established anti-racist tenets. At the same time, the coding allows for usefully variegated reception: those who are sympathetic to the racial message will find it there, while those who are not will be able to persuade themselves that it is not there.

In 2015, when this special issue was being planned, academic self-reflectiveness among race scholars seemed more the trend of the day, and not just in the U.S.A. Making the connection from the U.S.A. to the U.K., Paul (2014) observed: "A form of racial neo-liberalism is arguably unfolding in the UK – erasing and/or muting any explicit articulation of race from government policies and equality discourse" (707); he found it a challenge to "develop a language for having a sophisticated discussion on the ethical and political dilemmas associated with race that would not disable communication" (708). In 2017, as this special issue goes into production, López's more direct engagement with coded racial appeals seems more of the moment. As the discussion of the manifestos suggests, race is closer to the surface of political discourse now – it is, so to speak, *barely coded*. The papers below, written in the interim between 2015 and 2017, all find ways of articulating and analysing this barely coded language of race and racism effectively. Schierup, Ålund and Neergaard's contribution gives a careful account of the bio-political management through which race has surfaced in Swedish politics, and notes moments when explicit racial terms are rendered covert. Oliveri understands racialism as a form of governmentality (à la Foucault) in Italy, the contours of which become manifest when racialising and counter-racialising moves are considered together. Tyler contemplates the growing "state racism" in Europe (especially the Czech Republic) directed against refugees, by developing a concept of racial stigma. Virdee and McGeever locate racialization within a glaring erasure of the history of migration, which was inextricably entwined with race politics and policies, in recent Brexit debates. Murji's paper draws on framing analysis to explore accounts of riots in Britain, thereby sharpening the mechanics of racialization and de-racialization. With pedagogic practice in view, West-Pavlov understands racism as a freezing and polarizing of essentially fluid identities in response to political and economic upheavals. The insertion of colour-terms does the deliberative work of accentuating race within coded appeals in some of the contributions. De Genova brings out the barely concealed racism that dehumanizes the "black and brown bodies" of illegal migrants who die in attempting the Mediterranean crossing.

Giorgos and Elisavet present Greek anxieties about accommodating different groups of immigrants through a grid of "whitening" and "blackening" factors (with reference to Aihwa Ong). Pondering the results of the Brexit referendum, Seed pauses on pat explanations pointing to the "white working class" and recriminations about their xenophobia, and considers more complex and historically informed ways of understanding the referendum result.

Note

1. While the concept of race was invented to legitimize racism, those who bore the weight of such oppression have appropriated the category and infused it with an emancipatory vision to combat racism. In fact, one of the ramifications of the last cycle of protest (of anti-colonial revolt in the Global South accompanied by the anti-racist movements of the Anglo-American world) was its wounding of the project of legitimizing racism in the name of race (Virdee 2014). In its slipstream, however, have emerged cultural racisms and more recently the postracial moment, where the concept of post-racial serves to occlude the ongoing material force of racism and discrimination (see, for example, Lentin 2014; Valluvan 2016).

Acknowledgements

The authors are grateful to Michał P. Garapich, Carl-Ulrik Schierup, Achim Brosch and Prem Poddar for helping them understand and translate from the Polish, Danish and German manifestos discussed in this paper.

Disclosure statement

No potential conflict of interest was reported by the authors.

References

AfD. 2017. *Programm für die Wahl zum Deutschen Bundestag AM 24.* September. https://www.afd-goe.de/kandidaten/bundesprogramm/.

Castles, S. 2012. "Cosmopolitanism and Freedom? Lessons of the Global Economic Crisis." *Ethnic and Racial Studies* 35 (11): 1843–1852.

Chakravarty, P., and D. F. da Silva, eds. 2012. "Special Issue: Race, Empire, and the Crisis of the Subprime." *American Quarterly* 64 (3): 361–385.

DF. 2009. *Dansk Folkepartis Arbejdsprogram.* https://www.danskfolkeparti.dk/Arbejdsprogram.

Dymski, G. A. 2009. "Racial Exclusion and the Political Economy of the Subprime Crisis." *Historical Materialism* 17 (2): 149–179.

Fekete, L. 2009. *A Suitable Enemy: Racism, Migration and Islamophobia in Europe.* London: Pluto.

Fella, S., and C. Ruzza, eds. 2013. *Anti-racist Movements in the EU: Between Europeanization and National Trajectories.* Basingstoke: Palgrave Macmillan.

FPÖ. 2011. *Party Programme of the Freedom Party of Austria*. https://www.fpoe.at/themen/parteiprogramm/ (available in English)

Gillborn, D. 2013. "Interest-divergence and the Colour of Cutbacks: Race, Recession and the Undeclared War on Black children." *Discourse* 34 (4): 477–491.

Hall, S. 1997. "Race – The Floating Signifier (documentary)." Directed by Sut Jally. Northampton, MA: Media Education Foundation. https://www.mediaed.org/assets/products/407/transcript_407.pdf.

Ivery, C. L., and J. A. Bassett. 2015. "Introduction and Theoretical Overview." In *Reclaiming Integration and the Language of Race in a "Post-Racial" Era*, edited by C. L. Ivery and J. A. Bassett, 1–19. Lanham: Rowman and Littlefield.

Jackson, P. 1989. *Maps of Meaning: An Introduction to Cultural Geography*. London: Routledge.

Lentin, A. 2004. *Racism and Anti-racism in Europe*. London: Pluto.

Lentin, A. 2014. "Post-race, Post Politics: The Paradoxical Rise of Culture after Multiculturalism." *Ethnic and Racial Studies* 37 (8): 1268–1285.

Leonardo, Z. 2012. "After the Glow: Race Ambivalence and Other Educational Prognoses." In *The Power In/Of Language*, edited by D. R. Cole and L. J. Graham, 124–147. Chichester: Wiley-Blackwell.

Livola, M. M., ed. 2013. *Discourses of Immigration in Times of Economic Crisis*. Newcastle upon Tyne: Cambridge Scholars.

López, I. H. 2014. *Dog Whistle Politics: How Coded Racial Appeals Have Reinvented Racism and Wrecked the Middle Class*. Oxford: Oxford University Press.

NF. 2017. *144 Engagements Présidentiels Marine*. http://www.frontnational.com/le-projet-de-marine-le-pen/.

Paul, J. 2014. "Post-racial Futures: Imagining Post-racialist Anti-racism(s)." *Ethnic and Racial Studies* 37 (4): 702–718.

PiS. 2014. *Program Prawa i Sprawiedliwości*. http://pis.org.pl/dokumenty.

PVV. 2017. *Concept – Verkiezingsprogramma PVV 2017–2021*. http://www.pvv.nl/visie.html. English translation at https://www.geertwilders.nl/94-english/2007-preliminary-election-program-pvv-2017-2021.

Redclift, V. 2014. "New Racisms, New Racial Subjects? The Neo-liberal Moment and the Racial Landscape of Contemporary Britain." *Ethnic and Racial Studies* 37 (4): 577–588.

Rugh, J., L. Albright, and D. Massey. 2015. "Race, Space, and Cumulative Disadvantage: A Case Study of the Subprime Lending Collapse." *Social Problems* 62 (2): 186–218.

SVP. 2015. *Party Programme of the Swiss People's Party, 2015–2019*. http://www.svp-international.ch/index.php/en/about-us/svp-s-party-manifesto.

Taras, R. 2012. *Xenophobia and Islamophobia in Europe*. Edinburgh: Edinburgh University Press.

UKIP. 2015. *Believe in Britain: UKIP Manifesto 2015*. http://www.ukip.org/manifesto2015.

Valluvan, S. 2016. "What Is "Post-Race" and What Does It Reveal About Contemporary Racisms?" *Ethnic and Racial Studies* 39 (13): 2241–2251.

Virdee, S. 2014. *Racism, Class and the Racialized Outsider*. Basingstoke: Palgrave Macmillan.

Wise, T. 2010. *Colorblind: The Rise of Post-racial Politics and the Retreat from Racial Equity*. San Francisco, CA: City Light Books/Open Media Series.

Wyly, E., M. Moos, D. Hammel, and E. Kabahiz. 2009. "Cartographies of Race and Class: Mapping the Class-monopoly Rents of American Subprime Mortgage Capital." *International Journal of Urban and Regional Research* 33 (2): 332–354.

The "migrant crisis" as racial crisis: do *Black Lives Matter* in Europe?

Nicholas De Genova

ABSTRACT
We are currently witnessing a remarkable conjuncture between the escalation, acceleration, and diversification of migrant and refugee mobilities, on the one hand, and the mutually constitutive crises of "European" borders and "European" identity, on the other, replete with reanimated reactionary populist nationalisms and racialized nativisms, the routinization of antiterrorist securitization, and pervasive and entrenched "Islamophobia" (or more precisely, anti-Muslim racism). Despite the persistence of racial denial and the widespread refusal to frankly confront questions of "race" across Europe, the current constellation of "crises" presents precisely what can only be adequately comprehended as an unresolved *racial crisis* that derives fundamentally from the postcolonial condition of "Europe" as a whole, and therefore commands heightened scrutiny and rigorous investigation of the material and practical as well as discursive and symbolic productions of the co-constituted figures of "Europe" and "crisis" in light of racial formations theory.

"Illegal"/deportable/disposable ... dead

The first intimations of a European "migrant" (or "refugee") "crisis" arose amidst the unsightly accumulation of dead black and brown bodies awash on the halcyon shores of the Mediterranean Sea. Following the monumental shipwreck of 19 April 2015, in which as many 850 migrants and refugees were sent to their deaths, the accumulating momentum of a gathering storm of human mobility over both sea and land served to fix in place a newfound dominant common sense about a "crisis" of the borders of "Europe" (New Keywords Collective 2016). The putative crisis surrounding the influx of migrants and refugees in Europe – and the border spectacle that it generates (De Genova 2013) – has long been nowhere more extravagantly put on display than in the Mediterranean Sea, which is incontestably the veritable global epicentre of such lethal border crossings.[1] Human catastrophes at sea have transformed the maritime borders of Europe into a macabre deathscape (cf. Heller and Pezzani 2017; IOM 2014; Jansen, Celikates, and de Bloois 2015).

The brute *racial* fact of this deadly European border regime is seldom acknowledged, because it immediately confronts us with the cruel (post)coloniality of the "new" Europe. In the face of the inevitable and ever-more bountiful harvest of empire, past and present, the mobility of the vast majority of people from formerly colonized countries – indeed, the vast majority of humanity – has been preemptively illegalized (Andersson 2014; De Genova 2013, 2016; Karakayali and Rigo 2010; Scheel 2017). With the termination of the post-Second World War-era guestworker programmes, postcolonial labour migration from poorer countries assumed in the 1970s what was commonly the only permissible form, that of refugees fleeing persecution and seeking asylum (Karakayali and Rigo 2010). European states generally refuse to consider asylum applications lodged abroad, however, and there are ordinarily no provisions in their immigration guidelines for anyone to be given permission to travel to their countries to petition for asylum. Moreover, travellers from all of Africa and virtually all of Asia, as well as several Latin American and Caribbean countries, require visas for travel to any Schengen-zone country, for which the inordinate majority of prospective applicants cannot qualify (Scheel 2017).[2] Consequently, both labour migrants and refugees who cannot secure visas are compelled to first arrive on European territory as "unauthorized" asylum-seekers, and hence, as de facto "illegal migrants", who only thereafter may petition for asylum. Furthermore, the European asylum system has routinely denied the great majority of petitioners formal recognition as legitimate asylum-seekers, and ordinarily grants refugee status to less than 15 per cent of applicants.[3] Thus, the EU-ropean legal frameworks governing travel visas, migration, and asylum, together with the externalization of border policing and transportation carrier sanctions, preclude literally the vast majority of humanity from "legitimate" access to the European Union (EU). The fervent invention and fortification of a new border around the newly reunited "Europe" may therefore be understood to be nothing less than yet another re-drawing of the global colour line (De Genova 2016), and the institutionalization of what Étienne Balibar has tellingly suggested may be "a European 'apartheid'" ([1999] 2004, 43–45; 2001; cf. van Houtum 2010). Only in this stark racial light, therefore, can we adequately assess the fact that the EU, for the last two decades, has actively converted the Mediterranean into a mass grave.

Migrant lives/"Black" lives

Prior to the record-high death toll of 2016, untold tens of thousands of refugees, migrants, and their children have been consigned to horrific, unnatural, premature deaths by shipwreck and drowning, often following protracted ordeals of abandonment at sea.[4] Little surprise, in light of the racial materiality of the unrelenting conversion of European borders into a ghoulish death-scape, that one mode of critical response was to invoke an analogy with the premier slogan of contemporary African-American civil rights struggles in the United States – *Black Lives Matter* – by insisting that *Migrant Lives Matter*.[5] In a manner that is analogous but distinct from the outrageous fact that the proposition "Black Lives Matter" remains controversial in the United States, a European border regime that systematically generates and multiplies the conditions of possibility for mass migrant deaths compels us to reckon with the brute fact that the lives of migrants and refugees, required to arrive on European soil by "irregular" (illegalized) means, have been systema-tically exposed to lethal risks. Like the proposition "Black Lives Matter" in the United States, therefore, objective realities command that we admit that the proposition "Migrant Lives Matter" remains fundamentally in dispute in Europe. Furthermore, given that the horrendous risk of border-crossing death systematically generated by the European border regime is dispropor-tionately inflicted upon migrants and refugees from sub-Saharan Africa, we should be reminded here or Ruth Gilmore's poignant proposition that this indeed may be taken as the very definition of racism: "Racism", she contends, "…is the state-sanctioned or extralegal production and exploitation of group-differentiated vulnerability to premature death" (2007, 28). Hence, the poignant question of whether Black Lives Matter in Europe presents itself ever more urgently.

But why, and how exactly, has Europe so deftly managed to convert the precarious lives (and bodies) of migrants and refugees – disproportionately racialized as not-white, and in fact inordinately racialized as Black – into overtly de-racialized "migrant" lives? If migrant lives do arguably matter in Europe, why is it so persistently and perniciously difficult to recognize them as Black lives?[6] And if objective circumstances conspire to ensure that these lives truly do not matter – that these migrant lives are rendered utterly dispo-sable – does it not seem plausible, if not probable, that race has something to do with it?

It is noteworthy that we have also witnessed the emergence in Britain of a fledgling but spirited *Black Lives Matter* movement, explicitly dedicated to an anti-racist internationalist solidarity with the struggles against racist police brutality and murder in the United States, as well as elaborating a global analysis that links systemic racial oppression in the United States with racist policing and state violence in Britain. Still more pertinent, for present pur-poses, are efforts by the British movement to directly define anti-racist struggles in Britain – long associated with the politics of citizenship (much like in the United States) – to questions of: mass migrant (non-citizen) deaths during perilous crossings of the Mediterranean (not uncommonly fleeing geopolitical conflicts in which Britain has been implicated); abuses perpetrated during immigrant detention, incarceration, and deportation; state-sanctioned Islamophobia through putative antiterrorist programmes; and the escalation of post-Brexit anti-immigrant hate crimes.[7] Marking the fifth anniversary of the "lawful" London police murder on 4 August 2011 of an unarmed Black British man, Mark Duggan, which prompted riots across Greater London and numerous other English cities, the Black Lives Matter movement staged protests on 5 August 2016 in London, Birmingham, Manchester, and Nottingham, proclaiming: "This is a crisis." Notably, access roads to the London Heathrow and Birmingham airports were specifically targeted for civil disobedience because of their association with the detention and deportation of migrants, including the death under restraint of Angolan deportee Jimmy Mubenga in October 2010 (BBC News 2016a; see also BBC News 2016b). A similarly salutary development directly inspired by struggles in the United States is evidenced by the emergence of Berlin's *Ferguson Is Everywhere* campaign to denounce the killing of people of colour by German police.[8] Inevitably, these initiatives build upon more longstanding anti-racist struggles in Europe, such as the London-based Campaign Against Police and State Violence, Berlin's European Network of People of African Descent, Amsterdam's New Urban Collective, and the Parti des Indigènes de la République in France (Essif 2015). Nevertheless, it is unmistakable that the Black Lives Matter struggles in the United States have had a direct energizing effect on these parallel European movements. It is vital here to recognize these analogies and transversalities, and particularly salient that these trans-Atlantic reverberations have remained emphatically racial in their political self-understandings and critical analyses.

Anyone concerned with questions of race and racism today must readily recognize that they present themselves in a particularly acute way in the European migration context, haunted as Europe's borders are by an appalling proliferation of almost exclusively non-European/ non-white migrant and refugee deaths and other forms of structural violence and generalized suffering. Consequently, it is particularly crucial that we do the critical work of reconfirming the precisely *racial* specificity of what is so commonly and casually euphemized across Europe as "migrant" or "of migrant background". The mass deaths of non-European migrants and refugees systemically generated by the European border regime do not exhaust what is at stake in the present historical moment, however. We have witnessed a remarkable conjuncture between the acceleration and diversification of migrant and refugee mobilities, on the one hand, and the mutually constitutive crises of "European" borders and "European" identity, on the other, replete with reanimated reactionary populist nationalisms and racialized nativisms, the routinization of antiterrorist securitization, and pervasive and entrenched "Islamophobia" (or more precisely, anti-Muslim racism). Positing the idea of "racial crisis", Omi and Winant identified the police beating of Rodney King and the Los

Angeles rebellion in 1992 following the acquittal of the brutalizers as a watershed moment for racial politics in the United States ([1986] 1994, 145; cf. 1993). The same is plainly true once again for the contemporary Black Lives Matter movement's politicization of racist police killings inordinately perpetrated against African Americans across the United States. Analogously, we are challenged to discern the comparably momentous albeit multifaceted *racial* significance in the events of the last two years surrounding migration and refugee movements into and across Europe. The putative "migrant crisis" of Europe must be understood to be an historical moment of *racial crisis*.

In the European context, the very figure of *migration* is always already racialized, and anti-racist struggles are inevitably concerned at least in part with the racial conditions of (non-European) migrants – even as dominant discourses of migration in Europe systematically disavow and dissimulate race as such (Balibar 1991, [1992] 2002, [1999] 2004; De Genova 2010b, 2016; Goldberg 2006). Nonetheless, the European intellectual and political context, more generally, remains exemplary of "what happens when no category is available to name a set of experiences that are linked … to racial arrangements and engagements … a case study in the frustrations, delimitations and injustices of political racelessness" (Goldberg 2006, 335–336). This is what David Theo Goldberg has tellingly designated *racial Europeanism*. Specifically referring to the presumptive elision of the analytical concept of race with the essentialist conceits of race-ism, and the pervasive reduction of any question of "racism" in European contexts to the historical experience of the Nazi Holocaust, Goldberg demonstrates how "Europe's *colonial* history and legacy dissipate if not disappear" (2006, 336; emphasis added). Sanctimonious desires to renounce race as a residually race-*ist* article of faith, in other words, supply the dubious pretexts for an astounding postcolonial historical amnesia. Moreover, we are left with the peculiarly European paradox of an anti-racism without race, which is to say, an anaemic anti-racism that reverts to the purest liberalism: a mere politics of anti-discrimination, which in its refusal to interrogate the sociopolitical production of racialized distinctions, re-stabilizes the notion that racism is little more than a discriminatory hostility towards phenotypic and anatomical differences, and thus re-naturalizes race as "biology". Banishing race as a critical analytical category, in other words, risks forsaking any adequate account of the distinctly *European* colonial legacies that literally *produced* race as a sociopolitical category of distinction and discrimination in the first place.

Although race is systematically dissimulated if not actively disavowed in many European contexts, therefore, we find ourselves, in Michael Omi and Howard Winant's words, "compelled to think racially" – because "opposing racism requires that we notice race … that we afford it the recognition it deserves and the subtlety it embodies" ([1986] 1994, 159). Regarding the subtlety of race, it should be clear but deserves to be explicitly and emphatically affirmed that this proposition in no way upholds any anachronistic notion of race as a "natural" (quasi-biological, pseudo-objective) fact of genealogy. The pernicious power of racial distinction operates precisely through the *naturalization* of social inequalities, constructing them as putatively "natural" (phenotypic, anatomical, physiological, "biological") differences derived from common kinship and shared ancestry. But race is not a fact of nature; it is a sociopolitical fact of domination; indeed, race is the naturalized *effect* of a regime of domination orchestrated according to racialized distinctions and categories, which are themselves sociopolitical contrivances. Thus, race is not a fact of nature so much as a fact of racism, a fact of racialized domination, configured historically and continuously reproduced on a *global* scale – particularly the historically specific hierarchies of social power, wealth, and prestige enforced through violent and oppressive regimes of (European/colonial) white supremacy.

Whiteness as a racialized status ought not be reduced to any sort of simple synonym for Europeanness, as if there were a straightforward correlation of European origins and phenotypic "whiteness", or to put it more bluntly, as if whiteness were simply a matter of "colour". Indeed, the borders and divisions within Europe, or around which various notions of "Europe" have been contested, have themselves frequently been profoundly racialized ones. Foundational racialized distinctions and meanings, such as "white" or "Black", which were literally invented, imposed, and enforced through various iterations of the global regime of European/colonial supremacy, retroactively, have been made to appear as the transparent and self-evident ("natural") names for differences that only came to have the significance and gravity that they do because the particular forms of exploitation and domination that created them required and relied upon their naturalization.

Conversely, it is also necessary that we underscore the salience of the figures of migration and refugee movements into and within Europe for destabilizing, de-naturalizing, and de-essentializing yet again the pernicious persistence of encrusted and ossified racial nomenclatures. Hence, if we have the temerity to ask whether Black Lives Matter in Europe, we must nonetheless recognize that Blackness here must be conceived as more capacious than a mere synonym for African origin or ancestry alone. In other words, while never denying or disregarding the historical specificity of African experiences of white supremacy and the particularity for Africans and all people of African ancestry of being racialized as Black (cf. Chandler 2013, 2014; Gilroy 1993; Mbembe 2017), it is likewise instructive to recall that even for those who come to be racialized as Black, we must guard against naturalizing what is always an historically specific sociopolitical process of *producing* them as "Black". In this regard, Stuart Hall's reflections on his experience as a Black *migrant* are quite poignant:

I'd never called myself black ever in my life .... So it was a discovery for me, a rediscovery [in Britain] of the Caribbean in new terms ... and a rediscovery of the black subject .... I didn't choose that. I had no alternative. (Hall and Back 2009, 662)

In other words, although the centuries-old racialization of enslaved Africans and their descendants in the New World was indisputably a defining crucible for the global racial formation of Blackness, it was nonetheless the postcolonial migrant encounter with Europe that was, in Hall's account, tantamount to a migration into Blackness, a *re*-racialization, a subordination and subjection that was inextricable from the ongoing and unfinished business of (re-)producing racial distinctions and meanings. Thus, it is productive here to posit a conception of Blackness that exceeds the constrictions of the more rigid and conventional racial codifications that have been generated and sedimented historically.

If we are pressed in the present by the brutality of circumstances to examine the outlandish question of whether Black Lives Matter in Europe – and indeed, if we may posit the specifically *racial* question concerning the "migrant" or "refugee crisis" in and of Europe – such a line of inquiry must necessarily refer us to a Blackness that corresponds to the full range of racialized categories that white supremacy has orchestrated under the sign of negation. In other words, I refer here not to any supposedly "objective" or "natural" sort of (phenotypic, quasi-"biological") racial Blackness that might be more predictably attributed to people of African origin or descent in particular, but rather to the pronouncedly heterogeneous spectrum of all those categories of humanity that European imperialism unrelentingly produced as its colonized "natives". Hence, for present purposes, I am positing a more expansive, if provisional, understanding of Blackness as a racialized sociopolitical category that can be understood to encompass the full spectrum of social identities produced as specifically "not-white". In this respect, migration and refugee movements may be recognized as providing crucial sites for what Achille Mbembe has tellingly depicted as "the Becoming Black of the world", in which "the term 'Black' has been generalized" (2017, 6) and there is a "tendency to universalize the Black condition" (4).

"Terrorists"

Precisely when the public discourses of migrant–refugee "crisis" in Europe seemed to have reached an unsustainable crescendo over the summer months and through the autumn of 2015, and notably after the gruesome spectacle of mass deaths by shipwreck in the Mediterranean had receded in favour of the mass exodus over land across the Balkans of migrants and refugees (particularly those from Middle Eastern countries, with Syria, Iraq, and Afghanistan among the most prominent), the grisly spectacle of "terrorism" in Paris on 13 November 2015 supplied the catalytic event that could conjure anew the well-worn spectre of "Muslim extremism". The spectacle of "Islamist terrorism" of course had already prompted an unprecedented heightening of securitization following the attacks in Paris in January 2015, centred on the massacre at the offices of the anti-Muslim satirical magazine *Charlie Hebdo* (De Genova 2017). In those prior events, the culprits had been (racialized minority) European citizens. Ornamented now with a (fake) Syrian passport fortuitously deposited in the vicinity of one of the November bombings, however, the horrific bloodbath in the heart of urbane Europe was quickly conscripted to allege that the seemingly uncontrollable refugee influx was somehow providing cover for a nefarious ambush by the putative enemies of "civilization" itself, and that the refugee crisis truly represented a security threat, after all (De Genova 2007, 2010a). Notably, immediately following the events in Paris, within a few hours – and within days of having been branded a "lawless slum" that presented the risk of an "infiltration" of "guerrilla warfare" – the migrant and refugee camps at Calais were subjected to what appeared to be a vicious arson attack (Campbell 2015).

In the ensuing days, amidst the predictable (indeed, obligatory) speculations about a hydra-headed phantasm of "foreign fighters" and "homegrown extremists" travelling unhindered between combat zones in Syria and western European countries, France – long among the most stalwart advocates of European integration – stridently called for an unprecedented securitization of the external borders of the EU's Schengen zone of free mobility. Within a week of the events, amidst police raids against Muslim "suspects" across multiple countries, and various hysterical calls for mass internment, deportations, and the electronic monitoring of such alleged suspects, EU interior and justice ministers convened an emergency meeting and vowed to institute significantly tighter external border controls and expanded surveillance over human mobility, citizen and non-citizen alike. The urgent push to create new "hotspot" migrant and refugee reception and processing facilities (i.e. detention camps) at sites of illegalized border crossing (Garelli and Tazzioli 2016; Sciurba 2016), likewise, came now to be re-imagined as a matter of perimeter defence against terrorist infiltration, re-figured as vital strategic sites for "culling terrorist wolves from refugee sheep" (Lyman 2015). Despite the fact that all of the alleged culprits identified in the November attacks, as in the earlier attacks in January, were in fact (racialized minority) Europeans, therefore, the spectacle of terror nevertheless served quite effectively as a virtually unquestionable pretext for dramatically reinvigorated border enforcement. Despite the manifest absence of migrants or refugees in these events, in other words, the spectre of Europe's "homegrown" (disaffected, "second-generation") "Muslim extremist" *citizens* – routinely racialized as being "of migrant background" – served to re-confirm the pernicious affiliation between

26

migrants and refugees (as invasive foreign infiltrators) with the racialized threat of a corrosive and inimical pathology festering within the bosom of Europe.

"Sexual predators"

Following the violent events in Paris that served to re-energize the securitarian figuration of "the Muslim" as Europe's premier Other – a racialized condensation of *un*-reason, manifested as religious fundamentalism, fanaticism, and terrorism – the abrupt outbreak in January 2016 of a moral panic over multiple sexual assaults during the New Year's Eve festivities in Köln/Cologne promptly delivered up yet another instantiation of the ostensible Muslim Problem. Allegedly perpetrated by unruly mobs of young men, casually characterized as being "of North African or Middle Eastern appearance", the Cologne events reinvigorated the racialization of "Muslim" identity. In the face of these offences, the racialization of "Muslims"/"Arabs" (eagerly depicted as including recently arrived asylum-seekers) could now be represented in terms of unsavoury cultural differences that had to be excoriated and criminalized as transparently inimical to "European" norms of civility and moral decency. Revealingly, the eminent philosopher and cultural critic – and avowed ("leftist") Eurocentric[9] – Slavoj Žižek seized upon the refugee crisis as an occasion to unabashedly celebrate Europe, demanding: "Isn't the very fact that millions want to go to Europe proof that people still see something in Europe?" (2016b). Confronting the Cologne events, then, Žižek unsurprisingly adopted the condescending moralistic standpoint of European (white) supremacism: "Immigrant refugees", as he designated them,

> … are well aware that what they are doing is foreign to our predominant culture, but they are doing it precisely to wound our sensitivies. The task is to change this stance of envy and revengeful aggressiveness … they have to be educated (by others and by themselves) into their freedom. (2016a)

Making his commitment to a culturalist Europeanism still more emphatic, Žižek goes further:

> Europe needs to be open to refugees, but we have to be clear they are in our culture. Certain ethical limits … are non-negotiable. We should be more assertive toward our values … . Europe means something noble – human rights, welfare state, social programs for the poor. All of this is embodied in enlightenment of the European legacy. (2016b)

Discussing the wider question of the refugee "crisis", and exuding his characteristic flair for unapologetic authoritarianism, Žižek elsewhere contends:

> Europe should organize itself and impose clear rules and regulations. State control of the stream of refugees should be enforced through a vast administrative network encompassing all of the European Union … . Refugees should be

reassured of their safety, but it should also be made clear to them that they have to accept the area of living allocated to them by European authorities, plus they have to respect the laws and social norms of European states ... . Yes, such a set of rules privileges the Western European way of life, but it is a price for European hospitality. These rules should be clearly stated and enforced, by repressive measures (against foreign fundamentalists as well as against our own anti-immigrant racists) if necessary. (2015)

Replete with the obligatory critiques of the immanence of refugees to the havoc wrought by global capitalism and perfunctory gestures against neocolonialism as well as anti-immigrant racists, Žižek goes further still, and even transposes his advocacy of "repressive means" into a call for "military and economic interventions" (2015). More specifically, he has proposed the European "militarization" of migration management in the war-stricken sites from which refugees flee, in order to "organize airlifts and regulate immigration" in places such as Syria and Libya (2016b). That is to say, Žižek unreservedly advocates a militarist Eurocentrism with regard to the challenge of imposing an unprecedented control of the borders of "Europe" and all those who may become the presumptive beneficiaries of Europe's "hospitality". Notably, Žižek's insistence upon a recognition of the agency of the migrant–refugee Other merely becomes an occasion for projecting the migrant–refugee's subjectivity as an unsavoury and misguided one: "not just escaping from their war-torn homelands; they are also possessed by a certain dream ... offering themselves to become cheap precarious workforce, in many cases at the expense of local workers, who react to this threat by joining anti-immigrant political parties" (2015). Thus, he implies that it is the migrants and refugees themselves who are the real cause of such European excesses as far-right anti-immigrant racism, and consequently contends that refugees must be held to account for their own "responsibility in the crisis" (2016b).

Deemed to be dangerously deficient in terms of "European values", the presumptively culturally alien, newly arrived and unassimilated (and by implication, unassimilable) Muslim/Arab asylum-seekers were now re-figured, in the aftermath of the Cologne events, as probable sexual predators and potential rapists, suspected of dangerous and violent types of putatively "cultural" tendencies towards flagrant misogyny and "uncivilized" forms of deviancy and perversity. Thus, a menace previously fashioned as the rather more rarefied threat of terrorism could now be dramatically expanded to encompass virtually all Muslim men as potential criminals. Predictably, this anti-Muslim moral panic was laced with racial hysteria: images proliferated in the mass media in Germany of white women's bodies stained or otherwise graphically violated by black or brown hands (Lalami 2016).

Even the iconic innocent – Aylan Kurdi, the three-year-old Syrian refugee boy found dead on the Turkish shores of the Aegean Sea, whose image had catalysed an outpouring of sympathy and compassion – was now, just a few months later, callously denigrated in a cartoon published by the notoriously anti-Muslim French satirical magazine *Charlie Hebdo*. Under the titular heading "Migrants", the drawing depicts two lascivious pig-like (or ape-like) men with lolling tongues and out-stretched groping hands, chasing two women. An insert at the top the cartoon duplicates the famous image of Kurdi, laying face-down on the beach, drowned. The top of the page poses the purportedly comical riddle: "What would little Aylan have become if he had grown up?"; the answer appears at the bottom of the page: "Ass fondler in Germany". Plainly, the cynical and derisive insinuation was that even this helpless and harmless victim, by sheer dint of the barbaric moral deficiencies of his despised Muslim heritage, could only have inevitably become a vicious perpetrator, one more predatory miscreant, like all the rest of the Muslim migrant men alleged to have perpetrated the sexual assaults in Cologne. This abject Aylan, notably, was not the newly arrived "foreigner" – no longer the victimized refugee deserving of rescue by the self-styled humanitarian border regime (Andersson 2017; Garelli and Tazzioli 2017, forthcoming; Heller and Pezzani 2017; Pallister-Wilkins 2015; Tazzioli 2015a, 2015b) – but instead a menacing projection into the future: his moral turpitude was that of the purportedly irredeemable foreignness attributed to opportunistic "migrants" and the unassimilable "second generation", the incorrigible racialized minority, the presumptively oxymoronic European Muslim. Thus, the figure of the refugee – so recently fashioned as an object of European compassion, pity, and protection – was re-fashioned with astounding speed, first as the potential terrorist who surreptitiously infiltrates the space of Europe, and then as the potential criminal or rapist who corrodes the social and moral fabric of Europe from within.

Most significantly, the controversy around the Cologne events immediately authorized public debates over how recently arrived refugees and migrants could be expeditiously rendered deportable and promptly expelled. The rather selective logic of antiterrorist suspicion that had been mobilized for the purposes of more stringent (external) border enforcement, once confronted within the European interior with the palpable presence of recent arrivals of "Muslim" refugees and migrants, was promptly re-purposed as a considerably more expansive problem of internal law enforcement, emphatically conjoined to arguments for new powers to unceremoniously deport allegedly criminal asylum-seekers. Thus, nebulous and spectral affiliations are invoked to encompass refugees, ("illegal") migrants, smugglers, sexual deviants, religious fundamentalists, criminals, "homegrown" and international terrorists, and "foreign fighters" along an inchoate continuum of suspicion and contempt: the "fake" asylum-seeker therefore re-appears now not only as the actual (duplicitous) economic migrant, but also as the (deviant) rapist whose culture or morals are simply inimical to the "European" way of life, or as the (devious) terrorist who conceals himself among the genuine refugees in order to wreak havoc upon Europe. Above all, migrant and refugee mobilities and subjectivities have instigated for European authorities an epistemic and governmental dilemma regarding an amorphous mob composed simultaneously of people "in need of protection" shadowed by the spectre of predators or enemies against whom Europe itself must be protected. Hence, the "emergency" associated with the uncontrolled arrival of migrants and refugees quickly became not only a matter of border enforcement but also mundane policing, and signalled an incipient crisis not only of the borders of Europe but also of the entire fabric of the European social order.

"Muslims"

Importantly, the racialization of "Muslim" as a category of pronounced non-whiteness is an inherently equivocal one, encompassing a variegated spectrum of gradations of "colour" extending from the vaguely "off-white" through the gamut of "browns" and "blacks" (De Genova 2010a). Thus, "Muslim" operates as a racial condensation that is produced as inherently heterogeneous, while yet inimical to the white (Christian, "European") identity of "the West". Indeed, its racial productivity is predicated on precisely this phenotypic ambiguity: the racial instability of the figure of "the Muslim" is, consequently, always subject to suspicion, commanding antiterrorist surveillance and further investigation in the incessant securitarian police work of uncovering the potential "extremists" who supposedly refuse to be assimilated and are susceptible to "radicalization". In this respect, the European racial order produces and sustains a permanent suspicion and (at least) latent hostility towards "Muslims" in a manner that nonetheless appears to uphold the official "anti-racism" that has become an ideological fixture of post-Holocaust racial Europeanism. This ostensibly race-neutral ideological short-circuit is achieved through the hegemonic demand for "integration" on the parts of migrants and their European-born "second-generation" progeny, racially minoritized as being "of migrant background". As in the larger metaphysics of antiterrorism, the dominant theme has consistently been not an indiscriminate "clash of civilizations" against Islam as such, but rather a persistent and unrelenting impulse to sort and rank "Muslims" as "good" ones or "bad", "integrated" or "communitarian", "friend" or "enemy", "with us" or "against us" (De Genova 2007, 2010a, 2010b, 2017).

Consequently, specifically anti-Muslim formations of far-right racial nativism have abounded (Fekete 2004, 2009), from Anders Breivik's neo-medievalist campaign of mass murder in Norway, to the English Defence League, to Pegida (Patriotische Europäer Gegen die Islamisierung des Abendlandes) in Germany. What is perhaps most significant in these developments, however, is the capacity of these blatantly racist movements to dissimulate their racism with recourse to the contention that their particular grievances and animosity, rather than an indiscriminate antagonism to all people who are deemed to be racially different, are selectively reserved for "Muslims" and the phantasmic menace of "Islamization". The historical specificity of such anti-Muslim racism is clearly distinguished by its enunciation within the now-routinized ideological rubric of the so-called Global War on Terror. Not uncommonly, however, these forms of discrimination are justified through the liberal pretence of secularism. Here, we need only to recall recent campaigns to prohibit the construction of minarets and to aggressively target identifiably Muslim women through bans on various Muslim practices of gendered "modesty", from headscarves to "burkinis". Nonetheless, the complacent demand for "integration" consistently enfolds the Muslim Question within the broader parameters of a cultural politics of "European" identity that is inextricable from the present racial crisis.

Re-articulating "European"-ness through the "migrant crisis"

With this remarkable cross-contamination of divergent discourses of "crisis", we find ourselves in the presence of what Balibar has depicted as an "immigration complex", which induces "a transformation of every social 'problem' into a problem which is regarded as being posed *by the fact of* the presence of 'immigrants' or, at least, as being aggravated by their presence"—regardless of the problem in question (1991, 219–220; emphasis in original). Now, however, the typical and well-worn European immigration complex has been amplified and intensified into a migration–migrant–refugee–border "crisis", through which the figures of migration and refugee mobilities uncannily resonate and ramify with multiple overlapping sociopolitical formations of "emergency" (New Keywords Collective 2016). Most notably, in all of these manifold incarnations of the migrant–refugee "crisis", what is repeatedly reconfigured and reinstated is a more fundamental antagonism between "Europe" (and "Europeans") and the unsettling and invasive (or alternately, corrosive) alterity of diverse figures of putative non-Europeanness: "migrants", "refugees", "asylum-seekers", "foreigners", "minorities", "Muslims", and so on. That such figures tend to be overtly de-racialized and ostensibly race-neutral only amplifies the intensity of their persistent juxtaposition to the figures of "Europe" and "European" identity. Their heterogeneous origins and consequently their inherently diverse and divisive racializations are not immediately apprehensible as a unified racial formation. Nonetheless, the variety of these "minority" subjects in Europe become readily affiliated precisely because they tend to be newly (re-)racialized and subordinated according to such racially equivocal and thus expansive logics. Thus, they always coexist and overlap with overtly racialized and relatively exclusive terms, such as "Blacks" or "Arabs", for instance, while also presenting themselves in more inclusive and capacious terms, such as "Muslims" or "migrants" or indeed, persons "of migrant background". In this regard, anxious securitarian iterations of the Muslim Question are always anchored in a minoritizing discursive continuum that includes the more bluntly and indisputably racial category of Blackness as an inevitable bedrock of its ideological repertoire. Thus, we must begin to take stock of the multiple, inherently inconsistent and contradictory ways in which "European"-ness itself is (re-)articulated precisely as a *racial* formation of postcolonial whiteness (De Genova 2016).

The seemingly disparate or discrepant racialized flashpoints of Europe's multifarious "crisis" – from Lampedusa or Lesvos or Calais, to Paris or Brussels or Nice, to Cologne – have plainly not entailed the sorts of racial crisis instigated or provoked directly by racially self-conscious sociopolitical movements, such the Black Lives Matter struggles over the last few years, much less the Civil Rights and Black Power struggles of the 1960s and early 1970s in the United States and beyond. Obviously, apart from the promising but comparatively small-scale manifestations of organized anti-racist self-assertion, the recent events in the European context do not ordinarily articulate a coherent oppositional politics, if any. Nonetheless, their very existence has an objectively political character inasmuch as they are repeatedly made the object of moral panics and produced as a "problem" that is consistently posed in terms of what a nativist (white) *we* – the nation, "Europe", "the West" – will do with *them*. Thus, the succession of reiterations of a crisis of sovereign control over borders and the governmental impasse provoked by the autonomy of migrant and refugee movements has continuously been reconstructed not merely as an "integration" dilemma or an affront to national (or European) "culture", "values", or "civilization", but also as an outright menace to law and order and, to one degree or another, a security threat that purportedly legitimates a state of emergency. In this respect, these events have represented major disruptions in the "unstable equilibrium" of what Omi and Winant have incisively depicted as "the racial state" and its social order, and have commanded the requisite strategies and tactics of absorption and insulation through which to re-domesticate racial transformations and restabilize the dominant racial politics of the hegemonic sociopolitical order ([1986] 1994, 86–87). Comparable to the L.A. rebellion twenty-five years ago or the Black Lives Matter struggles today, then, but in ways that are still more variegated, convoluted, and equivocal, recent events in Europe signal a veritable racial crisis precisely because they "[intensify and reveal] the ambivalences, fault lines, and polarizations which characterize … racial identities today" (1993, 104–105), and likewise, summon forth tremendous political energies devoted to the re-articulation of their meanings and consequential salience ([1986] 1994, 89–91). This, indeed, is precisely what is at stake when one such as Žižek, hailing from Europe's pathologized Balkan borderland, pronounces, "*We* [Europe] have to be clear *they* are in *our culture* …. We should be more assertive toward *our values* …. Europe means something noble" (2016b; emphases added).

Here, we are reminded that all "Europeans" – those who may pretend to the status of not being "of migrant background" – are certainly *not* equally "European" or "white", nor are they "white" in the same ways. Like the racial formation of whiteness itself, the homogenizing character of a racial formation of "European"-ness (or European whiteness) is precisely devoted to obfuscating and suturing what are otherwise profound and consequential differences and inequalities. The constitutive contradictions and intrinsic antagonisms of Europeanness, in its real heterogeneity, are precisely what the homogenizing racial formation of whiteness serves to superintend and re-code. As with whiteness, so we may posit of "European"-ness: it has historically acquired a spurious semblance of integrity or coherence solely based on its presumptive derision for and subjugation of whatever is produced as *non*-European. Consequently, the production of "Europe" through the refortification of borders has become synonymous with the utter disposability of black and brown lives.

Notes

1. For a global overview of the escalation in migrant deaths, see IOM (2014) and the IOM's "Missing Migrants Project": http://missingmigrants.iom.int.
2. The Schengen Area, the European area free of border controls or passport checks for travellers from the 26 countries that are signatories of the Schengen Accord, includes 22 of the 28 EU member states, plus an additional 4 countries that are not EU members. The Schengen accord pre-dated the European Union, but was incorporated into the EU's Amsterdam Treaty of 1997, with provisions for some member states to opt out.
3. Even in the extended aftermath of the Arab Spring and ongoing civil wars in Syria, Afghanistan, Iraq, and Somalia, alongside political turmoil in Eritrea, in 2012, for example, first-instance "refugee" recognition across all EU member states was only 13.9 per cent, with 73 per cent of all asylum applications rejected outright (European Commission/Eurostat News Release [22 March 2013]: http://epp.eurostat.ec.europa.eu/cache/ITY_PUBLIC/3-22032013-BP/EN.PDF).
4. The most comprehensive database documenting migrant and refugee deaths during attempts to traverse the borders of Europe is 'The Migrants' Files", www.themigrantsfiles.com, a data project coordinated by Journalism++, which estimates the total number of European border deaths at more than 30,000. See also IOM (2014), Spijkerboer and Last (2014), and van Houtum and Boedeltje (2009), cf. IOM's "Missing Migrants Project": http://missingmigrants.iom.int.
5. This was the principal slogan of a protest on 25 April 2015 directed at the European Commission's offices in London, called by the Movement Against Xenophobia and supported by the Stop the War coalition, BARAC UK (Black Activists Rising Against Cuts), and Global Justice Now.
6. Notably, in their six-point platform of demands, the Movement for Black Lives (M4BL), a collective of more than fifty Black-identified organizations in the United States – where racial Blackness is presumptively affiliated with African-American U.S. citizens and tends to be systematically dis-articulated from "immigrants" – has nonetheless explicitly recognized that the criminalization of "immigrants" is disproportionately experienced by those migrants who come to be racialized as "Black". See https://policy.m4bl.org/end-war-on-black-people/.

7. See, in particular, the video call for a UK-wide #Shutdown racism/#Shutdown violence/#Shutdown borders protest on 5 August 2016, posted on the Black Lives Matter-UK Facebook page: https://www.facebook.com/BLMUK/home.
8. "Ferguson" refers to the police murder of African-American Michael Brown on 9 August 2014 in Ferguson, Missouri, a predominantly Black suburb of St. Louis where community outrage erupted repeatedly in both protests and rioting over an extended period (through the first anniversary of the killing in August 2015).
9. For Žižek's defence of Eurocentrism, see Žižek (1998), and remarks in Žižek and Horvat (2013, 56, 179).

Disclosure statement

No potential conflict of interest was reported by the author.

References

Andersson, Ruben. 2014. *Illegality, Inc.: Clandestine Migration and the Business of Bordering Europe*. Berkeley: University of California Press.
Andersson, Ruben. 2017. "Rescued and Caught: The Humanitarian-Security Nexus at Europe's Frontiers." In *The Borders of "Europe": Autonomy of Migration, Tactics of Bordering*, edited by Nicholas De Genova, 64–94. Durham, NC: Duke University Press.
Balibar, Étienne. 1991. "Racism and Crisis." In *Race, Nation, Class: Ambiguous Identities*, edited by Étienne Balibar and Immanuel Wallerstein, 217–227. New York: Verso.
Balibar, Étienne. (1992) 2002. "Is There Such a Thing as European Racism?" In *Politics and the Other Scene*, edited by E. Balibar, 40–55. New York: Verso.
Balibar, Étienne. (1999) 2004. "Droit de Cité or Apartheid?" In *We, the People of Europe? Reflections on Transnational Citizenship*, edited by E. Balibar, 31–50. Princeton, NJ: Princeton University Press.
Balibar, Étienne. 2001. "Outlines of a Topography of Cruelty: Citizenship and Civility in the Era of Global Violence." *Constellations* 8 (1): 15–29.
BBC News. 2016a. "Black Lives Matter Movement 'Needed in UK'." August 5. http://www.bbc.co.uk/news/uk-36982748.
BBC News. 2016b. "Black Lives Matter Protests Stop Cars and Trams Across England." August 5. http://www.bbc.co.uk/news/uk-england-nottinghamshire-36983852.
Campbell, Scott. 2015. "Calais Jungle Migrant Camp 'Set on Fire' after Hundreds Killed in Terror Attacks." *Daily Express*, November 14. http://www.express.co.uk/news/world/619361/.
Chandler, Nahum D. 2013. *Toward an African Future – of the Limit of the World*. London: Living Commons Collective.
Chandler, Nahum D. 2014. *X: The Problem of the Negro as a Problem for Thought*. New York: Fordham University Press.
De Genova, Nicholas. 2007. "The Production of Culprits: From Deportability to Detainability in the Aftermath of 'Homeland Security'." *Citizenship Studies* 11 (5): 421–448.
De Genova, Nicholas. 2010a. "Antiterrorism, Race, and the New Frontier: American Exceptionalism, Imperial Multiculturalism, and the Global Security State." *Identities* 17 (6): 613–640.

De Genova, Nicholas. 2010b. "Migration and Race in Europe: The Trans-Atlantic Metastases of a Post-colonial Cancer." *European Journal of Social Theory* 13 (3): 405–419.

De Genova, Nicholas. 2013. "Spectacles of Migrant 'Illegality': The Scene of Exclusion, the Obscene of Inclusion." *Ethnic and Racial Studies* 36 (7): 1180–1198.

De Genova, Nicholas. 2016. "The European Question: Migration, Race, and Postcoloniality in Europe." *Social Text* 34 (3) (Issue #128): 75–102.

De Genova, Nicholas. 2017. "The Whiteness of Innocence: *Charlie Hebdo* and the Metaphysics of Antiterrorism in Europe." In *After Charlie Hebdo: Terror, Racism, Free Speech*, edited by Gavan Titley, Des Freedman, Gholam Khiabany, and Aurélien Mondon. London: Zed Books.

Essif, Amien. 2015. "How Black Lives Matter Has Spread into a Global Movement to End Racist Policing: The Next Baltimore Could Be Somewhere in Europe." *In These Times*, June 29. http://inthesetimes.com/article/18042/.

Fekete, Liz. 2004. "Anti-Muslim Racism and the European Security State." *Race & Class* 46 (1): 3–29.

Fekete, Liz. 2009. *A Suitable Enemy: Racism, Migration and Islamophobia in Europe*. London: Pluto Press.

Garelli, Glenda, and Martina Tazzioli. 2016. "The EU Hotspot Approach at Lampedusa." openDemocracy. February 26. https://www.opendemocracy.net/can-europe-make-it/glenda-garelli-martina-tazzioli/eu-hotspot-approach-at-lampedusa.

Garelli, Glenda, and Martina Tazzioli. 2017. "Choucha Beyond the Camp: Challenging the Border of Migration Studies." In *The Borders of "Europe": Autonomy of Migration, Tactics of Bordering*, edited by Nicholas De Genova, 165–184. Durham, NC: Duke University Press.

Garelli, Glenda, and Martina Tazzioli. Forthcoming. "The EU Humanitarian War Against Migrant Smugglers at Sea." *Antipode*.

Gilmore, Ruth Wilson. 2007. *Golden Gulag: Prisons, Surplus, Crisis, and Opposition in Globalizing California*. Berkeley: University of California Press.

Gilroy, Paul. 1993. *The Black Atlantic: Modernity and Double Consciousness*. Cambridge, MA: Harvard University Press.

Goldberg, David Theo. 2006. "Racial Europeanization." *Ethnic and Racial Studies* 29 (2): 331–364.

Hall, Stuart, and Les Back. 2009. "At Home and Not at Home: Stuart Hall in Conversation with Les Back." *Cultural Studies* 23 (4): 658–687.

Heller, Charles, and Lorenzo Pezzani. 2017. "Liquid Traces: Investigating the Deaths of Migrants at the EU's Maritime Frontier." In *The Borders of "Europe": Autonomy of Migration, Tactics of Bordering*, edited by Nicholas De Genova, 95–119. Durham, NC: Duke University Press.

IOM (International Organization of Migration). 2014. *Fatal Journeys: Tracking Lives Lost During Migration*. Tara Brian and Frank Laczko, eds. Geneva: IOM. https://publications.iom.int/system/files/pdf/fataljourneys_countingtheuncounted.pdf.

Jansen, Yolande, Robin Celikates, and Joost de Bloois, eds. 2015. *The Irregularization of Migration in Contemporary Europe: Detention, Deportation, Drowning*. London: Rowman & Littlefield.

Karakayali, Serhat, and Enrica Rigo. 2010. "Mapping the European Space of Circulation." In *The Deportation Regime: Sovereignty, Space, and the Freedom of Movement*, edited by Nicholas De Genova and Nathalie Peutz, 123–144. Durham, NC: Duke University Press.

Lalami, Laila. 2016. "Who Is to Blame for the Cologne Sex Attacks?" *The Nation*, March 10. www.thenation.com/article/who-is-to-blame-for-the-cologne-sex-attacks/.

Lyman, Rick. 2015. "Regulating Flow of Refugees Gains Urgency in Greece and Rest of Europe." *New York Times,* November 25. http://www.nytimes.com/2015/11/26/world/europe/regulating-flow-of-refugees-gains-urgency-in-greece-and-rest-of-europe.html?emc=edit_th_20151126&nl=todaysheadlines&nlid=44765954.

Mbembe, Achille. 2017. *Critique of Black Reason.* Durham, NC: Duke University Press.

New Keywords Collective. 2016. "Europe/Crisis: New Keywords of 'the Crisis' in and of 'Europe'." *Near Futures Online.* New York: Zone Books. http://nearfuturesonline.org/europecrisis-new-keywords.

Omi, Michael, and Howard Winant. (1986) 1994. *Racial Formation in the United States: From the 1960s to the 1990s.* 2nd ed. New York: Routledge.

Omi, Michael, and Howard Winant. 1993. "The Los Angeles 'Race Riot' and Contemporary U.S. Politics." In *Reading Rodney King, Reading Urban Uprising,* edited by Robert Gooding-Williams, 97–114. New York: Routledge.

Pallister-Wilkins, Polly. 2015. "The Humanitarian Politics of European Border Policing: Frontex and Border Police in Evros." *International Political Sociology* 9: 53–69.

Scheel, Stephan. 2017. "'The Secret Is to Look Good on Paper': Appropriating Mobility Within and Against a Machine of Illegalization." In *The Borders of "Europe": Autonomy of Migration, Tactics of Bordering,* edited by Nicholas De Genova, 37–63. Durham, NC: Duke University Press.

Sciurba, Alessandra. 2016. "Hotspot System as a New Device of Clandestinisation: View from Sicily." openDemocracy. February 25. https://www.opendemocracy.net/can-europe-make-it/alessandra-sciurba/hotspot-system-as-new-device-of-clandestinisation-view-from-si.

Spijkerboer, Thomas, and Tamara Last. 2014. "Tracking Deaths in the Mediterranean." In *Fatal Journeys: Tracking Lives Lost During Migration,* edited by Tara Brian and Frank Laczko, 85–106. Geneva: International Organization for Migration.

Tazzioli, Martina. 2015a. "The Desultory Politics of Mobility and the Humanitarian-Military Border in the Mediterranean: Mare Nostrum Beyond the Sea." *REMHU: Revista Interdisciplinar da Mobilidade Humana* 23 (44). http://www.scielo.br/scielo.php?pid=S1980-85852015000100061&script=sci_arttext&tlng=es.

Tazzioli, Martina. 2015b. "The Politics of Counting and the Scene of Rescue: Border Deaths in the Mediterranean." *Radical Philosophy* 192. www.radicalphilosophy.com/commentary/the-politics-of-counting-and-the-scene-of-rescue.

van Houtum, Henk. 2010. "Human Blacklisting: The Global Apartheid of the EU's External Border Regime." *Environment and Planning D: Society and Space* 28 (6): 957–976.

van Houtum, Henk, and Frederk Boedeltje. 2009. "Europe's Shame: Death at the Borders of the EU." *Antipode* 41 (2): 226–230.

Žižek, Slavoj. 1998. "A Leftist Plea for 'Eurocentrism'." *Critical Inquiry* 24 (4): 988–1009.

Žižek, Slavoj. 2015. "We Can't Address the EU Refugee Crisis Without Confronting Global Capitalism." *In These Times.* September 9. http://inthesetimes.com/article/18385.

Žižek, Slavoj. 2016a. "The Cologne Attacks Were an Obscene Version of Carnival." *New Statesman,* January 13. http://www.newstatesman.com/world/europe/2016/01/slavoj-zizek-cologne-attacks.

Žižek, Slavoj. 2016b. "'EU Must Militarize Chaotic Immigration, Identify States Behind Middle East Crisis' – Zizek to RT." Interview with RT News. April 22. https://www.rt.com/news/340562-eu-refugee-policy-chaos-militarization/.

Žižek, Slavoj, and Srećko Horvat. 2013. *What Does Europe Want? The Union and Its Discontents.* London: Istrosbooks.

The hieroglyphics of the border: racial stigma in neoliberal Europe

Imogen Tyler ⓘ

ABSTRACT

In the summer of 2015, 1.5 million refugees arrived at Europe's borders. This article examines how and why this humanitarian crisis was transformed into a "racist crisis". It begins by recounting a highly publicized event in the Czech Republic which saw police forcibly removing hundreds of people from trains at midnight in the border town of Břeclav, before inking numbers on their arms and transporting them to detention centres. Thinking with this scene, the article develops the conceptual framework of "racial stigma" to capture some of the multiple practices that characterize border regimes in contemporary Europe. Racism, it argues, is the stigma machine of sovereign power in neoliberal Europe. The article concludes with some reflections on how Europe's current "racist crisis" reanimates both historical spectres of race and spectral geographies of racism.

Swim harder, darkie. See whether you can reach Europe. (in Čulík 2015)

During 2015, an unprecedented 1.3 million people applied for asylum in the 28 member states of the European Union (EU), Norway and Switzerland. This was "nearly double the previous high-water mark of approximately 700,000 [asylum] applications in 1992, after the fall of the Iron Curtain and the collapse of the Soviet Union" (Connor 2016). Those seeking protection in Europe were largely fleeing wars, conflicts and political oppression in Syria (over 50 per cent), Iraq, Afghanistan and Eritrea. Some arrived via Balkan land routes, but these borders were soon blocked and the vast majority made treacherous Mediterranean Sea-crossings (from Turkey and Libya). An estimated 3,771 people drowned in the Mediterranean in 2015 alone and in the summer of 2015, newspapers and news websites across the world were filled with photographs of drowned children and people desperately paddling towards shore on overloaded dinghies. In response to the growing humanitarian crisis at Europe's border, the German Office for

Migration and Refugees announced on the social media site Twitter on 25 August 2015 that they were "no longer enforcing #Dublin procedures for Syrian citizens".[1] What this meant for Syrian refugees on the ground was that if they could navigate a route to Germany, they would be guaranteed at least temporary leave to remain. This triggered "a million-man march through Europe" as hundreds of thousands of people caught in dire conditions at camps and transit zones across Europe's southern borders made their way north by foot, car, bus and train (Foster 2016). It was amidst this intensifying human and political drama that shortly after midnight on 1 September 2015, two trains drew to a halt in Břeclav, a town in the Czech Republic, close to the border with Austria and Slovakia.

Scene one: Břeclav railway station, Czech Republic

At midnight on 1 September 2015, a squad of Czech Alien Police boarded two trains in Břeclav and forcibly removed 214 people (115 men, 38 women and 61 children). The first train had arrived from Vienna shortly before midnight and the second shortly after midnight from Budapest, both bound for Germany. Czech government officials described the passengers removed from these two trains as "214 illegal migrants". The vast majority, over 90 per cent, were refugees from Syria and were just hours away from their German destination when the trains were intercepted by police, who moved through carriages checking people's documents. After escorting people from the trains, some in handcuffs, the police assembled people on the platforms and proceeded to use indelible pens to ink numbers on their arms and wrists. Kateřina Rendlová, a spokeswoman for the Czech Alien Police, stated that the inking of refugees was a means of keeping a record of family members: "We also write the code of the train they have arrived on so that we know which country we should return them to within the readmission system", adding, "we used to put the numbers on a piece of paper but they kept throwing them away" (Flemr 2015). The refugees were then packed onto buses destined for temporary camps in local school gymnasiums in south Moravia, where officials said they would be processed, before being transferred to remote rural detention centres.

Events at Břeclav were captured by the Czech News Agency photojournalist, Igor Zehl, and were posted on the associated press website. One photograph in particular caught the attention of international news editors: an image of a small child sitting on his mother's lap, his face folded into her body, while a Czech policewoman wearing blue plastic gloves wrote numbers on his arm (Figure 1). This image was printed in newspapers, published on news websites and shared across social media platforms around the world, provoking an international outcry from human rights organizations for the disturbing associations it elicited with the badging and tattooing of

Figure 1. Břeclav, South Moravia, Czech Republic, 1 September 2015. Source: Igor Zehl/ Associated Press © CTK / Alamy Stock Photo, copyright permission obtained.

Jews during the Second World War. As Ruth Dureghello, a Jewish community president in Rome, explained:

> It is an image we cannot bear, which recalls to mind the procedure at the entrance of Nazi extermination camps, when millions of men, women and children were marked with a number, like animals, and they were sent to die. (AFP & JTA 2015)

These allusions to the Nazi holocaust were not lost on far-right activists. Adam Bartoš, the leader of the fascistic Czech party the National Democracy Movement, used Facebook to call for the Břeclav "intruders" to "be concentrated in Theresienstadt" (2015a).[2] These views, as Jan Čulík (2017) has extensively detailed, were symptomatic of rising populist anti-refugee sentiments in the Czech public sphere. Indeed, it was not extremist minorities but rather the Czech President, Milos Zeman, who was the "major catalyst" for the crafting of "mendacious anti-refugee narrative[s]" (Čulík 2017). Zeman warned the Czech public that refugees were "Muslim invaders" who might bring infectious diseases into the nation and could harbour "sleeper cells" of Islamic terrorists (Schultheis 2015). The fear this generated was apparent in local responses to the detention of refugees in Břeclav. On 8 September, 350 people turned up to a meeting convened by the police, the Mayor and representatives from the Czech Government Ministry of the Interior to reassure the local population. Officials offered reassurances that refugees would be segregated from any contact with local people. "The conversation", reported a local journalist, "was refined and quiet. Only occasionally did the audience shout out statements such as *'It's too late. Europe has turned black'*" (Hrabal 2015, my translation, my emphasis).

Introduction

This article unfolds from Břeclav, "digging into" this scene in order to better understand "the rush of past racial 'debris'" it provoked (Amin 2010, 3, 6). Historical figures of "race" and latent forms of "race thinking" haunt Europe. Indeed, racism draws its "narrative energies" from existing grids of associations, from "semantic and iconic folds" that are deeply etched in the collective memories of people and places (Spillers 2003, 210). In this article, I explore how different genealogies of racism converged in responses to the "refugee crisis" as "migrants became a focus point" for public concerns "about European values and their crisis" (Gagyi et al. 2016). In what follows, I first briefly outline the political and economic context in which the Czech response to the "refugee crisis" emerged, and the histories of racism in the region which enabled this humanitarian crisis to be recast as a "racial crisis". I then consider the ways in which responses to the inking of refugees at Břeclav gave rise to "epidemics of racial stigma" in the wider context of news and social media responses. The article then examines the abject conditions endured by refugees in Czech immigration detention centres. It argues that the stigmatization of refugees (both literally and symbolically) legitimates illegal practices of dehumanization and degradation in detention. The article concludes with some reflections on how the "refugee crisis" animates historical spectres of racism. The afterword invites the reader to confront these ghosts by returning once more to Břeclav train station. The main argument of this article is that racism is a primary technology of statecraft in contemporary Europe. Whether performed with razor wire or crafted through words, borders are "racial assemblages" through which humanity is classified and disciplined into "humans, not-quite-humans, and nonhumans" (Weheliye 2014, 8). Racism is not only an accessory of border control; rather, in a more fundamental and material sense, *racism makes borders*.

Context: the Czech Republic and the Visegrád states

To begin, it is necessary to provide some context for those unfamiliar with the political situation in Eastern Europe. The Czech Republic is a nation of 10.5 million which joined the EU in 2004 as part of a group of former communist states, Hungary, Poland and Slovakia, which are known collectively as the Visegrád group. From the early 1990s, the Visegrád states were *transitioned* from Soviet-style command economies to neoliberal market economies.

This process involved the implementation of the 1993 Copenhagen criteria, a policy package involving rapid privatization of state-owned infrastructure and assets and the liberalization of labour and financial markets (Hamm, King, and Stuckler 2012). While the availability of cheap credit initially cushioned the impact of neoliberal reforms, this "shock treatment" injected economic inequality into the region: wage levels collapsed, workers' rights and welfare provisions were eroded, public services and infrastructures privatized (Blanden 2016). As a consequence, and particularly in the wake of the 2008 North Atlantic Financial crisis, there has been public disillusionment across the Visegrád states with the "so-called 'freedom' and capitalism" promised by EU membership (Biray 2015). This disenchantment has seen an electoral shift away from "democratic parties which embraced neoliberalism and austerity" to nationalist right-wing parties (Blanden 2016).

As Jodi Dean argues, the inequalities and insecurities introduced by "globalized neoliberal capitalism" require the simultaneous crafting of "racist, nationalist ethnocentrism" (Dean 2012, 40). On cue, as the humanitarian crisis at Europe's borders deepened, Visegrád politicians harnessed the animosities generated by growing economic inequalities in the region to nationalist fantasies of "ethnic security" through "border security". As Zeman put in his 2015 Christmas address to the nation: "I am profoundly convinced that we are facing an organized invasion and not a spontaneous movement of refugees". Visegrád politicians began to craft a geopolitical role for the region as a buffer zone against which (Western) Europe could be protected against this "incursion". Indeed, 2015 saw a rush of fence-building on Eastern borders, the opening of new camps to detain migrants, the formation by neo-Nazis of "human walls" against refugees on state borders and the formation of armed citizen militia groups, such as Hungary's state-funded "border hunters" and a 2,500 strong Czech vigilante border militia.

In the Czech Republic, a populist narrative emerged which, animating histories of German and Communist occupation, imagined the Czech people in an existential struggle against invading "foreign hordes". This struggle was explicitly framed as a "race war". For example, a news headline on 3 September 2015 quoted Czech Sociologist, Petr Hampl, stating, "We have the right to deal with the refugees as though they were aggressors. The traitors of the Czech nation are helping them to exterminate us like the whites have exterminated the Red Indians" (Čulík 2017). Explicit in these kinds of racial narratives was the idea that liberal Western European political leaders failed to understand the "genocidal" consequences of granting refuge to Middle Eastern, African and/or Muslim refugees. For example, an editorial in the Czech broadsheet newspaper Lidové Noviny, penned by "expert ethnologist" Mnislav Zelený-Atapana and titled, "Is a genocide against whites next for Europe?", argued that: "Mrs Merkel and those like her are basically undertaking an artificial mixing of the races in which the white race will be gradually liquidated and we Europeans will become black or brown. This is a genocide against white people" (Zelený-Atapana 2016). These ethnonationalist sentiments spilled onto the streets: On 12 September 2015, thousands gathered in Prague to protest against refugee arrivals, one of many such demonstrations across the country and wider region that year. Video footage of this protest captures a carnival atmosphere with young people, and families with children, carrying Czech flags and holding up banners carrying the demands, "Send them back!" and "Protect the borders". Many wore T-Shirts and face paint adorned with anti-Islamic and anti-refugee slogans, and crowds chanted in unison "Fuck Off, Islam".

It is important to note that Visegrád states are transition rather than destination countries for refugees. For example, in 2015 the Czech Republic granted refugee protection to a mere 71 people, out of a total of only 1,525 asylum applications. Indeed, these are states that habitually record negative net migration rates, as young people seeking higher wages migrate West. National policies in the region are designed to deter refugees and migrant workers, despite growing labour shortages. The small numbers of refugees straying onto Czech territory in the summer of 2015 were seeking only to cross the border. In practical terms, refugees and migrants are unlikely to be able to speak Czech or to have family, friends or other contacts to induce them to remain. What this tells us is that the inking and detention of the refugees at Břeclav were *orchestrated political theatre*. The refusal to let refugees continue unmolested on their journeys was an opportunity to demonstrate control over national borders. In particular, the timing of the detention of the refugees at Břeclav was designed to add weight to a Visegrád-wide negotiating position on a proposed EU quota system that would require states to accept an agreed number of Syrian refugees. A matter of hours after the detention of refugees at Břeclav, the Czech Interior Minister stated to journalists that he was interested in negotiating a "simplified procedure" with Berlin, which might allow refugees to travel unmolested across the Czech territory on the understanding that any quota scheme would be "unacceptable to the Czech government" (2015b).

Neighbouring Hungary, which under the leadership of *Viktor Orbán* has led the war against refugees in the region, had considerably more arrivals than the Czech Republic in 2015. On 2 October 2016, the Hungarian Government held a referendum on the EU quota system to share "the burden" of Syrian refugee settlement.[3] What was most significant about this referendum was the "gigantic wave of racist state propaganda" that preceded it, which ranged "from giant billboards to new elementary school textbooks, from the internet to hundreds of thousands of personal phone calls civil servants were forced to make to mobilize for the 'no' vote" (Tamás 2016). This campaign "cost Hungarian taxpayers the equivalent of over $18 million – or approximately $13,500 per asylum seeker Hungary has been asked to take"

(Gall 2016). It also marked state-funded racism on a scale not witnessed in Europe since the Nazi propaganda of the 1930s and 1940s. This was, in short, an eruption of state racism which liberal democracies further West had long sought "to freeze in the past" (Lentin 2016).

Genealogies of racism in Europe

As Magdalena Nowicka argues, "Eastern Europe remains a blind spot in theorizing racism in Europe" (Nowicka 2017). Under communist rule, while racism was widely *practiced* against racialized minorities, notably the Roma, *racism didn't officially exist.* Furthermore, even though the worst atrocities of the Second World War took place on Nazi-occupied Central and Eastern European soil (often with the collaboration of local populations), there was no acknowledgement of historical state racisms. Even while the material remnants of a more multicultural past were "hidden in plain sight", for example in formerly Jewish neighbourhoods and empty Synagogues, neither the genocides that took place during the Nazi occupation, nor the racial classification of Eastern Europeans as "Slavs", nor the expulsion of German-speaking citizens after the war, was understood through the lens of racism.[4] While the absence of racial genocide from official histories of Eastern European states has been partially revised since the fall of "the Iron Curtain", this process has been complicated by the ways in which ethnic forms of nationalism became associated with freedom from communist totalitarianism. Furthermore, it is not only that state racism has been historically repressed, but that racism per se as a topic of debate and concern continues to be marginalized within the Visegrád public sphere, including academic scholarship. As Nowicka notes in the Polish context, "the popular opinion, common also among Polish scholars [is] that 'the racial problem has never existed in Poland'" (Nowicka 2017, 4). What is now faced is a situation in which racism has emerged "starkly into the open", but is imagined as a "new" problem which originates from "outside" (Fella 2013, 212). In short, racism is imagined as a problem imported from the West. As Zelený-Atapana puts it:

> They started in the distant past colonialist division of the world and after WWII began to reap the rotten fruit as they opened borders to people of former colonies. We, however, not participate in [colonialism] and therefore we have no moral obligation to accept refugees. (Zelený-Atapana 2016)

It is important to note also that "race" is still popularly understood in Eastern Europe through the lens of scientific racism (Nowicka 2017). This was evident in "expert" responses to "the refugee crisis", where racist views about refugees were expressed not only in terms of religious and cultural differences (for example as Islamophobia), but also in terms of "biological differences". The persistence of these "older" forms of race thinking trouble liberal understandings of "European racism", which have been theorized almost exclusively from the perspective of "the West".

In Western Europe, "scientific" theories of race have been publicly discredited since the Second World War and there has been official acknowledgment of state racism through the memorialization of (some) past genocides, albeit primarily Nazi-era atrocities that took place on European soil. However, this commemoration of "racist crimes" occludes "the foundational relationship between the liberal political project and the racial-colonial domination within and despite which it developed" (Lentin 2017). Furthermore, as Lentin (2016) argues, if "real racism" is a thing of the past, the endurance of racism is imagined, and legislated against in Western Europe, as the aberrant behaviour of deviant individual racists. In the process, actually existing forms of institutional and state racism, including the ongoing exclusion of racialized citizens from the full rights and protections of citizenship, are occluded.

The convergence of post-communist and liberal regimes of racism in governmental responses to the "refugee crisis" was frequently imagined in liberal Western European commentary as a conflict between "backward" Eastern European racism and the "superior moral stance of humanitarianism" (Gagyi et al. 2016). By "freezing" racism geographically in the East, state racism against refugees and other racialized minorities was *orientalized* as a symptom of underdevelopment, a sign of the distance "they" must travel "to become liberal, humanitarian and modern Europeans" (Gagyi et al. 2016). This article does not seek to contribute to the stigmatization of Eastern Europe as "more racist" than "the West", or diminish the central role of Western European powers in enabling deaths at the borders. It is, however, interested in what we might learn from the conjunction of these different genealogies of racism. Not least, in terms of what these different registers of racism might teach us about the dramatic blossoming of neofascist politics in Western Europe in the same period. It is not only right-wing Visegrád politicians who have crafted and mobilized populist racisms as a means to make political capital "at home": This was evident in the UK Brexit campaign in 2016, where the two key themes of the leave campaign, namely "that immigration is unravelling" the nation and "anything foreign, except investment, is abhorrent" not only granted "a fillip to popular racism" but allowed "fully fledged state racism" to emerge (Sivanandan 2016). Indeed, while Hungary undertook a state-sponsored propaganda campaign against migrants in October 2016, the far-right United Kingdom Independence party used almost identical tactics and messages in its campaign to leave the EU. One of the most notorious posters in this campaign, titled "Breaking Point", and subtitled "We must break free of the EU and take back control of our borders", employed a photograph of refugees crossing the Croatia–Slovenia border in 2015 as "evidence" that "white" Europe was being "invaded" by brown migrants.

Penal stigma

> people no more fasten the stigma of race upon themselves than cattle sear the brand into their own flesh. (Fields and Fields 2014 , 102)

This article emerges out of a larger research project which draws on the long penal history of stigma, including material practices of penal tattooing, branding and badging and contemporary forms of symbolic violence, to reconceptualize stigma as a form of political power. Penal practices of marking the body are not only historically familiar forms of dehumanization, but also describe the original meaning of the word stigma. "Stigma" (στίγμα) was a common Greek noun meaning "a mark, dot, puncture", or "a sign", from the verb στίζω ("to puncture"). In Ancient Greece, and in the Roman Empire, the word stigma was used to denote marks on the skin made by tattooing, which then, as now, involved the use of needles and ink. A stigma was a tattoo acquired as a punishment. To be stigmatized was to have a crime written into your flesh. Common stigmas included "Thief!" or "Stop me, I'm a runaway", tattooed across the face. A stigma might also record a specific sentence, such as deportation from the city–state for a period of forced exile and a sentence to a labour camp (Jones 1987; Gustafson 2000). These humiliating penalties were reserved for non-citizens, slaves and other resident aliens. Indeed, stigmatization was sometimes employed en masse to generate new sources of slave labour for the vast economies and infrastructures of Empire through the tattooing of captured enemy soldiers during border skirmishes and expropriation of enemy territory. As an ink tattoo was almost impossible to remove and often difficult to conceal, being stigmatized curtailed your mobility, making both everyday movements through public spaces and journeys across borders treacherous.

The word stigma retains traces of this original meaning. *The Oxford English Dictionary* defines stigma as "a sign of severe censure or condemnation … *impressed* on a person" (OED 2014, my emphasis). However, in contemporary usage, stigma is generally understood as the state of "disgrace itself", rather than the *violent acts* of inscription, badging, marking or tattooing that this penal genealogy suggests (Goffman 1987, 11). Since the mid-twentieth century, we have become accustomed to thinking about stigma as a problem of social norms, which can be challenged and alleviated through compassion and education. As I detail at length in forthcoming work, this modern usage erases continuities between ancient and contemporary practices of penal stigmatization. In actuality, penal practices of stigmatization continued to be deployed over many centuries by European powers as terrorizing governmental technologies, from colonial practices of badging, tattooing and branding subjected populations overseas, through to the badging of the poor "at home". In uncoupling the meaning of stigma from this penal history, what we lose sight of is *stigmacraft*; the mechanisms through which stigma is produced, the processes through which it becomes attached to bodies, by whom and for what purpose. Holding to a reading of stigma as a material practice of dehumanization is also suggestive of how and why the penal tattoo became intertwined with the modern history of racism. As Stuart Hall argues, *race is a badge*, a political practice of classification which is inscribed in the body (Hall 1997). This history of racial stigma can be illustrated through a few brief but resonant twentieth-century historical examples.

The badge of race

German South–West Africa, modern-day Namibia, was a colony of the German Empire from 1884 until 1915. In areas under German control, all Africans over the age of 8 had to wear metal passes around their necks, which were embossed with the imperial crown, the magisterial district and a number. As in Ancient Greece, this badging was a form of stigmatization that both humiliated colonial subjects, and allowed colonialists better control over the slave labour force. When people resisted this badging, for example by discarding their tags during escape attempts, a system of ink tattooing was proposed (Olusoga and Erichsen 2010; Schaller 2013). Uprisings by the Herero against the colonial administration led in 1904 to the adoption of an extermination policy against the Herero and Nama people in the region. What followed was described by the then commander of German forces in South West Africa, Colonial General Lothar von Trotha, as "a racial war" (Bridgeman and Worley 2004, 27). By 1906, the German colonists had murdered 65,000 Herero people out of a total population of 80,000. Those who surrendered were branded with the letters "GH", for "Gefangene Herero" (imprisoned Herero), before being dispersed as slave labour on the farms of German settlers (Bridgeman and Worley 2004, 30). Alongside the use of penal tattoos, this genocide saw the development of concentration camps in the region and the arrival of German scientists to conduct genetic experiments on the population to evidence the emerging "racial sciences".

These colonial applications of penal stigma as "race branding" (Sarkin-Hughes 2010, 27) were developed when, as Frantz Fanon puts it, "Nazism transformed the whole of Europe into a veritable colony" (Fanon 2005, 27). The establishment and expansion of the Nazi Empire in Eastern Europe involved the creation of a vast, bureaucratic stigma machine for the classification of "racial enemies" (i.e. Jews, Gypsies and Slavs), "asocial" elements (i.e. the "work-shy", criminals, sexual deviants) and "useless eaters" (disabled people and "the mentally ill"). The identification and classification of these "aliens to the community" ("Gemeinschaftsfremde") and "pests harmful to the nation" ("Volksschädlinge") was grounded in the racist practices of penal stigma developed in the German colonies. This included SS

Stormtroopers branding people with swastikas as a terrorising punishment (Gedye 1939, 503), and the introduction of laws forcing Jews to wear distinguishing badges, most often a yellow star, in public places.[5] At labour and extermination camps, an elaborate system of badging was developed to distinguish different classes of prisoners. Those designated for slave labour at camps, rather than immediate death, were often stamped with ink signs on their forehead, and labour numbers were also frequently inked on the skin. At the Auschwitz complex, stigmatization extended to the ink tattooing of serial numbers upon the arms of Jewish inmates selected for work. The Czech holocaust survivor Ruth Elias recalls that although she had survived near-starvation in the Jewish ghetto of Theresienstadt, it was only when she lined up to be tattooed at Auschwitz that she understood that she was no longer considered a human being: "The numbers on our forearms marked our depersonalization" (Elias 1999, 109–110).

This penal genealogy teaches us that stigma, like "race", does not begin with a body "but with what that body was made to mean via the powerful grammars of capture" (Spillers 2003, 14). Furthermore, it reveals how "the badge of race" has long been employed as an othering practice, a *colouring device*, to dehumanize slaves, colonial subjects, non-citizens, refugees and migrants (Hall 1997). While stigma is not always racializing, racism is its pre-eminent form. Stigma as racism is a "hieroglyphics of the flesh" (Spillers 2003, 21). This genealogy of penal stigma haunts Břeclav.

Transnational racist responses to Břeclav

The British right-wing tabloid newspaper, *The Daily Mail*, hosts the most visited news website in the world, the *MailOnline*, which attracts a daily international readership of 12 million people. On September 2, the *MailOnline* featured Zehl's photograph of the child being inked by the Czech police in a news story titled "Fury as Czech police write numbers on arms of migrants 'like concentration camp prisoners'". This story attracted 4000 readers' comments, extending over 23 pages, with comments from readers in the UK, Ireland, USA, Australia, New Zealand, Canada, Spain and Singapore. Some readers responded – as invited by the use of scare quotes around "concentration camp" in the title – with outrage at the suggestion of any analogy between the inking of refugees hands and concentration camp regimes, insisting, for example, that, "it's no different than having your hand stamped as you enter a night club". Many more suggested that more penal forms of stigmatization should be used to manage refugees at Europe's borders.

They should write the id numbers on the forehead instead!

You could inject them with an RFID tag, at least you could track them!

Rubber stamp their foreheads instead!

They should be made to wear a yellow badge so that members of the public know who they are and know to stay well away from them.

With the numbers involved and the desperate deceit used by many of these people tattoos would be a more effective option. if they behave well give them a yellow star to wear too

Pigs ears are clipped and tagged #justsaying

Just because the J E W S don't like it we must comply!

Dig pits and machine gun the lot of them – Cheaper to use gas.

Well done Czech police … I'd brand them like cattle with a massive M on their foreheads!

Good idea – tattoo everyone with a barcode – easier to track

They should all be fingerprinted, DNA samples taken and photographed before tattooing i11eg@1 on their fore head [sic]

While it is easy to dismiss or disregard these kinds of discussion threads, they are important archives of everyday stigmacraft in contemporary media cultures. Our task, as Les Back suggests, is to "develop a radical attentiveness" to racist speech, to understand the "resonance and reach" of racist sentiments and conversations (Back 2008). The imagined anonymity of Internet forums, and devices such as the use of fabricated user names, offer users a license to break social taboos on racist speech, an opportunity to craft racism in extreme and virulent ways. Reading this discussion thread, it is evident there is enjoyment in provoking outrage, an intense pleasure in *being racist* with others in a community setting and by evading the censorship of forum moderators by, for example, placing spaces between letters in words like "J E W S". While some of the readers respond negatively to racist comments, for the majority the opportunity to be racist motivates their participation. As Kimberlé Crenshaw notes, "racism helps to create an illusion of unity through the oppositional force of a symbolic 'other'. The establishment of an Other creates a bond, a burgeoning common identity of all nonstigmatized parties" (Crenshaw 2010, 550).

The refugees arriving in Europe in the summer of 2015 are difficult to characterize in terms of a single religion, nationality or through racial colour lines. Perhaps, to account for the difficulty in fixing a singular "badge of race", the racism against refugees in the *MailOnline* thread conjures multiple figures and names: Muslims, Jews, Niggers, Arabs and Terrorists morph into one another. Most notably, Nazi-era anti-Semitic practices are repurposed as anti-Muslim racism: "I'd brand them like cattle with a massive M on their foreheads". The *graphic* character of racism is striking, with many posts imagining different ways of stigmatising refugees. Signs and words are imagined impressed, branded, tattooed upon migrant bodies, stressing the relationship between racism, writing and wounding uncovered in the genealogy of penal stigma. Also notable are the many calls for the segregation and confinement of these "waste populations" in concentration camps: "No one invited them to the Czech Republic!"; " Like roach infestation"; "Let the Germans set up some of their 'special' camps in Poland for them"; "We don't want them – go or be gone".

Scene two: Bělá-Jezová immigration detention centre, Czech Republic, 31 August 2015

Because the Czech Republic receives so few refugees, there are only three immigration detention centres in the Czech Republic. Coincidentally, on 31 August 2015, the very day that the refugees began the train journeys that ended at Břeclav, Anna Šabatová, the Czech Government's Public Defender of Rights, made an unannounced visit to the Bělá-Jezová detention centre, a former Soviet Army Barracks. Šabatová's subsequent report offers important insights into the abject conditions faced by those refugees bussed from Břeclav on their arrival in detention. Indeed, the situation she describes at Bělá-Jezová is so disturbing that it triggered responses from the EU and from Zeid Ra'ad Al Hussein, the United Nations High Commissioner for Human Rights.

When she arrived at Bělá-Jezová, the chief of the Czech Alien Police at the centre tried to refuse Šabatová, and the four lawyers and two interpreters accompanying her, access, and attempted to remove the cameras they had brought to document conditions, despite that the unannounced inspection of prisons and detention centres is a regular part of the role of Public Defender of the Rights (Šabatová 2015, 4). Having gained access, Šabatová begins her inspection report on Bělá-Jezová by noting that it had increased its capacity from 270 to 700 beds in a period of six months. During her visit on August 31, there were 659 people, including 147 children, detained there. Šabatová describes how a constant "demonstration of force" is maintained throughout the centre by the "presence of uniformed private security guards, police officers, riot police unit and police dogs". The refugees relay their feelings "of utter humiliation". They tell Šabatová that some of the police officers "handled them roughly, or spit in front of them" and that "private security guards allegedly called them terrorists". Šabatová notes that people are frequently handcuffed and that many, including children, have insufficient clothing and shoes to keep warm and clean. Some of those she spoke to had no hot meals, but were surviving on rations of bread and cheese. Others had no direct access to toilets or running water, and had to rouse guards to be released from the rooms in which they were locked each time they needed the bathroom. Detainees described being given mattresses that were filthy and infested with lice. People also describe being subject to humiliating strip and body cavity searches in front of families and children, ostensibly to make sure they are not hiding valuables; mobile phones, watches, shoelaces, belts and money were confiscated on their arrival. The anxiety of being detained in these conditions was "intensified by the fact that they are unable to contact their relatives. Many have no way to report back home that they are alive, or to try and find a relative with whom they have lost contact" (Šabatová 2015, 7). Indeed, people don't know when they will be released and some don't even know which country they are in. Despite the claims of police at Břeclav, that people were being inked as a means of keeping families together, Šabatová discovers that family members are frequently separated in different detention centres (see also Ahmed-Čermáková 2015). Amidst this litany of details, she pauses to note in her report:

> Simple description of the situation cannot fully convey the conditions in which these [people] were held, nor their psychological condition. … They often come to believe they have been deprived of their humanity and treated as a "herd of animals". (2015, 29)

In the most shocking passage, Šabatová details her discovery of an annexe in a forest behind the main detention centre where people were living in tents and transport containers confined inside wire fencing:

> The container units in the forest were "discovered" only at the very end of the inspection visit. When [we] arrived on these premises, some of the detained foreign nationals raised banners such as: "We are refugees, not prisoners!" and "Help us, please". These people saw themselves as "caged animals". (2015, 13)

To add to their humiliation, people are charged for their stay: ordinarily imprisoned for 90 days at a cost of €10 per person, per day. These charges are "levied" from confiscated cash and valuables. Many leave without any money left in their possession and are presented with a bill for their outstanding debts to the Czech Republic. This is a "final deterrent" as it is illegal to claim asylum in the Czech Republic if you are financially indebted to the government. People are frequently released without prior warning, without even a map, directions or transport to the nearest train station: "destitute in front of the gate of the camp, in the middle of the forest" (Ahmed-Čermáková 2015). They are forced to seek assistance from Czech volunteers in order to continue on their journeys to Germany. Perhaps, as one activist wryly notes, on the very same train "from which police dragged them two months ago in Břeclav" (Ahmed-Čermáková 2015).

Conclusion: spectres of fascism

With regard to the Czech Republic, the United Nations concludes that

the violations of the human rights of migrants are neither isolated nor coinci-
dental, but systematic: they appear to be an integral part of a policy by the
Czech Government designed to deter migrants and refugees from entering
the country or staying there. (United Nations 2015)

This article has attempted to demonstrate the role of what I term "racial
stigma" in this process, the ways in which racial stigmatization dehumanizes
people to the extent that it becomes possible to keep them caged and
hidden in transport units. The penal practices of stigma I have described are
also a reminder that it is impossible to imagine or think about "race and
crisis" in contemporary Europe without recourse to history. The tattooing of
refugees, their removal from trains at night, the fearful and racist responses
of local communities, the comments of *MailOnline* readers, with their advocacy
of yellow stars, tattoos and gas chambers, the humiliating practices of strip-
searching refugees, confiscating their valuables and the abject and hidden
conditions in which they are held, evoke ghosts of Europe's recent past. One
argument of this article is that contemporary political struggles over borders
pivot on "the seething presence" of these ghostly refugees – whether in calls
from the far-right to detain the Břeclav refugees in Theresienstadt, or in
claims that migrants are enacting "white genocide", or in more liberal forms
of memorialization that seek to freeze "real racism" in the past – or in "the
East" (Gordon 1997, 195). The thing about haunting, as Avery Gordon argues,
is that it "alters the way we normally separate and sequence the past, the
present and the future" allowing a "repressed or unresolved social violence"
to make itself known (Gordon 2011). The processions of people arriving at
the borders today are caught at the same railway stations, waiting rooms, platforms and train tracks, and are even detained in some of the same camps and
prisons, where refugees were gathered in the 1930s and 1940s. Reckoning with
these ghosts is important because they have something valuable to tell us
about the high stakes of Europe's current racist crisis. While conditions for
industrial scale genocide of the 1940s do not currently exist in Europe, the
ways in which we confront these spectres is a matter of life and death.

Scene three: Břeclav train station, 11 March 1938

At midnight on 11 March 1938, a train carrying refugees was halted at
Břeclav station. Drawing on eyewitness accounts, the British journalist
George Gedye described how events unfolded that night. Earlier that
evening Austrian Chancellor Kurt von Schuschnigg had resigned, surren-
dering Austria to annexation by the German Government. Jews, Communists, Catholics, Anti-Fascists and intellectuals scrambled to get on the
last train from Vienna to Prague in order to escape before the German
Army entered the city the following day. The train was supposed to
leave at 11.15 pm, but by 8 pm "thousands of people were pushing each

other, squeezing themselves into the train while demanding to depart immediately" (Gedye 1939, 301). Before it was able to pull out of the station, Nazi Stormtroopers boarded the train "running through the carriages, armed with dog whips", looting and terrorizing passengers (301). Finally, the train departed. Then, 20 minutes into its journey, it was stopped in the middle of the countryside by the SS who proceeded to "go through the train with a fine-toothed comb" (301). Men, women and children were dragged out and herded into vans. "Those who remained were plundered quite openly of everything in their possession – money, jewellery, watches and furs" (301). After some hours, "the trembling survivors found themselves moving off towards Břeclav and safety", every moment "an agony for those who feared to be held up again" (301). Finally, they could see the lights of Břeclav, they had reached the safety of Czechoslovakian territory. The Czech police boarded and announced that all passengers with Austrian passports were to leave the train. The refugees were moved to a guarded waiting room, where they saw from a window that the train they had arrived on was departing for Prague without them. After some hours, Břeclav's Chief of Police came into the waiting room and announced that all Austrian nationals were to be returned to Vienna. As Gedye notes, "one of those who was there and managed by a ruse to escape told me later in Prague that the scenes that followed this announcement were too painful for him to recall" (301). Some of those forcibly returned to Vienna that evening, escaped by departing at Austrian towns en route, taking off on foot into surrounding forests. The rest were returned by train to Vienna, where they were locked in a waiting room at the train station for twelve hours, and were subject to further interrogation by the SS. Some were later released, others went "straight to Dachau" (301). By the autumn of 1938, Břeclav was annexed to Nazi Germany. Renamed Lundenburg, its local Jewish population was soon expelled. Its railway station became a node on the transnational train network used to deport Jews to Theresienstadt and extermination camps in Eastern Europe. Over the next few years, refugees halted at Břeclav on 11 March 1938 would return to this border town on special transports – this time their trains travelled straight on through to their final destinations.

Notes

1. The 1990 Dublin Convention, updated by the 2003 Dublin II regulation and the 2013 Dublin III regulation, stipulates that asylum applications should ordinarily be processed in the first country of arrival.
2. Established by the Nazis in 1941, Theresienstadt was a Jewish ghetto near Prague and a major departure point for the concentration camps in Eastern Europe.

3. While the turnout for the referendum was under 50 per cent, which made the result legally invalid, 98 per cent of those who participated voted against the admission of refugees to Hungary, enabling Orbán to claim an ideological victory.
4. As Frankl (2003) details in the Czech context, when the "final solution" when taught in schools and textbooks was remembered as German-orchestrated mass killings perpetrated against all citizens, and especially communists, who, it was claimed, had most fiercely resisted fascism.
5. The yellow star resurrected much older forms of badging Jewish people in Europe, which can be traced back to the eighth century.

Disclosure statement

No potential conflict of interest was reported by the author.

Funding

This work was supported by Leverhulme Trust (Philip Leverhulme Prize).

ORCID

Imogen Tyler 🆔 http://orcid.org/0000-0002-4823-2404

References

AFP & JTA. 2015. "Czech Police Stop Marking Refugees with Numbers." *Times of Israel*, 3 September. http://www.timesofisrael.com/numbers-on-refugees-arms-recall-holo caust-jewish-leaders-say/.

Ahmed-Čermáková, Martina. 2015. "Strach a hnus v Bělé-Jezové." http://a2larm.cz/ 2015/09/strach-a-hnus-v-bele-jezove/.

Amin, Ash. 2010. "The Remainders of Race." *Theory, Culture & Society* 27 (1): 1–23.

Anon. 2015a. "Czech Extremist Adam Bartoš: Put the Refugees in a Former Nazi Concentration Camp." http://blisty.cz/art/78865.html.

Anon. 2015b. "Minister Signals Possibility of Allowing Refugees to Cross Czech Territory to Germany." http://www.czech.cz/en/Vie-Travail/Minister-signals-possibility-of-allowing-refugees.

Back, Les. 2008. "An Ordinary Virtue." *New Jewish Thought*. http://www.newjewishthought.org/AnOrdinaryVirtue.html.

Biray, Kurt. 2015. "Communist Nostalgia in Eastern Europe: Longing for the Past." *OpenDemocracy*. https://www.opendemocracy.net/can-europe-make-it/kurt-biray/communist-nostalgia-in-eastern-europe-longing-for-past.

Blanden, Adam. 2016. "Central and Eastern Europe as Playground of a Conservative Avant-garde." *OpenDemocracy*. https://www.opendemocracy.net/can-europe-make-it/adam-blanden/central-and-eastern-europe-as-playground-of-conservative-avant-garde.

Bridgeman, Jon, and Leslie Worley. 2004. "Genocide of the Hereos." In *Century of Genocide: Critical Essays and Eyewitness Accounts*, edited by Samuel Totten, William S. Parsons and Israel W. Charny, 15–51. New York: Routledge.

Connor, Phillip. 2016. "Number of Refugees to Europe Surges to Record 1.3 Million in 2015." *Pew Research Centre*. http://www.pewglobal.org/2016/08/02/number-of-refugees-to-europe-surges-to-record-1-3-million-in-2015/.

Čulík, Jan. 2015. "Prague Springs to Intolerance." *POLITICO*. August 2. http://www.politico.eu/article/prague-springs-to-intolerance/.

Čulík, Jan. 2017. "Why is the Czech Republic So Hostile to Muslims and Refugees?" *EuropeNow*. http://www.europenowjournal.org/2017/02/09/why-is-the-czech-republic-so-hostile-to-muslims-and-refugees/#_edn34.

Crenshaw, Kimberlé Williams. 2010. "Race, Reform and Retrenchement." In *Theories of Race and Racism: A Reader*, edited by Les Back and Jon Solomos, 549–560. London: Routledge.

Dean, Jodi. 2012. *The Communist Horizon*. London: Verso.

Elias, Ruth. 1999. *Triumph of Hope: From Theresienstadt and Auschwitz to Israel*, Translated by Margot Bettauer Dembo. New York: John Wiley & Sons.

Fanon, Frantz. 2005. *The Wretched of the Earth*, Translated by Richard Philcox. New York: Grove Press.

Fella, Stefano. 2013. "Conclusion: Understanding European Racisms." In *Anti-Racist Movements in the EU: Between Europeanisation and National Trajectories*, edited by Stefano Fella and Carlo Ruzza, 209–240. London: Palgrave Macmillan.

Fields, Barbara, and Karen Fields. 2014. *Racecraft: The Soul of Inequality in American Life*. London: Verso.

Flemr, Jan. 2015. "Czech Police spark uproar by tagging refugees with numbers." *Times of Israel*, September 2. http://www.timesofisrael.com/czech-police-spark-uproar-by-tagging-refugees-with-numbers/.

Foster, Peter. 2016. "One year ago, Angela Merkel dared to stand up for refugees in Europe. Who else even tried?" *The Telegraph*, August 24. http://www.telegraph.co.uk/news/2016/08/24/one-year-ago-angela-merkel-dared-to-stand-up-for-refugees-in-eur/.

Frankl, Michal. 2003. "Holocaust Education in the Czech Republic, 1989–2002." *Intercultural Education*, 14 (2): 177–189.

Gagyi, Agnes, Tamás Gerőcs, Linda Szabó, and Márton Szarvas. 2016. "Beyond Moral Interpretations of the EU 'Migration Crisis': Hungary and the Global Economic Division of Labor". *LeftEast*. http://www.criticatac.ro/lefteast/beyond-moral-interpretations-of-hu-eu-migration-crisis/.

Gall, Lydia. 2016. "Hungary's War on Refugees." https://www.hrw.org/news/2016/09/16/hungarys-war-refugees.

Gedye, George. 1939. *Fallen Bastions. The Central European Tragedy*. London: Victor Gollancz.

Goffman, Erving. 1987. *Stigma: Notes on the Management of Spoiled Identity*. New York: Simon & Schuster.

Gordon, Avery. 1997. *Ghostly Matters: Haunting and the Sociological Imagination*. Minneapolis: University of Minnesota Press.

Gordon, Avery. 2011. "Some Thoughts on Haunting and Futurity." *Borderlands* 10 (2). http://www.borderlands.net.au/vol10no2_2011/gordon_thoughts.pdf.

Gustafson, Mark. 2000. "The Tattoo in the Later Roman Empire and Beyond." In *Written on the Body: The Tattoo in European and American History*, edited by Jane Caplan, 17–31. Princeton, NJ: Princeton University Press.

Hall, Stuart. 1997. "Race the Floating Signifier." *Media Education Foundation*. http://www.mediaed.org/transcripts/Stuart-Hall-Race-the-Floating-Signifier-Transcript.pdf.

Hamm, Patrick, Lawrence King, and David Stuckler. 2012. "Mass Privatization, State Capacity, and Economic Growth in Postcommunist Countries." *American Sociological Review* 77 (2): 295–324.

Hrabal, Michal. 2015. "Kdy si ty stany odvezete? ptala se žena na setkání s lidmi z ministerstva." http://breclavsky.denik.cz/zpravy_region/kdy-si-ty-stany-odvezete-ptala-se-zena-na-setkani-s-lidmi-z-ministerstva-20150908.html.

Jones, C. P. 1987. "*Stigma*: Tattooing and Branding in Graeco-Roman Antiquity." *Journal of Roman Studies* 77: 139–155.

Lentin, Alana. 2016. "Racism in Public or Public Racism: Doing Anti-Racism in 'Post-Racial' Times." *Ethnic and Racial Studies* 39(1), 33–48.

Lentin, Alana. 2017. "Learning from Lisa Lowe." http://www.alanalentin.net/2017/03/03/learning-from-lisa-lowe/.

Nowicka, Magdalena. 2017. "'I don't mean to sound racist but … ' 'Transforming racism in transnational Europe'." *Ethnic and Racial Studies*, [electronic pre-print].

Olusoga, David, and Casper Erichsen. 2010. *The Kaiser's Holocaust. Germany's Forgotten Genocide and the Colonial Roots of Nazism*. London: Faber and Faber.

Oxford English Dictionary [online]. 2014. 2nd rev. ed. Oxford: Oxford University Press.

Šabatová, Anna. 2015. "Facility for Detention of Foreigners Bělá-Jezová: Evaluation of Systematic Visit." Public Defenders of Rights, Ombudsman. http://www.ochrance.cz/fileadmin/user_upload/ochrana_osob/ZARIZENI/Zarizeni_pro_cizince/Report_Bela-Jezova.pdf.

Sarkin-Hughes, Jeremy. 2010. *Germany's Genocide of the Herero: Kasier Wilhelm II, His General, His Settlers, His Soldiers*. Cape Town: UCT Press.

Schaller, Dominik. 2013. "The Genocide of the Herero and Nama in German South-West Africa, 1904-1907." In *Centuries of Genocide: Essays and Eyewitness Accounts*, edited by Samuel Totten and William Parsons, 89–114. New York: Routledge.

Schultheis, Silla. 2015. "The Refugee Policy of the Visegrád Countries: 'No one invited you'." September 15. https://cz.boell.org/en/2015/09/15/refugee-policy-visegrad-countries-no-one-invited-you.

Sivanandan, A. 2016. Foreword. "Racial Violence in the Brexit State". *Institute for Race Relations*. http://www.irr.org.uk/app/uploads/2016/11/Racial-violence-and-the-Brexit-state-final.pdf.

Spillers, Hortense. 2003. *Black, White, and in Color: Essays on American Literature and Culture*. Chicago, IL: University of Chicago Press.

Tamás, G. M. 2016. "Anti-Immigration Referendum Sunday in Hungary". *OpenDemocracy*. https://www.opendemocracy.net/can-europe-make-it/g-m-tam-s/anti-immigration-referendum-sunday-in-hungary.

United Nations. 2015. "Zeid Urges Czech Republic to Stop Detention of Migrants and Refugees." October 22. http://www.ohchr.org/EN/NewsEvents/Pages/DisplayNews.aspx?NewsID=16632&LangID=E#sthash.t6NZThkI.dpuf.

Weheliye, Alexander. 2014. *Habeas Viscus: Racializing Assemblages, Biopolitics, and Black Feminist Theories of the Human*. Durham, NC: Duke University Press.

Zelený-Atapana, Mnislav. 2016. "Je na řadě genocida bělochů v Evropě?" *Lidovky*. http://www.lidovky.cz/diskuse-je-na-rade-genocida-belochu-v-evrope-fe0-/nazory.aspx?c=A160718_135549_ln_nazory_mct.

Racism, Crisis, Brexit

Satnam Virdee and Brendan McGeever

ABSTRACT
This article offers a conjunctural analysis of the financial and political crisis within which Brexit occurred with a specific attentiveness to race and racism. Brexit and its aftermath have been overdetermined by racism, including racist violence. We suggest that the Leave campaign secured its victory by bringing together two contradictory but inter-locking visions. The first comprises an imperial longing to restore Britain's place in the world as *primus inter pares* that occludes any coming to terms with the corrosive legacies of colonial conquest and racist subjugation. The second takes the form of an insular, Powellite narrative of island retreat from a "globalizing" world, one that is no longer recognizably "British". Further, the article argues that an invisible driver of the Brexit vote and its racist aftermath has been a politicization of Englishness. We conclude by outlining some resources of hope that could potentially help to negotiate the current emergency.

People are trapped in history, and history is trapped in them. (Baldwin 1984, 119)

Introduction

The neoliberal consensus in Europe, crafted over three decades by conservative and social democratic political parties alike, has been dramatically unsettled amid the most severe financial crisis since the Great Depression of the 1930s. The resultant imposition of austerity has aggravated existing social inequalities between classes (Piketty 2014), producing a marked polarization in politics. And it is the hard right, first and foremost, that has capitalized on these developments. From Sweden to Switzerland, from Belgium to

Bulgaria, a tide of reactionary populism is sweeping across the European mainland which demands nothing less than a restoration of a mythical golden age of sovereign nation-states defined by cultural and racial homogeneity (Inglehart and Norris 2016).[1]

Britain has not been inoculated from this economic and political turbulence, the most striking manifestation of which has been Brexit. On 23 June 2016, Britain voted narrowly to secede from the transnational formation of the EU by 52–48 per cent. This relatively unexpected victory for Brexit led many to go in search of possible explanations. Some claimed it was driven by those same social forces that had voted for the United Kingdom Independence Party (UKIP) at the 2014 European Parliament elections, that is, "the vote for Brexit was delivered by the 'left behind' … pensioners, low skilled and less well educated blue-collar workers and citizens who have been pushed to the margins" (Goodwin and Heath 2016, 13). While exit polls confirmed that around two-thirds of those who voted in social classes D and E chose to leave the EU (Ashcroft 2016), we should also note that the proportion of Leave voters who were of the lowest two social classes was just 24 per cent (Dorling 2016). Leave voters among the elite and middle classes were crucial to the final outcome, with almost three in five votes coming from those in social classes A, B and C1 (Dorling 2016). Additionally, age seems to have been central to the Brexit vote. While 62 per cent of 25–34 year olds chose to Remain, 60 per cent of those aged 65 and over voted to Leave. In sum, it is too simplistic to suggest that Brexit constituted the revolt of the "left behind"; rather, what needs to be understood is how the campaign to Leave managed to successfully cohere a significant cross-class coalition of middle-aged and older men and women.

What often gets elided in discussions of Brexit is the presence of what we might term "internal others" against whom the nation has often defined itself, including, most notably, racialized minorities and migrants (see, for example, Habermas 2016). In this article, we focus on the place of race and racism in the crisis that led to Brexit. We offer a conjunctural analysis informed by four questions. First, what do the social and political circumstances resemble if viewed with a greater attentiveness to questions of race and racism? Second, how did they arise? Third, what social forces are sustaining them? And, fourth, what forces are available that could help alter the currently dominant direction of travel?

We begin by examining the discursive dimensions of the Leave campaign. We show that the campaign's narrative was underscored by two contradictory but inter-locking visions. The first was a deep nostalgia for empire, but one secured through an occlusion of the underside of the British imperial project: the corrosive legacies of colonialism and racism, past and present. The second was a more insular, Powellite narrative of retreating from a globalizing world that is no longer recognizably "British". What gave these visions such traction, we contend, was that they carefully activated long-standing racialized structures of feeling about immigration and national belonging.

Having mapped out the core narratives of the Leave campaign, we then move on to an explanation for why the current crisis in Brexit Britain has been so overdetermined by racism. We focus, in particular, on the politics of Englishness.[2] As an invisible driver of Brexit, we show how this Englishness is characterized by two inter-related phenomena. The first is a striking confluence between English national feeling and the longing for Empire. The ease with which both nation and empire can sit together, we suggest, is one of the salient but unspoken dimensions of Brexit and its racist aftermath. We locate the second characteristic of contemporary manifestations of Englishness in the structural decline that Britain has undergone during the neoliberal era. Experiences of downward mobility, alongside the persistence of class injuries, we contend, have produced a politics of nationalist resentment. Coming in the wake of a momentous working class defeat, Englishness has been reasserted through a racializing, insular nationalism, and it found its voice in the course of Brexit. Finally, we draw this discussion of racism, crisis and Brexit to a close by outlining some resources of hope that might help us to navigate the current emergency.

Brexit, racism and the erasure of history

The case for Brexit was built around two distinct organizational formations. The first, Vote Leave (henceforth VL) – the official referendum campaign in favour of exiting the EU – was made up in the main of right-wing Conservative leaders such as Boris Johnson, Michael Gove, Liam Fox and Daniel Hannan as well as a sprinkling of Labour MPs including Gisela Stuart, Kate Hoey and Frank Field. Also part of this campaign was the lone UKIP MP, Douglas Carswell. The second, Leave.EU (henceforth L.EU) – the unofficial referendum campaign in favour of exiting the EU – was primarily a UKIP-led project founded by Aaron Banks and Richard Tice and fronted by then UKIP leader Nigel Farage.

A central feature of both campaigns was the emphasis they placed on reinstating the sovereign will of the British people, exemplified in VL's campaign slogan "Let's take back control". What such a deceptively simple demand signalled to the public was the desire of VL advocates to wrest back power from an EU that in the words of Boris Johnson had become "ever more centralizing, interfering and anti-democratic … . The independence of this country is being seriously compromised. It is this fundamental democratic problem – this erosion of democracy – that brings me into this fight" (Johnson cited in *Conservative Home*, May 9, 2016).

Significantly, this message of regaining democratic control over the affairs of the nation was entwined with a second argument that pointed to the economic and political returns that would arise from detaching Britain from a trading bloc that was in economic decline. And juxtaposed to the image of EU decline and over-reach was the portrait of an otherwise recovering capitalist world economy that Britain would once again re-join as an independent sovereign state. For VL advocates like Johnson, long-standing ties with kith and kin from the Old Commonwealth of Canada, Australia and New Zealand (as well as the US) along with the renewal of one-to-one trading relationships with India and China – so unforgivably sacrificed by the decision to join the EU in 1973 (Johnson 2016) – could now be re-established. Some, like the historian Linda Colley, were quick to draw the inference that this was nothing less than a vision crafted by, and for, "nostalgics in search of a lost empire" (Colley cited in *The Financial Times*, April 22, 2016). And such nostalgia surfaced in early 2017 following Secretary of State for International Trade Liam Fox's plans to boost trade links with African Commonwealth countries, which Whitehall officials branded as "Empire 2.0" (cited in *The Times*, March 6, 2017).

Yet clearly, Britain is not going to constitute a new Empire, no matter how much the architects of Brexit may wish they were able to. Instead, the work that empire is doing here is more discrete, and even subliminal. That is to say: Brexit draws on deep reservoirs of imperial longing in the majority population. When Prime Minister Theresa May (2016) gave her first speech following the vote to Leave, she made reference to a "Global Britain" no less than seventeen times. We contend that the allure of this "Global Britain" acquires resonance among large swathes of the Eurosceptic population in part because of its association with Empire 1.0. That is, to speak of a Global Britain is to not only suggest how great Britain can be in the future, but also to invoke warm collective memories of a now lost world where Britain was the global hegemon of the capitalist world economy. It is to remind that population of those glory days of economic, political and cultural superiority, where everything from ships to spoons were marked with a *Made in Britain* stamp.

Given this, one might have expected some sober deliberation and reckoning with the underside of the actual British Empire project of yesteryear from the VL campaigners, perhaps an acknowledgement of the unequal nature of the colonial relationship based on subjugation and legitimized in the name of scientific racism. Or even a coming to terms with the scars – both material and psychic – left on those stigmatized populations over the course of four centuries, and, of course, how this legacy of Empire continues to shape the uneven development of global capitalism in the present, forcing parts of these populations to migrate to western economies as a racialized reserve army of labour (Virdee 2014). However, hardly a single word has been spoken to this effect. Instead, the Brexit campaign and the subsequent Global Britain project are made more alluring precisely through the erasure of the racist underside of the actual Empire project of yesteryear. By effecting an artificial rupture

59

between Britain's historical past and its possible future, the VL architects circumvent having to confront the corrosive legacy of colonialism legitimized in the name of racism (including how it shapes lives into the present). In doing so, they also make the new project that much more palatable through an evasion of any discussion of its potential underside. Not only does this vision of an independent global Britain occlude racism, it also exhibits an inability to come to terms with the realities of a twenty-first century global capitalism whose epicentre has shifted decisively towards Asia (Arrighi 2009). The VL campaign was in many ways, then, an exemplar episode of postcolonial melancholy (Gilroy 2004) – a narrative crafted by, and for, those who have still not come to terms with the loss of Empire and the resulting decline in global prestige suffered by the British state (see also Ashe 2016).[3]

Insular nationalism: the Powellitte L.EU campaign

If the VL campaign was led by individuals like Boris Johnson who fantasized about re-establishing Britain as a global hegemon (i.e. Britain as the best in the world), many of the key leaders of L.EU articulated a narrative of British nationalism that was more insular and Powellite in tone (i.e. Britain for the British). At the centre of this perspective were concerns around immigration. According to Nigel Farage – the figurehead of L.EU – the EU had done great harm to Britain by facilitating uncontrolled immigration: "Open-door migration has suppressed wages in the unskilled labour market, meant that living standards have failed and that life has become a lot tougher for so many in our country" (Farage cited in *The Express*, June 21, 2016).

This construction of the migrant as economic threat to the domestic working class was married to a second set of representations that understood the migrant as security threat to the British population. This latter construction comprised three distinct elements. First, the terrorist attacks in France and Belgium and the onset of the migration to Europe of displaced Syrians and others escaping war in 2015 and 2016 were purposely linked by Farage to make the argument that the "EU's open borders make us less safe" (Farage cited in *The Express*, April 22, 2016). This sleight of hand then allowed him to suggest that by getting "our borders back, our democracy back" through exiting the EU we could also restrict the entry of such "undesirables" and make Britain safe again. The second element integral to this construction of migrant as security threat was that leaving the EU would effectively prevent refugees from seeking sanctuary in Britain since it would no longer be party to EU diktat. This argument was made most powerfully in the lead-in to the June 23 vote L.EU's "Breaking Point" poster, which pictured Middle Eastern refugees queuing at Europe's borders. The subheading read: "We must break free of the EU and take back control." This was a message of "island retreat" (Winter 2016): if Britons voted leave, they could successfully keep such people from entering the country. And third, when recently arrived migrants were alleged to have committed a series of sexual assaults in Germany – a country which accepted almost a million refugees in 2015 – L.EU campaigners contributed to a moral panic that understood refugees as 'sexual predators', reinforcing the message that remaining in the EU would place British women at risk.

Such representations and narratives acquired traction in everyday life because they dovetailed so neatly with long-standing repertoires of negatively evaluated representations accompanying the on-going racialization of the figure of the Muslim (Meer 2012). That is, while many believed the focus of the UKIP-inspired Brexiteer's ire was mainly white Europeans from the mainland undercutting British workers, it was clear to many within that formation itself that breaking with the EU and "taking back control of our borders" also represented an important opportunity to limit the numbers of Muslims entering Britain, Muslims whose culture many of them believed was incompatible with being British. Until the launch of the "Breaking Point" poster, many in the commentariat failed to appreciate the full toxicity of the L.EU campaign theme of controlling immigration, in part because they appeared to take at face value the careful avoidance of the language of race by L.EU advocates. As a result, it sometimes appeared that their suggestion to control borders was simply a pragmatic response to growing economic and political insecurity.

But the central mechanism through which the L.EU campaign succeeded in side-stepping media accusations of racism was by detaching their anti-migrant narrative from the history of immigration to Britain, and particularly its racialized reception. Throughout the course of the twentieth century, from the arrival of Jewish migrants from the Tsarist Empire to the migration of Caribbean and Asian migrants, there has always been a sustained cross-class coalition of social forces opposed to their presence in Britain (Solomos 2003). Ideologically, this opposition was cohered and mobilized through narrations of the nation that effectively made such groups incompatible with membership of the state on the grounds that they were not Christian (in the case of Jews) or not white (in the case of Asians and Caribbeans) (Virdee 2014).

However, Leave campaigners understood – in the way that much of the liberal media did not – that because this history of immigration to Britain had been so thoroughly racialized over time, a reservoir of latent racism could be activated through the production of appropriately coded language about immigration. That is, one could obey the formal rules of post-racial thinking (Lentin 2016) while at the same time signalling to your intended public that the Brexit project was precisely about keeping the nation Christian and white. That is why those regimes of representation that portrayed migrants as the bearers of alien customs and practices were sufficient to place them beyond the boundary of what it meant to be British. In these neo-racisms, culture takes the place of pseudo-biology, but secures the same intended outcome of generating public support for the permanent exclusion of migrants from membership of the imagined national community.

It is important to remember that these twin and inter-locking racializing visions of Empire and insular nationalism derived their political power by being situated within a broader narrative that postulated the Leave cam-paigners as the last authentic representatives of the British people. EU migration, said Farage, might benefit those sections of "the establishment" with their "cheaper nannies and chauffeurs, but it isn't in the best interests of ordinary British workers" (Farage cited in *The Express*, April 22, 2016). According to this vision, to support exit from the EU, to pull up the drawbridge on migration, was actually to be a democrat, a democrat that wished to restore the right of British people to determine their own destiny. This is what was signified by the demand to "take our country back".

Making sense of Brexit

If confirmation were needed that the case for Brexit was intimately bound up with questions of race, it was to be found in the wave of racist hate unleashed against migrants as well as the long-established black and brown British. Komaromi (2016) found that more than 6,000 racist hate crimes were reported to the National Police Chiefs Council (NPCC) in the four weeks after the refer-endum result was declared. Incidents ranged from physical assault and prop-erty damage to verbal abuse. One individual recalled being referred to as "dirty paki scum" and taunted about how "pakis need to be rounded up and shot". A Sikh radiographer recounted how a patient asked "shouldn't you be on a plane back to Pakistan.? We voted you out." In 51 per cent of the incidents, perpetrators referred specifically to the referendum in their abuse, with the most commonly involved phrases including "Go Home" (seventy-four stories), "Leave" (eighty stories), "fuck off" (forty-five stories). These were followed up by statements such as "we voted you out", "we're out of the EU now, we can get rid of your lot", "when are you going home?", "shouldn't you be packing your bags?" And then, in August 2016, six teenage boys were arrested in Harlow, Essex, for a brutal street attack on an eastern European migrant after he was heard speaking Polish in the street. The man subsequently died. What is striking about this wave of racist violence was the way its perpetrators made little attempt to distinguish between black and brown citizens and white European migrants – in their eyes, they were all outsiders.

How could it come to pass that the first formal break from the thirty-year neoliberal consensus in Britain was marbled through with such racism and violence? How was such a political terrain crafted that saw a majority of the British population vote for Brexit visions that were stained through with a desire to recover former glories associated with Empire, on the one hand, and the promise to pull up the proverbial drawbridge in order to drastically reduce migration on the other?

By disaggregating the vote for Brexit across the four nations, it quickly becomes apparent how uneven support for it was. In particular, support was markedly higher in Wales (52.5 per cent) and England (53.4 per cent) than in Scotland and Northern Ireland, where Remain had majorities of 62 and 55.8 per cent, respectively (BBC 2016). A comprehensive analysis of the place of racism in the Brexit vote across Britain would have to account for the specificities of the relationship between race and nation in each of these four contexts, and such an analysis lies beyond the scope of this paper (though for a brief overview, see McGeever 2015). In the remainder of this article, we want to place particular emphasis on England and the politics of Englishness, and suggest that they form a crucial (though not all-encompassing) insight into what happened on June 23, 2016 and its aftermath. Eighty-seven per cent of Leave votes were cast in England, and as such there is a compelling case to centre the English story in Brexit. Further, 79 per cent of those who identify as "English not British" voted Leave as did 66 per cent of those who identified as "more English than British" (Ashcroft 2016). We contend that the Brexit vote in England cannot be understood without accounting for the invisible driver of Englishness. This particular vision of Englishness, we suggest, is characterized by two inter-related phenomena. First, the ease with which it can sit within a deep-rooted nostalgia for the British imperial project, and second, its articulation of a new politics of resentment underscored by structural decline and class decomposition. Both these arguments require explication.

Englishness: empire, decline and class decomposition

The relationship between race and nation in England is intimately bound up with Empire. The colonization of a quarter of the world fostered a long lasting, expansionist worldview among the ruling elites in Britain. This had its own "blowback" at home through the consolidation of a colonial racism that came to define British politics. Crucially, this racism was further secured through working class incorporation into the imperial nation through the representative structures of the British state, including the Labour Party. Though a British-wide development, this colonial racism had a very specific and deep-rooted impact on the formation of English nationalism and English national identity (Hall 2000; Kumar 2003; MacPhee and Poddar 2007). Englishness was arguably submerged within the British imperial project during the era of expansion in the eighteenth and nineteenth centuries, so close was their historical association. As Perry Anderson once provocatively put it, the imperial moment "saturated" England in a "matrix it has retained to this day". The "motifs of Empire" swept across English society, Anderson argued, and "set" its "ideological horizons" (1964, 34–35). The racializing capacities of Englishness were further developed in the moment of decolonization: the arrival of migrants from India and the Caribbean was marked by a re-imagining of the nation in which both England and Britain were defined by a shared cross-class allegiance to whiteness (Knowles 2008; Tyler 2012; Virdee 2014). It was in this vortex that English nationalism derived the dimensions and referents that would define it in the decades to come, and they have come into view in the blowback of Brexit and its racializing consequences.

However, racism in post-Brexit England has its moorings not just in the "aching loss" of Empire (Gilroy 2004, 95), but also the structural decline that Britain has undergone since the late 1970s and the onset of neoliberalism. The politics of Englishness today asserts itself against a backdrop of Britain's comparatively marginal position in the world economy. Moreover, the defeat of the social movements in the 1980s and the accompanying delegitimizing of socialist politics have left a working class profoundly disaggregated by region, nation and ethnicity. In this sense, it is the transformations of the 1980s rather than the austerity programmes since 2008 that bear heaviest on our present moment (Davies 2016).

Significantly, the period of working class defeat under the Conservatives led by Thatcher was accompanied by the loss of alternative class frames of resistance, including those that re-imagined the working class as multi-ethnic. Although the organizations of the working class and the left more generally have a long history of imbrication in the politics of racism in England, these organizations have, at the same time, provided limited but nevertheless important cultures of solidarity that have in turn played a key role in re-imagining black and brown migrants (and their British-born descendants) as part of the working class (Virdee 2014). Under Conservative rule, the politics of class and the language of solidarity that had underpinned working class politics were significantly weakened. The historic settlement of post-1945 Britain that labour, to a limited degree, was to be protected from capital was reversed (Hall 1987, 17). These defeats in turn profoundly diminished those countercurrents of anti-racist class politics, including those aligned to the politics of blackness (Shukra 1998).

In recent years, therefore, the prospect (and reality) of downward mobility has produced class injuries and collective experiences that have been recast through the politics of *ressentiment* (Ware 2008). Whereas thirty-five years ago labour and anti-racist movements could meaningfully intervene, today the realignment of British politics has (in England, at least) left the terrain wide-open to the right, ranging from the neoliberal mainstream to its far-right outriders. In this context, decline, though necessarily a multi-ethnic process, is experienced in a racialized frame and is increasingly responded to by some sections of the working class through the politics of resentful English nationalism (Fenton 2012). The realignment of politics to the right has therefore created an environment in which racism can be more readily articulated since it resonates with the cultural and political logic of our time.

This racializing nationalism has borne a particularly defensive character since the 2008 crisis. It is defined not by imperial prowess or superiority, but by a deep sense of loss of prestige; a retreat from the damaging impact of a globalized world that is no longer recognizable, no longer "British". The decline of empire, then, has not led to the overcoming of the English imperial complex, but its retraction into a defensive exclusionary imaginary: we are under siege, it is time to pull up the drawbridge. As we have identified above, this was one of the defining features in the discursive architecture of the Leave campaign (L.EU). As Hall once put it, "Englishness has always carried a racial signature" (Hall 2000, 109). We are hearing its familiar refrains in these crisis-ridden post-Brexit times.

These new coordinates of Englishness are evident not just in the language of the Leave campaign, but in large-scale survey data that show the extent to which the main drivers of political Englishness are Euroscepticism and concern about "immigration" (Wyn Jones et al. 2013, 22, 26; Jeffery et al. 2016). Indeed, it is the racialized question of "immigration" that is arguably now defining the conversation around Englishness. In the 1980s and 1990s, public concern about "immigration" remained relatively low, with no more than 10 per cent of the population seeing it as a key issue during this period. Since 2000, however, the hardening of attitudes has seen that figure rise dramatically to 30–40 per cent (Duffy and Frere-Smith 2014, 8), such that by 2006 "race and immigration" were recorded as the most important issues facing the country (CRE 2006, 5). The toxicity of the EU Referendum has deepened these trends, and brought us to what we would now define as a state of emergency. Racism has become normalized in both elite political discourse and practice and everyday life, dramatically diminishing the spaces for Britain's racialized minorities to breathe and live life free from hate.

This is the context in which an emboldened racist nationalist right has emerged. The inter-locking features of racialized nationalism, anti-immigrant sentiment and Euroscepticism – identifiable across the whole of Europe (Condor and Fenton 2012, 386) – have particular resonance in England. The unprecedented electoral breakthrough of UKIP in the 2015 General Election shows that English nationalism now provides a dominant framing for this racism. Although ostensibly a Unionist party, the UKIP project has been predi-cated on a distinct politicization of Englishness (Hayton 2016). This is reflected not only in the composition of the UKIP vote (more than 90 per cent of the party's 3.8 million votes in 2015 were cast in England), but in recent attitudinal studies of those voters, who strongly identify as English rather than British (Wyn Jones et al. 2012, 33; Hayton 2016, 406). In 2015, the party was able to gain traction by tapping into a sedimented racist nationalist populism that has been a feature of the English social formation for a number of decades. Such racism gains traction not simply through the circulation of racist ideas within mainstream political discourse, but because such ideas have been part of the lived habitus of the English social formation for so long. The racialized codes of belonging that have come to shape dominant understandings of Englishness over the past century have always been met with contestation by emergent currents of anti-racism (Virdee 2014; Ashe, Virdee, and Brown 2016), but they continue to assert themselves in the popular imaginary. Unlike the anti-racist left, politicians such as former UKIP leader Nigel Farage have very little work to do: he can parachute into a constituency and let racism do its work, since he is able to draw not just on the "mainstream political consensus", but on active and long-standing forms of consciousness. Their trace and resonance is to be found in "popular inventories" (Hall 1979, 20), and the racist Right know exactly where to look. And in Brexit Britain, they keep returning for more.

Racism, crisis and the "political mainstream"

The racism of Brexit Britain, however, does not begin and end with UKIP (whose vote has since declined following a hard-right turn by the Conservatives in 2017). Despite elite hand-wringing and moral opprobrium levelled at the racist violence that followed Brexit, it is difficult to make sense of how the racially charged Leave campaigns could have succeeded without also naming Labour and Conservative complicity in manufacturing the social and political conditions for this momentous decision. While Brexit added an accelerant on those conditions and allowed racism to flourish, it did not create them. Instead, they were birthed under the tenure of New Labour. The riots in the Northern English mill towns during the summer of 2001 combined with the rapidly changing geo-political situation in the aftermath of 9/11 and the war in Iraq were formative moments in the consolidation of a new racialized enemy within – "the Muslim" (Kundnani 2007). Significantly, some of the dominant components of this modality of racism draw with increasing regularity on feminist and gay discourses of liberation – suitably de-fanged and shorn of their emancipatory potential. The effect has been to increasingly legitimize claims that "Muslim culture" and the Muslim presence more generally were in some sense incompatible with modern British values of tolerance and diversity. As a result, femonationalist and homonationalist ways of thinking aided the consolidation of a new consensus on race and difference (see, for example, Puar 2007; Farris 2017) in which anti-Muslim racism formed an intrinsic justification for the Labour and subsequently

Conservative elite turn away from multiculturalism, and towards an assimilatory nationalism (Back et al. 2002). Indeed, multiculturalism itself – denoting state recognition of cultural and ethnic diversity within a nation-state – has been alleged to perpetuate feelings of separation and racial division (David Cameron cited in *The Independent*, February 4, 2011).

And then, when the British economy spiralled into depression as part of the global economic collapse of 2008, New Labour remained resolutely committed to the neoliberal settlement and steadfastly refused to budge from stringent austerity. Alongside this, the Labour administration increasingly entwined the continuing and very real pain suffered by its working class constituency (ranging from wage freezes to the cutting back of welfare benefits) to questions of immigration. Then Labour Prime Minister Gordon Brown, for example, proposed reducing the numbers of migrants amid the economic crisis and resulting austerity with his deployment of what was hitherto a slogan of the far-right by promising to train "British workers for British jobs" (Brown cited in *The Telegraph*, June 6, 2007). Unconvinced of New Labour's fealty to limit immigration, the public turned instead to a Tory-Liberal coalition government which accepted the premise of the Brown argument and promised to reduce migration to the tens of thousands from its current levels of 300,000 per year.

After Brown's demise in 2010, the then incoming Labour leader Ed Miliband continued the downward spiral of racializing national politics with his attempts to consolidate an anti-migrant working class vote through his embrace of the tenets of Blue Labour. Blue Labour's intellectual founders such as Maurice Glasman spoke of the "paradoxes of Labour's tradition" arguing that it needed to "address the crisis of its political philosophy and to recover its historic sense of purpose" by "rebuilding a strong and enduring relationship with the people" (Glasman et al. 2011, 9–11). And this was to be achieved through a re-emphasis on Labour's socially conservative roots and an approach that emphasized concern for "family, faith, and flag" (Sandbrook cited in *The New Statesmen*, April 7, 2011). While this is certainly one side of the story of the Labour movement, it neglects to mention its more emancipatory underside that helped make Labour more attentive to concerns around race (Virdee 2014) and gender (Moore 2011). Additionally, what Blue Labour supporters fail to recognize is the increasingly multi-ethnic nature of the contemporary English working class and how their rhetoric is likely to only appeal to certain categories of workers, particularly those most concerned about questions of race, immigration and Europe. Such an approach culminated in the course of the 2015 general election campaign, where New Labour had as one of its five election pledges a commitment to control immigration, and had the confidence to sell mugs which invited us to vote for them because of such a pledge (see Bush in *The New Statesman*, March 28, 2015).

However, by then Labour was already lagging in the slipstream of a racializing narrative defined increasingly by the so-called establishment outriders of UKIP whose leader Nigel Farage claimed, openly, that "the white working class was in danger of becoming an underclass" because of immigration (Farage cited in *The Daily Mail*, April 2, 2014).

Across the political spectrum from New Labour to Conservative, a powerful narrative has become dominant which understands that the principal losers from globalization, and particularly migration, were a social category referred to as the "white working class" (May 2016). And this message has been amplified over and over again by the right-wing press who deploy this category for their own instrumental ends, particularly for eroding support for multiculturalism (Runnymede Trust 2009). As a result, the white working class – a descriptive and analytic category whose origins lay in social science research – has over the course of this decade-long crisis been brought to life as a collective social force in the Thompsonian sense (1991), such that some working class men and women now understand and make sense of the real economic pain they suffer through such a racialized frame of white working class victimhood (Ware 2008).

This construction of the white working class has led to a number of deleterious developments in the field of politics. First, it has helped cohere and then shift those parts of the working class most enamoured of such an identification into the camp of the anti-immigrant right, that is, they have come to invest politically in understanding themselves (i.e. the white working class) as the main victims of globalization. Second, by juxtaposing the category white working class to immigrant, such a narrative not only privileged one stratum of Britain's working class over the other on the grounds of citizenship, it also erased those parts of the working class who were black and brown Britons. And through this sleight of hand, the lived experiences of those whose economic austerity was overlain by race and gender discrimination were simply elided (Emejulu and Bassel 2015) and closed off from public scrutiny and debate. Third, and related, this had the effect of further dividing the multiethnic working class on racial lines, and in doing so submerged those other explanations for working class pain – the austerity imposed by Labour and Conservative elites alike. This has helped neuter (but not rule out) the possibility of a united working class challenge to neoliberal rule.

Conclusion

Williams (1989, 118) once remarked that "[t]o be truly radical is to make hope possible, rather than despair convincing". Where, then, might we locate the resources of hope today? Alongside the mapping of the powerful structuring force of racism within the English working class, Virdee (2014) has recently drawn our attention to how, throughout the nineteenth and twentieth centuries, including most recently in the 1970s and 1980s, there were periods of multi-ethnic class solidarity when parts of the English working class collectively suppressed expressions of racism and, on occasion, actively rejected it altogether. However, the current conjuncture is distinguished from that of the 1970s and 1980s by the disappearance of the working class subject as a collective social force accompanied by the hollowing out of a socialist culture, growing class disidentification (Skeggs 1997), and the decline of the labour and anti-racist movements more generally (Virdee 2015). Potential collective agents against racism in Britain today are not easily identifiable, but a tentative portrait of possibilities can nevertheless be sketched.

We write these words in the aftermath of the June 2017 General Election result which saw the Labour Party of Jeremy Corbyn secure 40 per cent of the vote – the highest Labour vote since Tony Blair won office in 1997, and the biggest increase since the Attlee government of 1945. This represents a further unsettling of the neoliberal consensus, but in contradistinction to Brexit, it has been crafted on a left terrain. Labour's manifesto – *For the Many, Not the Few* (2017) – not only set out a vision of opposition to austerity, it also struck a defiantly optimistic tone, of how to do politics differently. What was striking about its discourse was the ways in which it tried to alter the terms of debate by positing collectivism over individualism, of state regulation and intervention in the market, and a more expansive vision of class that encompassed black and brown British working people as well as those defined as white. At the same time, we are cognizant of the limits of Corbynism. Debates around immigration and antisemitism, for example, are far from resolved. Moreover, the re-emergence of this more solidaristic form of politics must combine more thoroughly with those social groups concerned with overcoming the structuring force of racism if they are to avoid the tendency to reduce inequalities arising from racism to those of class.

We believe there are grounds for optimism. Deposited within sections of the black and brown populations of England are memories of collective resistance. From the workplace strikes against discrimination led by the Indian Workers Association to the black struggles against state and street racism (Sivanandan 1982), it was autonomous collective action that helped turn the tide against such sustained exclusion and violence. And just like then, any push back against the exclusionary narrowing of Englishness today will more than likely involve those who directly incur the injuries of racism. The emergence of anti-racist movements including Black Lives Matter UK, Rhodes Must Fall, certain Decolonial initiatives and the formation of refugee support networks hint at the possibility that we may be entering a new period of sustained collective action against racist discrimination, as well as class inequalities.

In a more everyday sense, there is also hope to be found in the very fact of contemporary multi-ethnic life in Britain. We are, to put it simply, much more entangled in each other's lives than was once the case. For example, nearly one in ten people in England and Wales are involved in so-called mixed relationships, and nearly half of these are with someone from the majority "white" population (ONS 2011). The retreat of collectivism that has come to define the neoliberal era has also been accompanied by the emergence of an everyday multicultural reality, particularly among younger generations. Those who are under thirty-five grew up in the slipstream of the anti-racist struggles of the 1970s and 1980s. They encountered a Britain transformed by the very real gains of the anti-racist movement that preceded them (equality provisions at work, multicultural education in schools, an established anti-racist civic culture and so on). However much of these gains are being rolled back by the austerity programme of recent years, their imprint is traceable in the ease with which many young people handle the lived realities of multi-ethnic life in Britain, especially urban England where the vast majority of Britain's minority populations live. In this sense, the anti-racist victories of the past have their returns in the present, even though the political conjuncture is markedly different.

Gilroy has written confidently about how the "convivial metropolitan cultures of the country's young people" may serve as a "bulwark against the machinations of racial politics" (2004, 131–132). Additionally, in his study of South London, Back found that young whites vacated both whiteness and Englishness on account of the inability of these identifiers to speak to the multi-ethnicity that is forged at the everyday level (1996, 134–138). He also found that young black youths were "preparing the social ground where a reworked aesthetic of Englishness can exist free of racially exclusive terms of reference" (1996, 159). These observations led Back to optimistically predict a future in which racialized Englishness would no longer be tenable and would be rendered "almost meaningless" by such emergent new multiculture (1996, 250).

Some qualifications, however, need to be registered to these important insights. First, the racialized politics of English nationalism appear to be gaining ground in precisely those areas of England where there are relatively low levels of migration and less evidence of the kind of multiculture that Gilroy and Back describe (Dodds 2015). There are questions, then, about the representativeness of London as a case study for anti-racist resources of hope. Second, as a phenomenon that can be traced back to the 1990s, the multicultural sensibility that both Back and Gilroy speak to has not yet been tested, in a political sense. It is not clear then how durable the lived multiculture produced in the aftermath of the anti-racism of the 1970s and 1980s will prove to be, particularly in a juncture where the racist right are in the ascendency and the infrastructure of anti-racist resistance appears hollowed out and in long-term retreat.

There are resources of hope, but time is running out – we are at five minutes to midnight.

Notes

1. The cases of Greece, Spain, Portugal and arguably Scotland are in this sense exceptions in an otherwise rightward drift of politics in Europe.
2. The ways in which the crisis has unfolded in Scotland and how this intersects with questions of race and racism will be traced in a forthcoming article by the authors.
3. Such wilful ignorance on the part of the VL campaign not only occluded racism, but another dimension of the Empire story: namely, the wave of decolonial revolt that systematically dismantled the British Empire piece by piece in the name of democracy and freedom, such that between 1945 and 1965 the number of people under British colonial rule fell from 700 million to 5 million (Virdee 2014).

Acknowledgements

We would like to thank the three referees as well as Matt Dawson, David Featherstone, David Feldman, Bridget Fowler, Emma Jackson, Gareth Mulvey and Helge Petersen for their helpful comments on an earlier draft of this article.

Disclosure statement

No potential conflict of interest was reported by the authors.

Funding

We are grateful to the Economic and Social Research Council (ESRC) Centre on Dynamics of Ethnicity [award number ES/K002198/1] for supporting this research.

References

Anderson, P. 1964. "Origins of the Present Crisis." *New Left Review* 1 (23): 26–53.
Arrighi, G. 2009. *Adam Smith in Beijing*. London: Verso.
Ashcroft, M. 2016. "How the United Kingdom Voted on Thursday … and Why." http://lordashcroftpolls.com/2016/06/how-the-united-kingdom-voted-and-why/.
Ashe, S. 2016. "UKIP, Brexit and Postcolonial Melancholy." *Discover Society*, Issue 33, June. http://discoversociety.org/2016/06/01/ukip-brexit-and-postcolonial-melancholy/.
Ashe, S., S. Virdee, and L. Brown. 2016. "Striking Back Against Racist Violence in the East End of London, 1968–1970." *Race and Class* 58 (1): 34–54.
Back, L. 1996. *New Ethnicities and Urban Culture: Racisms and Multiculture in Young Lives*. London: UCL Press.
Back, L., M. Keith, A. Khan, K. Shukra, and J. Solomos. 2002. "New Labour's White Heart: Politics, Multiculturalism and the Return of Assimilation." *The Political Quarterly* 73 (4): 445–454.
Baldwin, J. 1984. *Notes of a Native Son*. Boston, MA: Beacon Press.
BBC. 2016. "EU Referendum Results." Accessed December 2, 2016. http://www.bbc.co.uk/news/politics/eu_referendum/results.

Bush, S. 2015. "Labour's Anti-immigrant Mug: The Worst Part Is, It Isn't a Gaffe." *New Statesmen*, March 28. http://www.newstatesman.com/politics/2015/03/labours-anti-immigrant-mug-worst-part-it-isnt-gaffe.

Commission for Racial Equality. 2006. *Race Relations 2006: A Research Study*. London: CRE.

Condor, S., and S. Fenton. 2012. "Thinking Across Domains: Class, Nation and Racism in England and Britain." *Ethnicities* 12 (4): 385–393.

Davies, W. 2016. *Thoughts on the Sociology of Brexit*. The Brexit Crisis: A Verso Report. https://www.versobooks.com/books/2352-the-brexit-crisis.

Dodds, L. 2015. "Mapped: Where Is UKIP's Support Strongest? Where There Are No Immigrants." http://www.telegraph.co.uk/news/politics/ukip/11539388/Mapped-where-is-Ukips-support-strongest-Where-there-are-no-immigrants.html.

Dorling, D. 2016. "Brexit: The Decision of a Divided Country." *British Medical Journal* 354.

Duffy, B., and T. Frere-Smith. 2014. *Perception and Reality. Public Attitudes to Immigration*. London: IPSOS-MORI Social Research Institute.

Emejulu, A., and L. Bassel. 2015. "Minority Women, Austerity and Activism." *Race & Class* 57 (2): 86–95.

Farris, S. 2017. *In the Name of Women's Rights: The Rise of Femonationalism*. Durham, NC: Duke University Press.

Fenton, S. 2012. "Resentment, Class and Social Sentiments about the Nation: The Ethnic Majority in England." *Ethnicities* 12 (4): 465–483.

Gilroy, P. 2004. *After Empire: Melancholia or Convivial Culture?* London: Routledge.

Glasman, M., J. Rutherford, M. Stears, and S. White, eds. 2011. "The Labour Tradition and the Politics of Paradox." Soundings.org.uk, 9–11.

Goodwin, M., and O. Heath. 2016. "The 2016 Referendum, Brexit and the Left Behind: An Aggregate-level Analysis of the Result." *The Political Quarterly* 87 (3): 323–332.

Habermas, J. 2016. "Core Europe to the Rescue: A Conversation with Jürgen Habermas about Brexit and the EU Crisis." *Social Europe*. https://www.socialeurope.eu/2016/07/core-europe-to-the-rescue/.

Hall, S. 1979. "The Great Moving Right Show." *Marxism Today*, January.

Hall, S. 1987. "Gramsci and Us." *Marxism Today*, June.

Hall, S. 2000. "Interview." In *Rethinking British Decline*, edited by R. English and M. Kenny, 106–116. London: Macmillan Press.

Hayton, R. 2016. "The UK Independence Party and the Politics of Englishness." *Political Studies Review* 14 (3): 400–410.

Inglehart, R., and P. Norris. 2016. *Trump, Brexit and the Rise of Populism*. Working Paper Series 26. Boston, MA: Harvard Kennedy School.

Jeffery, C., A. Henderson, R. Scully, and R. Wyn Jones. 2016. "England's Dissatisfactions and the Conservative Dilemma." *Political Studies Review* 14 (3): 335–348.

Johnson, B. 2016. "Boris Johnson's Speech on the EU Referendum: Full Text." *Conservative Home*, May 9. http://www.conservativehome.com/parliament/2016/05/boris-johnsons-speech-on-the-eu-referendum-full-text.html.

Knowles, C. 2008. "The Landscape of Post-imperial Whiteness in Rural Britain." *Ethnic and Racial Studies* 31 (1): 167–184.

Komaromi, P. 2016. *Post-referendum Racism and Xenophobia: The Role of Social Media Activism in Challenging the Normalisation of Xeno-racist Narratives*. http://www.irr.org.uk/news/post-referendum-racism-and-the-importance-of-social-activism/.

Kumar, K. 2003. *The Making of English National Identity*. Cambridge: Cambridge University Press.

Kundnani, A. 2007. *The End of Tolerance: Racism in 21st Century Britain*. London: Pluto Press.

Lentin, A. 2016. "Racism in Public or Public Racism: Doing Anti-racism in 'Post-racial' Times." *Ethnic and Racial Studies* 39 (1): 33–48.

MacPhee, G., and P. Poddar. 2007. *Empire and After: Englishness in Postcolonial Perspective*. New York: Berghahn Books.

May, T. 2016. "Statement from the New Prime Minister Theresa May." *Prime Minister's Office*, July 13. https://www.gov.uk/government/speeches/statement-from-the-new-prime-minister-theresa-may.

McGeever, B. 2015. "Nationalism and Anti-racist Strategy after the 2015 General Election." *New Left Project*. http://www.newleftproject.org/index.php/site/article_comments/nationalism_and_antiracist_strategy_after_the_2015_general_election.

Meer, N. 2012. "Racialization and Religion: Race, Culture and Difference in the Study of Antisemitism and Islamophobia." *Ethnic and Racial Studies* 36 (3): 1–14.

Moore, S. 2011. *New Trade Union Activism*. London: Palgrave Macmillan.

Office for National Statistics. 2011. *2011 Census Analysis: What Does the 2011 Census Tell Us about Inter-ethnic Relationships?* http://www.ons.gov.uk/peoplepopulationand community/birthsdeathsandmarriages/marriagecohabitationandcivilpartnerships/articles/whatdoesthe2011censustellusaboutinte rethnicrelationships/2014-07-03.

Piketty, T. 2014. *Capital in the 21st Century*. Boston, MA: Harvard University Press.

Puar, J. 2007. *Terrorist Assemblages: Homonationalism in Queer Times*. Durham, NC: Duke University Press.

Runnymede Trust. 2009. *Who Cares about the White Working Class?* London: Runnymede Trust.

Shukra, K. 1998. *The Changing Pattern of Black Politics in Britain*. London: Pluto Press.

Sivanandan, A. 1982. *A Different Hunger*. London: Pluto Press.

Skeggs, B. 1997. *Formations of Class and Gender: Becoming Respectable*. London: Sage.

Solomos, J. 2003. *Race and Racism in Britain*. Basingstoke: Palgrave Macmillan.

Thompson, E. P. 1991. *The Making of the English Working Class*. London: Penguin.

Tyler, K. 2012. *Whiteness, Class and the Legacies of Empire: On Home Ground*. London: Palgrave.

Virdee, S. 2014. *Racism, Class and the Racialized Outsider*. London: Palgrave Macmillan.

Virdee, S. 2015. "Anti-racism, Working Class Formation and the Significance of the Racialized Outsider." *New Left Project*. http://www.newleftproject.org/index.php/site/article_comments/anti_racism_workingclass_formation_and_the_significance_of_the_racialized.

Ware, V. 2008. "Towards a Sociology of Resentment: A Debate on Class and Whiteness." *Sociological Research Online* 13 (5). http://www.socresonline.org.uk/13/5/9.html.

Williams, R. 1989. *Resources of Hope*. London: Verso.

Winter, A. 2016. "Island Retreat: 'On Hate, Violence and the Murder of Jo Cox'." *Open Democracy*, June 20, 2016. https://www.opendemocracy.net/uk/aaron-winter/island-retreat-on-hate-violence-and-murder-of-jo-cox.

Wyn Jones, R., G. Lodge, A. Henderson, and D. Wincott. 2012. *The Dog that Finally Barked: England as an Emerging Political Community*. London: Institute for Public Policy Research.

Wyn Jones, R., G. Lodge, C. Jeffrey, G. Gottfried, R. Scully, A. Henderson, and D. Wincott. 2013. *England and Its Two Unions: The Anatomy of a Nation and Its Discontents*. London: Institute for Public Policy Research.

Rioting and the politics of crisis

Karim Murji

ABSTRACT
This article draws on selected explanatory accounts of rioting that occurred in England in 2011 for the purpose of illustrating the ways in which scholarly critiques frame quite different senses of what kind of "crisis" the riots represented. On one side, the riots are understood within a "race and policing" frame placing them in a line of continuity with events across time and space and in an ongoing crisis of racial subjugation. In direct contrast, another side treats the riots as a crisis of post-politics, in which nihilism has replaced purposive political action. While different types of politics are centred in both approaches, they differ remarkably in relation to racism, with the latter treating race as epiphenomenal. These frames are instances of how critical scholarly understandings draw on events, and it is argued they miss potentially far-reaching senses of "crisis" that can be drawn out of some aspects of rioting.

At least since the influential and groundbreaking book, *Policing the Crisis* (Hall et al. 1978), race and policing issues have commonly been interconnected as a site of crisis in academic analyses. Rioting in the U.K. in the early 1980s deepened that nexus, and for many years this has been a prism through which most riots or violent disorder has been understood (Benyon and Solomos 1987; Keith 1993; Smith 2013). By understood I am referring not to media commentary or to public debate, although it may also occur there, but to academic and scholarly coverage of events in the 1980s and since that has made racialization a predominant approach to think through disorder and policing (Holdaway 1996; Keith 1993; Rowe 1998). The racial connection of the 2011 riots as primarily another instance of this history is due to its perceived echoes of events from the 1970s and 1980s when there were riots at the Notting Hill Carnival, and then in various inner cities, most notably Brixton in 1981 (Scarman 1981) and Brixton and Broadwater Farm in 1985 (Gifford 1986). In this vein, riots became an episodic but familiar part of the

British landscape that made them an archetypal form of protest or mobilization associated with race issues and racial minorities. Yet, while the 2011
riots seem to speak to this history (Smith 2013), some interpretive frames
can also erase race in curious ways, and the 2011 events are notable for the
scholarly expression of a counter-view in which the riots were treated as
marking a crisis of "post-politics" and in which race and racism are given no
or very limited significance.

In setting these out as two prominent "ways of seeing" (Berger 1972), my
purpose is threefold. First, to highlight how events are captured for particular
ends in critical scholarship, either as a sign of continuing racism policing or of
the state of politics. Those ends are not illegitimate and they may even
account for some aspects of riots, but their explanatory overreach is a
problem. They lack specificity to times and places as they attempt to "shoe-
horn" disparate events into somewhat singular frames, which itself signals
the limits of these accounts. The sources included here appear in conventional
academic publications such as books and journal articles; it also draws official
reports, blog posts and social media. In Hammersley's (2014) terms, they are
explanations, and go beyond description, because they infer or claim to know
the causes of rioting. My aim is not to offer a counter-narrative of what "really
happened" in August 2011; timelines and a sense of how events unfolded are
available in Morrell et al. (2011) and the Riots, Communities and Victims Panel
report (2012). Second, while riots are often not amenable to any comprehensive account, their "critical" framing often does not allow for qualifiers or
explanatory limits. This is about more than language and terminology.
Rioting, as a set of messy and dispersed events in which the agency and identity of actors are disputed, lends itself to this argument, but it is also evident in
the ways that race is made significant. Even where race is centred, it is done in
a way that lends weight to some kinds of connections while obscuring others,
as I will show later. Third, I suggest that this argument may bear a wider claim
about what is "a" or "the" crisis. What if instead of seeing the events as a "race
crisis" or a "post-political crisis" it was called something else, for instance, a
"legitimacy crisis"? The intended echo of Habermas (1975) here is instructive.
Habermas' concern with tendencies of capitalist and liberal welfare states
perhaps matters less here than his more general invocation of a legitimation
crisis as a decline in or loss of confidence in the administrative and leadership
capabilities of the state. Viewed in this light, riots and protests may be thought
of as small instances that reflect failures of policing and of politics, though in a
different manner to the accounts of the events to be discussed.

Frames and framing are commonly applied in media studies (Fairhurst and
Sarr 1996) and employed in an analogous way, as in Butler (2009) who uses it
to suggest how a frame is a device to identify what is being brought to attention, or into the centre of the analysis or explanation. It is this sense of framing
I am relying on here, but for the purpose of drawing attention to partialities in

scholarly analysis. While mainstream media accounts provide a "preferred reading" of such events, my contention is that scholarly appraisals are also forms of preferred reading, even when they are cast as oppositional readings against an orthodoxy. They have a built-in diagnostic that instead of challenging "mainstream" views re-tread well-established tropes and perspectives that riots provide a pretext or a headline for. Hence, this article is not a "reading of the riots" that occurred in 2011, but rather a characterization of two prominent ways those events were framed. It does not try to cover every reading or analysis of the riots, but it is not based on a merely random selection either. The sources covered are selected for the purpose of the position being presented, but they are also among the main or key examples of the two types to be discussed. These two different "ways of seeing", or framing, interpreting, capturing and explaining riots, are the primary focus of this article. Although there are stark differences between them, they are not intended to be seen as simple opposites. In Badiou (2012), for instance, there are traces of both in his portrayal of riots, protests, urban social movements and the "Arab spring" as connected to police/state racism, as well as to apolitical consumerist looting. Similarly, Clover's (2016) reading also contains elements of both.

So while the article does discuss the 2011 riots, it draws on them for a specific purpose. I provide a brief overview only for some context. Like violent disorders in the U.S.A. in 2014–16 (Camp and Heatherton 2016), the 2011 riots are commonly said to have started from the fatal shooting (hence calling them "trigger" events is hardly appropriate in the circumstances) by Metropolitan police officers of Mark Duggan, a young man of mixed race origins in August 2011, in Tottenham, north London. While the police claimed Duggan had a gun and an illegal firearm was found, it was some distance from the car he was in. Community anger over the shooting led to a protest at the local police station which tipped over into widespread disorder and some looting in the area. Violent disorder continued into the next day, and subsequently there were riots, including looting, across various parts of north, east, south and west London. Riots of varying scale and intensity also occurred in other cities such as Birmingham, Bristol, Liverpool and Nottingham on the following days (Communities and Panel 2012; Morrell et al. 2011). This short account signals that while events began from the police shooting of a black/mixed race male in an ethnically and racially mixed area of London, rioting also occurred in other English towns and cities that have less notable African-Caribbean populations. Some parts of the cities where riots occurred have undergone significant gentrification in recent decades in ways that cut across race and class lines in multiple ways. Thus, the August 2011 riots "were different phenomena in different cities and even in different parts of the same city" (Home Affairs Committee 2011, 3).

"Only connect": a crisis of race and policing, and beyond

Probably the most common and recognizable scholarly trope employed in understanding the riots is by "connecting" them to other times and places, and this established a "causative chain" between here/now and then/there. Connecting can also work by way of contrast, which I mention at the end of this section. In the main, connecting occurs through contextualization or comparison, and it is generally done in a critical vein to imply or to assert continuity between past and present, or between different places, commonly ones with established and recent histories of race conflict. Linking or connecting the events of 2011 across time and space to other "similar" times and places is illuminating in terms of how racial connections are imagined and made, across time and space, and consequentially to the same or similar kinds of underlying causes, usually racism and/or racially discriminatory policing, or in extended forms, to social and economic inequality. It can be seen just in the titles of two short articles: Jefferson's (2011) "Policing the Riots: From Bristol and Brixton to Tottenham, via Toxteth, Handsworth etc"; and Tyler and Lloyd's (2015) "From Tottenham to Baltimore", which references the riots in the U.S. city following the funeral of an African-American man, Freddie Gray, who had died from spinal injuries a week after being taken into custody by the police. These titles exemplify the "from X to Y" type connection made between the 2011 riots and other places and other times; thus, connections are made temporally as well as in spatial terms, as Jefferson (2011) invokes places that were at the centre of "race" riots in the 1980s.

In each case, whether within Britain or across the Atlantic, the common thread is racism, and policing and social justice/inequality. Jefferson connects 2011 to places and a time – the context of the 1980s riots – in predominantly or recognizably, black or African-Caribbean population areas, some of which were designated as "symbolic locations" for policing where police–community conflict had become entrenched and routine (Keith 1993). Tyler and Lloyd (2015) make a more contemporaneous but transatlantic connection between racially unjust policing in England and in the U.S.A., that, for Kelley and Tuck (2015), is "the other special relationship" between the two nations. In these accounts, the "spark" that can light a fire and move from low-level to violent disorder is embedded in the everyday contacts between the police and black people. In spite of changes to police procedure and policy around key issues such as stop and search in the decades since the 1980s (Hall, Grieve, and Savage 2009), it remains a key aggravating feature of everyday interactions. Social and economic inequality provides the context that shapes these encounters and experiences. "Connecting" brings out such ways of understanding the 2011 riots as a moment of crisis, where a crisis is a rupture in time and space, but also one that has deep roots and histories that connect the antagonistic relationship of race and policing in urban locations. Thus, there is both a continuous crisis, as well as episodic crises that take an expressive form, such as rioting. Empirical evidence of statistical disproportionality and complaints about police harassment, including the use of the "sus" law historically, and stop and search (or stop and frisk in the U.S.A.) it is plays a key part in this argument about "endless pressure", where black people, often male and young, are simultaneously over-policed as "criminals" but under-protected (McGhee 2005) as victims with regard to gun and knife crime, particularly in large cities like London.

While "from Tottenham to Baltimore" represents the "X to Y" style of connecting places, a notable feature of 2011 is not the link from X to Y, but rather of X to X, "from Tottenham to Tottenham", as it were. This form of connection is revealing for the ways claims are framed, as well what is obscured or overlooked. The "X to X" connection is to violent disorders in broadly the same area, at Broadwater Farm in 1985 (Gifford 1986; Keith 1993). The close co-location of these two events, even spread over 36 years, speaks powerfully to a sense of ongoing racialized inequality, as well as unresolved problems with policing. In both 2011 and 1985, the events are connected to the deaths of black people in contact with the police, which itself is a matter of concern over more than five decades (Athwal and Bourne 2015). In this light, the riots in Tottenham in 2011 were not "meaningless" violence but an event haunted by the riot of 1985. The connection between them was commonly reported in the media, by commentators and other analysts. Tottenham was referred to as a place with a history of riot, a history made more charged because the 1985 riot involved the death of a police officer PC Keith Blakelock, a point that was also prominent in a verbatim play on the riots (Slovo 2011).

While racism and policing is the core of the frame, the analysis within it can be stretched to invoke a broader political–economic crisis. A near-contemporaneous example of this is found in Internet sites such as Ceasefire magazine and in Elliot-Cooper's (2011a) blog posts that begin with policing and then expand to wider policy issues that make the riots a case of "redefining the political". In September 2011, his starting point is comments made by rioters of the police as a lawless, "institutionalised gang" in inner city areas, a term itself invoking the notion of the police as an "army of occupation" in black areas in the late 1970s (Keith 1993). He views the police in blunt terms as part of the repressive state apparatus, being "used by the state to control and repress, not maintain stability or uphold justice", on behalf of "a state machine which racialises, impoverishes and dehumanises" black communities (Elliot-Cooper 2011a). Later, drawing from the voices of people on the street, he notes that "young people affected by the uprising ... offer their own analysis of the political ... on unemployment, the cuts to EMA[1] and youth services, police powers, media and political corruption, poverty and racism." This extension beyond policing is an indication of how riots come to be linked to poverty, inequality and political–economic issues. While in the second frame to be discussed looting is seen as failed consumerism, for Elliot-Cooper (2011b) it is purposive in a way that implicitly draws on moral economy (Thompson 1971). Thus, the stores targeted, such as JD Sports and Footlocker, are seen as both purveyors of desirable brands and consumer capitalism, but also as a form of (symbolic) violence toward poor people in deprived areas who find that the goods are well beyond their reach (Millington 2016). On other sites and in social media, there was a suggestion that these shops were targeted because of their exploitative approach in paying minimum wages and refusing to employ local people. Widening the frame from rioting to political diagnosis is seen in other sources also. Tyler (2013), for instance, links it to the abjection and stigmatization of the poor in the U.K. under neo-liberal economic policies; others emphasize widening social inequality as a key factor linking and underlying rioting in history (Grover 2011) and casino finance capitalism (Monaghan and O'Flynn 2011).

The analyses in the connecting frame exemplify narrower and wider claims, where the latter draws in critiques of capitalism, the financial crisis and economic inequalities, while the former looks more to factors such as policing and community conflict. In terms of level, these diagnoses can be pitched at local, national and/or global issues. Locality perspectives usually highlight local police/community relations in specific places, often ones with racialized associations, as in Jefferson (2011), though Elliot-Cooper (2011a, 2011b) goes beyond that. National views draw attention to the restructuring of the welfare state, increasing poverty and the politics of austerity, as in Tyler (2013), while global analyses centre casino capitalism, the banking crisis and neo-liberalism. Tyler's (2013) approach also aims to suggest the intersections between these levels analytically. However, all of these contain the common problem of structuralist analysis: how to link the "objective" social and economic conditions with the "subjective" motives, understanding and actions of individuals and groups. "Political" intentionality and readings may apply to some people and events in some places, but is the explanatory reach intended to encompass all events or just particular ones? Even when applied to specific places, such as Tottenham, which can be closely contextualized in terms of local histories of policing, experience of inequality and a widening gap between rich and poor, is the explanation pitched at the level of the riot as a whole, or can it include the diversity of actions and actors that took part in that? The messiness of riots, even in one location, tends to evade any neatly bounded explanations.

Resolutions to that problem include viewing the actions of rioters as "proto-politics" (Millington 2016), or by invoking a sense of latency in their consciousness or experience via the concept of habitus, as Akram (2014) does. Taking politics to refer to the contestation of the uneven distribution of power and resources, Akram identifies the key problem as the gap between the sense of grievance expressed by rioters – and their general demographic profile as people from socially deprived backgrounds – and the lack of an explicit political strategy or even any great sense of engagement with politics. Akram (2014, 383) argues that

> grievances and motivations are stored until they are triggered in the rioter's habitus. This means that, whilst individuals may have concerns about issues, they may not feel able to do anything about them, or there are few channels to do so. However, the riot, or its triggering events, represents an opportunity for stored grievances to be expressed, because the riot represents a rupture in the habitus.

Like others (e.g. Badiou 2012), this places great weight on a "triggering" event, without developing a model of how that is communicated, understood, deployed and invoked in events. It draws on the "flashpoint" models of disorder (Waddington 1992), but displays the same key shortcoming: why or how is it that many, or even daily, possible flashpoints do not lead to riots? Moreover, its focus on the spectacular and expressive forms of violent disorder prioritizes that over ongoing and everyday low-level social disorder, or "slow rioting" (Waddington, Jobard, and King 2011). Hence, while connecting by comparison in a diagnostic vein is not implausible, it can lack specificity to times and places, as well as how far it applies to individuals and groups. It requires a better link or connection between everyday "endless pressure" – daily and routinized experience, both current and remembered, of police and racial discrimination – and large-scale disorders. While an explanation or a frame cannot cover everything, its partialities – the selective nature of what gets connected to what – as well as its focus ought to be a reason to pause before asserting connections with any deep-seated confidence.

In terms of crisis politics, the connecting frame proffers a critique – of policing, austerity politics and/or neo-liberalism – but that overlooks, I argue, a potentially more modest but maybe also more powerful critique. To illustrate this, I need to spell out a connection that is not commonly evident in writings on the 2011 riots. The "X to X" connection of Tottenham in 2011 is to Broadwater Farm in 1985, as already stated. However, a different connection between 2011 and 1985 provides another narrative of crisis. The protests that followed the Duggan killing eerily echoed the events surrounding the police shooting of a black woman, Cherry Groce, at her home in Brixton in 1985, in a raid where the police were targeting her son (details of this event appear in various sources on the 1980s riots cited). That shooting also led to a protest around the local police station and, eventually, disorder. The connection between these two events can be used to propose that the start of the 2011 riots has less to do with everyday policing but instead the rarer, but highly consequential, use of firearms. In both cases, it is possible that police action in the wake of the shootings could have prevented or contained rioting. The common failure in the two situations was that of the police to draw on and implement their family liaison procedures that required them to communicate with and support the Duggan/Groce families. The inadequate response of the Metropolitan Police in the immediate aftermath of Duggan's death contributed directly to the mood of the organized protest at Tottenham police station on 6 August 2011. Poor or non-existent communication with the family of Mrs Groce was undoubtedly a factor in Brixton in 1985. In other words, in terms of policy, this speaks to an institutional failure. It could be called a crisis in light of the fact that by the time of Tottenham in 2011, it is hardly something the police can claim to be surprised about since, in between those decades, the most high-profile issue of race and policing was their poor handling of and dealings with the family of Stephen Lawrence after he was stabbed in 1993; those shortcomings were central to Macpherson's (1999) path-breaking formal finding of the police as being institutionally racist.

After Macpherson, family liaison techniques became a focus for policy improvement through sustained critical incident or "crisis management" training (Hall, Grieve, and Savage 2009). Despite that, around a key and long-standing concern – race relations in an inner city location such as Tottenham – ineffectual family liaison and critical incident management signal a sense of policy and institutional failure, or even crisis. Elaborating this viewpoint still puts events squarely within a race and policing frame, but as an alternative way of connecting events and issues, it produces a significantly different analysis of "crisis". It offers an institutional prescription that is lacking in most scholarly accounts, though the issue of family liaison is clearly identified as a community concern and a police mistake in the Home Affairs Committee (2011) report. Extending it as I have done so suggests that the crisis that Tottenham 2011 represents is or could be about legitimacy in the Habermasian sense that institutions of state cease to function effectively. In terms of the argument of this article, the other crucial point is that a largely overlooked and "minor" policy theme opens the way to a far-reaching critique.

Other connections not made or underplayed are also revealing for the way the "race narrative" of the 2011 riots is constructed. While in terms of race, there are aspects of 2011 that can be plausibly linked to 1981 and 1985, other events in between those decades are remarkably muted. For instance, the 2011 riots are generally not read in relation to riots in 2001 in northern English towns, which were mainly associated with people of South Asian descent, nor to "white" riots in places such as the Blackbird Leys estate in Oxford in 1991. In other words, connecting to the 1980s emphasizes some places and neglects others, setting up a preferred narrative that forms the race and policing connection. Furthermore, the stress on place continuity overlooks considerable demographic shifts and changes in a locality such as Tottenham. The arrival and settlement of newer and different migrant communities make the area super-diverse to an extent, as reflected in the make-up of both rioters and victims, including the local Turkish/Kurdish shop-keepers who used self-defence campaigns to protect their property (Lewis et al. 2011). Areas such as Gloucester, Enfield, and Ealing, which also witnessed rioting and all have very mixed populations, also call into question a strong race narrative of the 2011 riots. Drawing attention to these absences, over-sights and different geographies is not to undermine "connecting" but to point to its selectivity. In other cases, however, connecting is undercut through a method of contrasting the 2011 riots with other disorders. For some, earlier riots and in different places, disorder, even involving violence, was understandable as a political protest, as in the 1960s Civil Rights demon-strations in the U.S.A. By contrast, the 2011 events are said to lack any substan-tial cause; they are a form of misguided or defective rage, and this is the nub of the post-political frame.

"Shopping for free": the crisis of post-politics

The most obvious contrast with the preceding frame, which aims to identify some kind of political intentionality in rioting and read that in light of histories of racist over-policing and against conditions of inequality, would be one in which any political intentionality is denied. Such responses are usually a "knee jerk" law and order reflex, as in the comment of the Mayor of London, Boris Johnson: "Its time we stopped hearing all this (you know) nonsense about how there are deep sociological justifications for wanton criminality and destruction of peoples' property" (cited in Hammersley 2014, 123, n 10). Along with the similar tone taken in the first reaction of the Prime Minister, such statements are widely quoted (some of which can be found in Hammers-ley 2014; Kelley and Tuck 2015) in critical approaches as a sign of how out-of-touch and predictable such responses are, not least as they repeat similar words made in regard to rioting in the 1980s (Benyon and Solomos 1987; Rowe 1998) and before that to "race and crime" generally (Hall et al. 1978). While they are familiar, it is not the case that they always fit into a simple nar-rative. Even in August 2011 when the riots occurred, the Prime Minister and Leader of the Opposition both condemned violence but also suggested there were complex causes behind the riots, and such change over time is commonly overlooked (Hammersley 2014). Moreover, while "right wing" reac-tions do blame feckless families and welfare dependency, they can also be more nuanced than that. For instance, Iain Duncan Smith, the Secretary of State for social welfare, a politician commonly regarded as being on the "hard right" of the Conservative Party, wrote in 2011 that:

> while we have to be tough on the perpetrators and on the gangs, we also have
> to ask ourselves what lies behind this. We cannot simply arrest our way out of

these riots … The riots have provided a moment of clarity for all of us, a reminder that a strong economy requires a strong social settlement, with stable
families ready to play a productive role in their own communities. The challenge
of our generation is to reforge our commitment to reform society so that we can
restore aspiration and hope to communities that have been left behind.[2]

The appeal to "stable families" and restoring "aspiration" is quite different
from the political and policy prescriptions that come out of the preceding
frame, but it is not the same as denying any politics in riotous disorder. In
Duncan Smith's view of "communities … left behind", there is a suggestion
that governments bear some responsibility for that, as well as markets or
their own actions. The "integration" strategy (Casey 2016) that flows from it
is a mixture of punitive as well as welfare measures that does responsiblize
people in poverty (Tyler 2013), but it is not merely about more "law and
order", not least as in the period since 2010 a Conservative-led government
had been reducing police resources.

Demands for more policing, tougher sentences and punishment is a
common refrain in rioting of all kinds and usually linked to right wing and
authoritarian politicians and commentators. Such enforcement/police-led
perspectives appear to contrast with more "social democratic" responses
that stress "repair", in the form of community building, better education,
housing and welfare and even, at times, anti-racism. Yet, Duncan Smith's
words cut across that to an extent. While there can be quite large differences
of emphasis and inflexion, the responses of left and right do overlap. Scarman's (1981) report into Brixton disorders, for instance, can be read as a
liberal document that recommended better community facilities and bridge
building between the police and black communities, as well as heralding a
decade of increasing "tooling up" by the police in preparation for more
violent disorder. In spite of the many critical objections to Scarman at the
time, in Hall's (1982) incisive reading the report did not conform to any
simple liberal/reactionary divide. He saw that it contained elements of both
and also marked an attempt at a new kind of settlement. Hence, there is
some continuity between left and right views as well as less predictability
about what is "left" and what is "right" in readings of rioting. Three decades
on, responses to the 2011 riots also demonstrate that. A denial of politics in
the 2011 riots appears in the report of the Labour-led Parliamentary Home
Affairs Committee (2011, 31), for instance. It observed that though there
could have "been an element of disengagement" among some of those
involved in the riots, but it adds that, "unlike some events in the past, including the riots in the 1980s, there does not seem to be any clear narrative, nor a
clear element of protest or clear political objectives". This does rather beg the
question of what "clear" means in relation to 2011. Contextualized as a matter
originating from a black death in contact with the police, there are clear links
from 1985 to 2011. The spread of riots to many other places may lack the

"clear narrative" the Committee refers to, but to wilfully fail to recognize race as a starting point seems to be a determinedly narrow and self-limiting outlook. It also displays the contrast method where the 2011 events are cast unfavourably in relation to previous events. Politics "then" is invoked to rule out politics "now"; thus, it is not the absence of politics per se but a matter of how it is conceived.

If the 1980s was the decade of monetarism, by the twenty-first century the master category is neo-liberalism, particularly in light of the banking and financial crisis from 2008 (Harvey 2012). This context produces two almost diametrically opposite points of view. In one, rioting is a kind of, maybe nascent, political activity against poverty and inequality, as in the preceding frame, while in another perspective, the 2011 riots are seen as marking an absence of politics, or a "post-political" reaction of failed rage by defective consumers. It is typified by Bauman's (2011) widely quoted remarks about the events: "These are not hunger or bread riots. These are riots of defective and disqualified consumers ... We are all consumers now, consumers first and foremost, consumers by right and by duty". Building on this, Žižek (2011) commented that the riots were, more than anything else, "a manifestation of a consumerist desire violently enacted when unable to realise itself in the 'proper' way – by shopping." For Žižek, the events "contain a moment of genuine protest" but it "is impotent rage and despair masked as a display of force". Thus, in Žižek as well as in Bauman, there is a sense that there are "objective" economic conditions that require political protests against capitalism, but the form the riots took – directionless violent disorder whose main goal was to acquire desirable consumer goods through looting – is not an expression of that.

The crisis of post-politics is a time or an era where alternative political imaginaries, as well as faith in the capacity of the state to effect progressive change, have been ruled out of court under neo-liberal domination; in this context, the legitimation crisis is the failure of left political leadership. The most developed exposition of the "shopping for free" perspective is in Treadwell et al. (2013) and Winlow et al. (2015). Taking their cue from the view that the dominance of neo-liberal and managerialist logics have undermined leftist political strategy against capitalism, their analysis follows Žižek in seeing rioters as post-political subjects incapable of collective action and driven by individualism and consumerism, or what they describe as the "shallow pleasures and distractions of consumer culture". It is significant that is not disorder per se that underlies their objection as they do view earlier riots and protests as expressions of political grievances: "In previous eras, the marginalized subject was ... active in ... political collectives ... [and] able ... to articulate [its] rage onto the real socio-economic, ethical and political causes of dissatisfaction". However, unlike what they see as the solidaristic politics then, now "it seems almost impossible for a potential collective of marginalized subjects to construct a universal political narrative that makes causal and contextual sense of their own shared suffering and offers a feasible solution to it" (Treadwell et al. 2013, 1–2).

Once again, there are conditions that call for political reaction, so it is the disorganized form of that in rioting that these authors see as symptomatic of post-politics. This covers misguided street politics, a lack of alternative ideologies to neo-liberal capitalism, and a failure to think of solidarity in class terms, rather than what they call "protests … structured in relation to the needs and wants of specific micro-communities" (Winlow et al. 2015, 203). This speaks to their rejection of cultural politics and the politics of difference, in which race is a form of "identity politics", promoted by some leftists. In this regard, the riot becomes a metaphor for a futile politics:

> In many cases, no progressive politics exists within the frame of the riot, and there is no seductive image of an ideological alternative for people to rally around. Instead, the riot is driven forward by an incoherent rabble of pissed-off individuals incapable of joining together to form a genuine political community. In the context of the post-political present, the riot is more a depressive acting out of deep, objectless frustration and anger than a concerted proto-political intervention demanding change. In most cases, the only vague hope we have been able to identify among contemporary rioters is the desire to be re-included into the very socio-economic system that excluded them in the first place. (Winlow et al. 2015, 203)

Their argument is based on some empirical work with rioters, though other empirical research questions their analysis. Newburn et al. (2015) observe that looting is a usual rather than an exceptional feature of riots. The stress on it by Treadwell et al. (2013), Winlow et al. (2015) and Žižek (2011) enables them to draw on it for the purpose of an argument about the nature of disaffected consumer capitalism among rioters whose purpose is just to be "included" as capitalist subjects. Yet, drawing on the more comprehensive LSE/Guardian study which interviewed around 270 people in the first phase (Treadwell et al. (2013) interviewed 30 people, by comparison), Newburn et al. (2015) show that rioters do express a mixture of motives, including dissatisfaction with politics and the police. Reducing that to, or focusing only on the desire to acquire free goods is to miss such views; using Thompson's (1971) "moral economy", Newburn et al. (2015) also suggest that the targets of looting are not random and violence can be understood as directed in some cases.

While Winlow et al. (2015) call for alternative political imaginaries, their "pessimistic" view of any political solidarities in rioting is symptomatic of a kind of "narrative of decline". Nostalgia is one form of cultural pessimism that Bennett (2001) identified as a trope in which a nation or culture, or in this case, political agency, is regarded as in irreversible decline. Its invocation may say more about the psychic disposition of those who reach for or appeal to "genuine political community", "universalism" and a seeming harking back to class politics, without difference. Treadwell et al. (2013) acknowledge that riots are messy and complex, but their refusal to see in at least some part of rioting elements of solidarity and collective action is to adopt a blinkered view of what counts as politics. New social movements, such as Occupy, also fail their test, though, like Harvey (2012), they do see elements of hope in some political alternatives such as the Syriza movement in Greece. For Harvey also, the 2011 riots are a poor relation to "real" politics because they bear no relation to "various glimmers of hope and light around the world" such as the movements in Spain and Greece, Latin America. Unlike the London rioters, Harvey maintains that the latter movements can "see through the vast scam that a predatory and feral global capitalism has unleashed upon the world" (157). Thus, these writers bemoan the decomposition of class politics and look to it as a basis for anti-capitalist movements. In doing so, they adopt a rather race-blind view of such politics and the intersections of race and class (Virdee 2014). While I have proposed that the "race and policing" frame makes too much of race, in a way that overlooks rioting in places and at times that do not fit that narrative, in post-politics, there is a stark reversal where race and racism are either absent or epiphenomenal. In spite of the messiness of riots, their varying locations and the multiracial composition of rioters, there is evidence that encounters with the police are an aggravating factor, as to an extent is inequality among and within definable demographic groups (Lewis et al. 2011; Newburn et al. 2015). It is arguable if the actions are directed in the ways that some see (Akram 2014; Millington 2016) but to treat them as "race-blind" and as directionless consumerism is, perhaps bizarrely for a high-level perspective, to miss the bigger picture by focusing on some details.

Conclusion

In selecting and assessing two ways the 2011 riots have been framed the purpose of this article was to treat them as analyses that centre or decentre race, provide contrasting senses of what the politics of rioting amount to and convey varying notions of what crisis the events are viewed as a symptom of. Although elements of both forms of explanation can be found in the *post hoc* accounts of rioters, these approaches share the common problem of any unqualified treatment of what goes on in riots, of accounting for variation across time and place, as well as the diversity of individuals and groups; this makes both more tenuous as explanations. The "race and policing" frame can make some credible links between past and present and "here" and "there"; however, the associations made reveal a preferred narrative that supports some sense of continuity but is less adept at addressing social, policy and demographic changes over time. The racial signification of rioting in the 1980s is powerful, but then as in 2011, the heterogeneous nature of cities and issues around over-policing and social injustice extend beyond race. Race is clearly necessary in understanding some of what occurred in 2011 but it is not sufficient; the same also applies to the police/ policing. The "post-political" frame highlights nihilism and looting in the riots but it does so at the expense of overstating the latter as routine, not exceptional. More importantly, it does not give due weight to the grievances about policing and sense of injustice that rioters did express (Lewis et al. 2011). It wilfully neglects the politics of race and racism that has been prominent since the 1980s in order to buttress a view of failures in organized politics, in which "identity politics" is itself seen as a cause.

Reflecting briefly on the U.S.A., there is a strong case to view recent (2014–16) events there as a race crisis if race is constitutive of and an inescapable feature of the events. The centrality of racialized experience and subjugation is undeniable because of the local and national histories of racism and racially unjust policing, which has formed the basis of the now well-known and transnational campaign Black Lives Matter.[3] That race is at the core is evident as even those who want to deny that racism is the issue lean on racialized explanations, such as the absence of father figures or poor parenting in black communities. While there are traces of such a narrative or analysis to be made in Britain, race is more crucial to some times and places, but not necessarily to all locations that witnessed rioting.

While rioting as example lends itself to a case against totalizing approaches, my wider argument is about styles of critical scholarly analysis that fit such events into a preferred framework or narrative, and as signs of some type of crisis. Readings of all riotous assembly could be criticized in this way but my point is more specific. The two frames provide varying definitions of the issue or problem; they are too broad in their sweep but also too narrow, in stressing some things and ignoring or overlooking others. If read through a "legitimacy crisis" perspective, the connecting frame casts light on the continuing problems of policing, but with little sense that the issues identified, such as stop and search, have been widely researched and subjected to policy changes; what comes after or out of all that remains an unanswered question. By pointing to an alternative connection – between Brixton 1985 and Tottenham 2011 – I have indicated how a/the crisis could be framed differently, as an institutional problem. This more modest analysis provides, I argue, a far-reaching critique of police policy. Meanwhile in post-politics, the failures of legitimacy lie with political leaders and organizations that mean rioters are directionless and selfish actors. Whether, some years on, the social movements criticized in this perspective, as well as the "glimmers" of hope they perceive, do or do not represent alternatives to capitalism is a question that goes well beyond rioting. Public disorders such as the 2011 riots are treated largely a symbol or a metaphor for a wider argument that is unconvincing in terms of specifics, such as "shopping for free", while, in general, it is unanchored from the place(s) or context(s) of rioting. To make sense of events as a "crisis", whether continuous or periodic, calls for an analytical gaze that can resist the temptations of grand narrative claims as a form of critique, and instead be alert to what is and is not continuous over time as well as how, and if, places can be linked.

Notes

1. EMA refers to the Education Maintenance Allowance that was withdrawn by the 2010–15 UK coalition government.
2. In *The Times*, 15 September 2011.
3. See http://blacklivesmatter.com/.

Acknowledgements

The author thanks the three anonymous reviewers for their comments and engagement with the paper. The author is grateful to the editors of this special issue for their help, and especially to Suman Gupta for including him in the Leverhume Trust funded series this issue comes out of.

Disclosure statement

No potential conflict of interest was reported by the author.

References

Akram, S. 2014. "Recognizing the 2011 United Kingdom Riots as Political Protest: A Theoretical Framework Based on Agency, Habitus and the Preconscious." *British Journal of Criminology* 54: 375–392.

Athwal, H., and J. Bourne, eds. 2015. *Dying for Justice*. London: Institute of Race Relations.

Badiou, A. 2012. *The Rebirth of History: Times of Riots and Uprisings*. London: Verso.

Bauman, Z. 2011. "The London Riots – On Consumerism Coming Home to Roost." *Social Europe Journal*, 9 August.

Bennett, O. 2001. *Cultural Pessimism: Narratives of Decline in the Postmodern World Edinburgh*. Edinburgh: University Press.

Benyon, J., and J. Solomos, eds. 1987. *The Roots of Urban Unrest*. Leicester: Scarman Centre.

Berger, J. 1972. *Ways of Seeing*. London: Penguin.

Butler, J. 2009. *Frames of War: When if Life Grievable?* London: Verso.

Camp, J., and C. Heatherton, eds. 2016. *Policing the Planet: Why the Policing Crisis Led to Black Lives Matter*. London: Verso.

Casey, L. 2016. *A Review into Opportunity and Integration*. https://www.gov.uk/government/uploads/system/uploads/attachment_data/file/575973/The_Casey_Review_Report.pdf.

Clover, J. 2016. *Riot. Strike. Riot: The New Era of Uprisings*. London: Verso.

Communities, Riots, and Victims Panel. 2012. *After the Riots*. http://webarchive.nationalarchives.gov.uk/20121003195935/http://riotspanel.independent.gov.uk/wp-content/uploads/2012/03/Riots-Panel-Final-Report1.pdf.

Elliot-Cooper, A. 2011a. "Redefining the political". https://ceasefiremagazine.co.uk/the-anti-imperialist-12-1/11 Sept 2011 The UK riots: redefining the political.

Elliot-Cooper, A. 2011b. "Advertising as a form of violence". https://ceasefiremagazine.co.uk/anti-imperialist-12-2/18 Sept 2011.

Fairhurst, G., and R. Sarr. 1996. *The art of Framing*. San Francisco: Jossey-Bass.

Gifford, T. 1986. *The Broadwater Farm Inquiry: Report of the Independent Inquiry Into Disturbances of October 1985 at the Broadwater Farm Estate, Tottenham*. London: Karia Press.

Grover, C. 2011. "Social Protest in 2011: Material and Cultural Aspects of Economic Inequalities." *Sociological Research Online* 16 (4).

Habermas, J. 1975. *Legitimation Crisis*. Boston, MA: Beacon Press.

Hall, S. 1982. "The Lessons of Lord Scarman." *Critical Social Policy* 2: 66–72.

Hall, S., C. Critcher, T. Jefferson, J. Clarke, and B. Roberts. 1978. *Policing the Crisis: Mugging, the State and Law and Order*. London: Macmillan.

Hall, N., J. Grieve, and S. Savage, eds. 2009. *Policing and Legacy of Lawrence*. Devon: Willan.

Hammersley, M. 2014. *The Limits of Social Science*. London: SAGE.

Harvey, D. 2012. *Rebel Cities: From the Right to the City to the Urban Revolution*. London: Verso.

Holdaway, S. 1996. *The Racialization of British Policing*. London: Macmillan.

Home Affairs Committee. 2011. *Policing Large Scale Disorder: Lessons From the Disturbances of August 2011*. London: The Stationery Office.

Jefferson, T. 2011. "Policing the Riots: From Bristol and Brixton to Tottenham, via Toxteth, Handsworth, etc." *Criminal Justice Matters* 87: 8–9.

Kelley, R., and S. Tuck, eds. 2015. *The Other Special Relationship: Race, Rights, and Riots in Britain and the United States*. New York: Palgrave.

Keith, M. 1993. *Race, Riots and Policing*. London: UCL Press.

Lewis, P., T. Newburn, M. Taylor, C. Mcgillivray, A. Greenhill, H. Frayman, and R. Proctor. 2011. *Reading the Riots: Investigating England's Summer of Disorder*. London: The LSE and The Guardian.

Macpherson, W. 1999. *The Stephen Lawrence Inquiry*. London: The Stationery Office.

McGhee, D. 2005. *Intolerant Britain? Hate, Citizenship and Difference*. Maidenhead: Open University Press.

Millington, G. 2016. "'I Found the Truth in Foot Locker': London 2011, Urban Culture, and the Post-Political City." *Antipode* 48 (3): 705–723.

Monaghan, L., and M. O'Flynn. 2011. "More Than Anarchy in the UK: 'Social Unrest' and its Resurgence in the Madoffized Society." *Sociological Research Online* 16 (4).

Morrell, G., D. Scott, D. Mcneish, and S. Webster. 2011. *The August Riots in England Understanding the Involvement of Young People*. London: NatCen.

Newburn, T., K. Cooper, R. Deacon, and R. Diski. 2015. "Shopping for Free? Looting, Consumerism and the 2011 Riots." *British Journal of Criminology* 55: 987–1004.

Rowe, M. 1998. *The Racialization of Disorder in Twentieth Century Britain*. Aldershot: Ashgate.

Scarman, L. 1981. *The Brixton Disorders 10-12 April 1981*. London: HMSO.

Slovo, G. 2011. *The Riots*. London: Oberon.

Smith, E. 2013. "Once as History, Twice as Farce? The Spectre of the Summer of '81 in Discourses on the August 2011 Riots." *Journal for Cultural Research* 17 (2): 124–143.

Thompson, E. P. 1971. "The Moral Economy of the English Crowd in the Eighteenth Century." *Past and Present* 50: 76–136.

Treadwell, J., D. Briggs, S. Winlow, and S. Hall. 2013. "Shopocalypse Now: Consumer Culture and the English Riots of 2011." *British Journal of Criminology* 53 (1): 1–17.

Tyler, I. 2013. "The Riots of the Underclass? Stigmatisation, Mediation and the Government of Poverty and Disadvantage in Neoliberal Britain." *Sociological Research Online* 18 (4): 1–10.

Tyler, I., and J. Lloyd. 2015. "From Tottenham to Baltimore, Policing Crisis Starts Race to the Bottom for Justice", *The Conversation*, 1 May 2015. http://theconversation.com/from-tottenham-to-baltimore-policing-crisis-starts-race-to-the-bottom-for-justice-40914.

Virdee, S. 2014. *Racism, Class and the Racialized Outsider*. Basingstoke: Palgrave Macmillan.

Waddington, D. 1992. *Contemporary Issues in Public Disorder*. London: Routledge.

Waddington, D., F. Jobard, and M. King, eds. 2011. *Rioting in the UK and France*. Abingdon: Taylor and Francis.

Winlow, S., S. Hall, J. Treadwell, and D. Briggs. 2015. *Riots and Political Protest: Notes From the Post-Political Present*. Abingdon: Routledge.

Žižek, S. 2011. "Shoplifters of the World Unite." *London Review of Books* 19 August, 28–29.

"Race" and the upsurge of antagonistic popular movements in Sweden

Carl-Ulrik Schierup, Aleksandra Ålund and Anders Neergaard

ABSTRACT

Across a crisis-stricken Europe battles rage for post-neoliberal hegemony, with "race" and "austerity" as central signifiers. One of the places where the frontlines are most pregnant is Sweden; long perceived as a role model for its welfare state, cultural equity and social equality. Sweden is, however, facing social conflicts following in the tracks of a deep transformation in terms of welfare cuts, racialization and growing social polarization, targeting in particular a disadvantaged migrant and post-migrant population. On that background, the paper focuses on the upsurge of mutually antagonistic popular movements – "racist" and "anti-racist". We use Sweden as an exemplary case of Europe's present Polanyian moment, reminiscent of the 1930s. Yet, current upheavals expound, the authors claim, a different configuration of crisis and racism as well as a dissimilar utopia for the imagineering of nation and community.

Introduction

By the second decade of the twenty-first century, at a moment marked by the reality of extensive immigration and a multiethnic social reality, speech on good governance in the EU has become dominated by the hailing of ima-gined mono-cultural nations. This is a common-sense racializing discourse, which has for decades been present as an influential political stratagem in European politics. But it has come to dominate a wide realm of public-political debate across the European Union, especially after the 2008 financial crash underscored a search for legitimacy for austerity politics through a discourse blaming "immigration", cultural pluralism and the racialized subaltern Other for the decline of citizenship, welfare and social cohesion.

This new-old racializing nativism is a toxic terrain which the political main-stream increasingly shares with extreme-right anti-immigration movements and parties across Europe. These appear, on their part – in spite of their philosophical roots and present-day political agendas bordering on fascism – increasingly successful in cleansing their public-political stigma of "racism". By successfully positioning itself neither to the right, nor to the left, but as *both right and left* (e.g. Holmes 2000), and foremost the "true" representation of the nation, this contemporary populism potentially appeals to broad categories of European populations, suffering economic insecurity, social crisis and identity loss. It can appeal to parts of a traditionally conservative and nationalist right, frustrated by perceived threats to national self-esteem represented by globalization, Europeanization and transnational migration. But explaining all ills through migration and alien cultures also vies for the allegiance of parts of the traditional left, frustrated with the denigration of the welfare state and the precarization of work. In the process, "Culture" has systematically been fabricated into what Ernesto Laclau (2005) calls "a floating signifier" with a plastic capacity of gluing together the multitude of disparate and often contradictory political claims embraced by a multifaceted contemporary European racism. Such a deployment of "culture" is not confined to the extreme right, but is a shared heritage and contemporary reality of Western democracy. Albeit clad in the unsullied robe of "culture", "the problem of the color line", which Du Bois (1903, 13) once called "the problem of the Twentieth Century", persists at the threshold to the twenty-first. Its differentiating signifiers of "color, bone and hair" now figure as (mostly) invisible, but no less important, subscripts. They continue to direct the bio-political management of imagined racial difference through the politics of outer and inner border control and securitization, policies of counterinsurgency, of urban segregation, and of discriminatory social and labour market policies.

This is the general context in which an ominous transformation of our present has unfolded, also in Sweden for long famed for its exemplary social model, regarded as merging extended rights of citizenship with a politics freed from nativist obsession. In the booming reformist spirit of the mid-1970s, new policies had been conceived in terms of "Equality, Partnership and Freedom of Choice", confidently rephrasing the revolutionary 1789 trinity into a credo of an inclusive welfare society: a particular Swedish "exceptionalism" (Schierup and Ålund 2011). It was specifically designed to offer a ramified body of substantial rights of citizenship for all – civil, political, cultural, social and labour rights – independently of ethnic identity or national origin. It included fast access to full formal citizenship for newcomers and inaugurated a solidaristic policy of asylum and refugee reception. It was supposed to guarantee empowerment to migrants and ethnic minorities of migrant background through principled and actual access to democratic participation on the basis of their unique historical experience and cultural identity. While there has always been a remarkable gap between professed ideals and another reality, from the spring of 2016, this former showpiece of socio-cultural inclusionism and public welfare had come to stand virtually inflamed by a cynical right–left game of thrones. It threatens to pragmatically dispose of what still remains of a model Swedish exceptionalism's moral political foundations in the dustbin of history (Ålund, Schierup, and Neergaard 2017).

Sweden is still a country with a privileged position in the international division of labour. It is a country for which a continued open migration and asylum policy would combine allegiance to humanitarian ideals with forward-looking opportunities for filling gaps in the labour market, for boosting economic dynamism, for redressing a crisis in an undermanned welfare institutional system and for successfully combating a looming demographic crisis; yet despoiled through the breakdown of the broader solidarities needed for pursuing long-term goals of sustainable economic development and a resuscitated social welfare (Schierup and Scarpa 2017). But a looming dismantling of the country's welfare system can now be conveniently hidden behind a smokescreen of "the refugees". Thus, the "refugee" or "migration crisis" is the symptom of a deeper structurally and institutionally grounded crisis of solidarity. It is about a trajectory driven by neoliberal austerity politics, which, since the mid-1990s, has made Sweden the OECD member with the fastest growth of social inequality. A deepening inequality has been produced through the politics of deregulation, privatization and changes in the taxation regime favouring the well off and skinning the already disadvantaged on the margins of the social welfare system – a dismantling of the social fabric. It has produced precarization of work, citizenship and livelihoods (Schierup and Scarpa 2017). Taken together, all of this is generating an existential insecurity and a crisis of the polity and of identity. It is a state which has – using a concept coined by the historian Karl Polanyi ([1944] 2001) in his analysis of the economic and political crisis of the 1930s – been driven by a destructive "commodification" of labour, money, and urban and rural environments. In *The Great Transformation*, he suggests that this will, in turn, breed a contentious countermovement aiming to "re-imbed" the unregulated market in protective social institutions.

This is not the place to review a huge contemporary academic debate on the work of Polanyi, its insights, weaknesses and flaws. Suffice here to emphasize, with Michael Piore (2008), that although the theories that have guided deregulation and globalization today are the "direct descendants of the laissez faire ideas that guided globalization a century ago", the kind of state-driven social policies that emerged from the Great Depression of the 1930s have largely been discredited. Given the erosion of citizenship and a waning faculty of the nation state to uphold protective social institutions, in the era of globalization, the Polanyian problematic of "society" versus the "market" needs to be critically revised to meet the challenges posed by a new matrix of social development. Nancy Fraser (2013) for one emphasizes the centrality of Polanyi's analysis, but argues that it is neither analytically nor normatively sufficient to focus on this "double movement" of social protection *versus* commodification. She points in her reception of The Great Transformation to a distinction between an "oppressive protection", embodied in étatist social policies versus an "emancipation from domination" represented by claims and practices of an array of "new social movements"; a "triple movement", in addition to market-driven "commodification" and "social protection" embodied in state institutions. Notwithstanding their often ambivalent relation to both market and state, new social movements represent struggles for emancipation, Frazer claims, aiming at unmasking power asymmetries and exposing contradictions resting in state-driven social protection and the oppressive effects of uncontrolled markets.

Seeing marketization, social protection and emancipation as three movements, we argue, facilitates an analysis of today's contestations of political hegemony in Sweden. From this perspective, we interrogate in the following pages a Swedish scenario that intimates driving forces of social movements of today – albeit subject to different global and local conditions – similar to those of a composite global countermovement against a disruptive rule of financial capitalism and an unbridled market economy that swept across the world of the 1930s. As in the 1930s – with Stalinism, Fascism and Social Democracy – today's countermovement embraces a diversity of actors and possibilities.

Using the case of Sweden and focusing on the upsurge of mutually antagonistic popular movements – "racist" and "anti-racist" – this article discusses a situation in which a neoliberal development, marking Sweden since the beginning of the 1990s, is becoming challenged by counterhegemonic movements. While exposing different visions of the future, we see these movements as counterpoised hallmarks of the contemporary crossroad for the development of Swedish society. We analyse, in the first part of the paper, the shifting racial discourse of the extreme-right radical party, the Sweden Democrats and the articulation of the party's advance with the current political conjuncture in Sweden. In the second part of the article, we examine a politically articulate new urban justice movement carried forth by young Swedes from migrant backgrounds. We ask whether this movement of "the Rest" within "the West"[1] may harbinger a brighter future that merges the heritage of a seemingly exhausted social democratic project with the incipient movement of young Swedes in ways that could transgress the oppressive racializing dynamics that was always present in the "Swedish Model", but which has been exacerbated with the surge of the extreme right today?

Countermovement or cow deal? A brown–blue alliance in the making

Today, in many states of Europe as in the European Parliament, extreme right, racist and fascist parties have grown. While gaining support for a number of reasons, as anti-globalist and flag-bearers for a growing distrust of the political system, the central interpellation of the Extreme Right Parties (Fennema 1997) operates through the construction of racialized or ethnicized "Others" – the Muslim, the Roma, the black or the "Migrant" in general – threatening the nation and the people.

In a critique of much of the established research, Mudde (2010) stresses the close relationship between the populist radical right and mainstream Western political democracy, arguing that "the key difference is not to be defined in kind, i.e. by fundamental opposition (i.e. antithesis), but in degree, i.e. by moderate versus radical versions of roughly the same views. Moreover, the typical right populist attitudes and ideas are not marginal under normal conditions; they are fairly widespread, if often in a more moderate form than expressed by the populist radical right parties" (Mudde 2010, 1178). While Mudde eschews naming these parties racist, he uses empirical data demonstrating that racism is alive and pungently present in Europe.

Expanding Mudde's analysis, we argue that racisms are intrinsically part of the social formation of European states. In understanding the manifestation of racisms, Stuart Hall's (1997) approach to race as a floating signifier provide tools for a further analysis. In a Swedish context, in which the concept of "race" has generally been abolished in usage following the Second World War (Holocaust) and the 1960s (decolonization and the U.S. civil rights movement), race has lingered on in unspoken forms, that every now and then have resurfaced in public discourse. A major mode in which race has been expressed in what we would call the mainstream politics is a racialization of refugees and immigrants related to the contemporary neoliberal project of commodification based on an *exploitative racism*. It points back to both the legacy and the covert forms of the geopolitics of racism represented by colonialism, imperialism and neo-colonialism (Mulinari and Neergaard 2017; cf. Fennema's discussion of colonial racism 2005).

Through migration, Sweden, like most other European states, has become increasingly diverse in terms of the national origin of its population, ethnic identity and religious affiliation. With reference to the "peril of migration", the imaginary threat of cultural diversity to social solidarity and cohesion of the nation state has, in turn, become a lynchpin for contemporary parties spanning what Fennema (1997) differentiate as protest, racist and extreme-right positions and propelling racializing politics across the continent. One example is the rapid upsurge of the Sweden Democrats (Mulinari and Neergaard 2017).

Sweden for long did not harbour any successful Extreme Right Party, barring the short-lived rise and fall of the party, *New Democracy* 1991–94 (Rydgren 2002) accompanied by street-level neo-Nazi and overtly racist movements (Pred 2000). In 2010 the Sweden Democrats entered parliament with the support of close to 6 per cent, and in the general election of 2014 the party more than doubled its support (13 per cent). If a general election were to be held as this is written, the Sweden Democrats would, according to the polls, be the second largest part in parliament. It is a party that grew from remnants of old Nazi alignments, racist and neo-Nazi organizations (Block 2001). The parliamentary breakthrough in 2010 was propped up by an inter-pellation mainly revolving around a perceived "Muslim threat" to Sweden's national cultural and social fabric (Hellström 2016). It was driven by major media breakthroughs, representing cultural incompatibility in line with what Fennema designates as racism through quasi-biological attributes (2005, 9). One was an op-ed piece published in the leading daily tabloid newspaper framing Muslims and Islam as the most serious threat to Sweden since the Second World War. Another was a propaganda film aired on national TV and uploaded on YouTube.[2] It pitted an elderly white "Swedish" woman against "Muslim" women wearing Burkas and surrounded by many children. It projected an image of how decreasing welfare for elderly "Swedes" was a direct effect of immigration by culturally incompatible "Muslims" portrayed in quasi-biological attributes.

Despite the cloaked albeit prevalent racism of Sweden Democrats repre-sentatives, popular support is increasing for the Sweden Democrats. With the party's strategic position in parliament, it has become able to destabilize Swedish politics. It purports a political project that in some aspects questions globalization and neoliberalism. It may be about nostalgia for an idealized (ethnically or racially "pure") Swedish "People's Home"; a national welfare state that once was, or more correctly, imagined (Norocel 2016). The migrants are seen as pollution and the destruction of what is truly Swedish, while the established left, imagined as ranging from socialists and social democrats to feminists and anti-racists, are seen as betraying Sweden and the ideals of the nation and the family. Thus, the destruction of the nation through immi-gration and the import of foreign cultures with a particular focus on Islam are at the core of the party's political imagination. The Janus-faced combination of being both racist against migrants, framing race through culture and other-ness, and at the same time, a self-presentation as being anti-racist through expelling some members resorting to a discourse of biological racism and/ or violence is we contend a successful strategy based on skilfully juggling race as a floating signifier.

The question remains, however: why now and why with such rapidly growing success?

We contend that the rise of Sweden Democrats is only partially based on fruitful efforts to distance the party from the crude and overt racism of its own past, flagging overt biological signifiers of "race", and replacing them with a more covert racism communicated through subtler metaphors of "culture". Parallel to this strategy of cleansing its official image, which it shares with other extreme-right parties in Europe, representatives and individ-ual members of the Sweden Democrats continue to disseminate a more traditional overt and crude racism, especially through social media. An example is a Sweden Democrats municipal representative and lay judge asking on Facebook "Can someone place themselves on the Öresund bridge with a machine gun" in a situation where thousands of refugees were entering Sweden through the bridge applying for asylum.[3] While a more overtly aggressive racism is mostly directed against Muslims or migrants in general, at times it does also entail anti-Semitism as in the case of a member of Parliament using the classic idea of Jews controlling media, or another laughingly recounting a story in which Nazi work colleagues are kicking lambs at a slaughter house pretending that they are Jews.[4] This, apparently, is not affecting the party's standing in opinion polls negatively. Despite this, or perhaps more accurately through the combination of a Janus-faced approach – explaining that everything that has gone wrong is caused by migration and migrants – the Sweden Democrats have forged an interpellation that seemingly presents an option for a population in search of an alternative to the visionless politics of the present. This appears, in effect, ironic in the sense that while being basically a one-issue party, its dogma is interpreted as an answer to everything. In this sense, the Sweden Democrats may be seen as a parliamentary manifestation of a contemporary "Polanyian" countermovement. A social movement oscillating in emphasis between anti-establishment and anti-immigrant protest, single-issue racist and extreme-right positions (Fennema 1997), but with racism and welfare nostalgia as salient. However, it is becoming an increasingly powerful movement organization through successfully articulating two main positions, merged into a composite counterstrategy for, allegedly, combating the destruction of Sweden. On the one hand, the idea of disembedding the nation from globalization and a supranational EU and, on the other hand, excluding non-deserving "others" from its welfare system or its territory altogether.

The rapidly increasing entry of refugees to Sweden in 2015 has been used actively in the propaganda of the Sweden Democrats. Not only has the party linked refugees to an alleged destruction of Sweden as a nation, but actively attempted to mobilize violent direct action among citizens (Mulinari and Neergaard 2017). While Sweden Democrats staunchly define themselves as neither left nor right, and enjoy a sturdy and increasing electoral support particularly among working class men, in parliamentary politics they are slowly positioning themselves more and more to the right, weaving together racism, authoritarianism and increasingly neoliberalism. In some of the most central left–right conflicts concerning privatization and profits in public finance welfare, labour market legislation, reduced taxation and concerning preferred government, the party has aligned itself with the major right-wing party, *Moderaterna* (Wingborg 2016). The formal cordon sanitaire around the Sweden Democrats, formerly devised by all other parliamentary parties, has broken down with the announcement of *Moderaterna* that they are prepared to negotiate with Sweden Democrats, together with increasing cooperation on the municipal levels.

On the background of right-wing parties bleeding potential voters to the Sweden Democrats, a Social Democratic and Green Party government in minority, and an unprecedented number of refugees seeking asylum in Sweden, in 2015 the scene was finally set for a dramatic policy shift, toppling an established left–right compact on a comparatively generous refugee policy. Thus, in October 2015 the government struck an agreement with the four right-wing parties concerning refugee and integration policy. Breaking with a principled policy of granting permanent residence following refugee status, temporary residence permits were made the rule, with the explicit purpose of limiting the number of asylum seekers. Possibilities for family unification have been dramatically curtailed. At the same time, future possibilities for permanent residence permits have been linked to labour market integration and family unification and to earning a substantial income through reforms, which in effect directly push refugees into low-wage service work and which breaks with established norms and practices in providing public subvention for job-openings to employers without collective agreements. Asylum policy has, in effect, been adapted to the global apartheid of policies of temporary and circular migration. In November 2015, the Social Democratic and Green Party government announced even harsher refugee and integration policies, preventing refugees from the very opportunity to use the right to apply for asylum. While the neoliberal *Centerpartiet* voted against this latter reform, there was just one party – the Left party – voting against the reforms of refugee and integration policy as a whole (Neergaard 2017).

Despite scorning the Sweden Democrats as racist and neo-fascist, the Social Democratic and Green government's rupture with decades of Swedish policies for asylum and integration – in the span of less than a year – has made some of the Sweden Democrats' political claims part and parcel of the Swedish migration-policy regime. Furthermore, it has underscored the image of immigration as a threat to Sweden. Nevertheless, the Sweden Democrats continue, in chorus with parts of the old mainstream political right, to propagate further restrictive measures, arguing that deserving "natives" must be treated differently from non-deserving, culturally deviant "foreigners", in order to protect the claims of the former to the scarce resources of a crisis-ridden welfare state in a hardening globalized world (Mulinari and Neergaard 2017; Wingborg 2016).

The party has attracted increasing electoral support through refocusing "cultural" racism towards Muslims and Roma migrants, which increasingly is not only aligning with the established right-wing parties, but increasingly also with the public opinion as expressed in polls (Wingborg 2016). At the same time, there is the continued rhetoric of the traditional core of the party, especially through party linked blogs, web journals and in social media, infused with a more blatant and overt racism. Is it possible to understand this development in a Polanyian frame? A historical analogy may help. Like in the case of the alliance of the National Socialists with German big capital in the 1930s – after the purge of the party's militant left wing, the SA Stormtroopers – the position of the Sweden Democrats is ambiguous and opportunistic, reflecting a dual challenge. On the one hand, it is mobilising support as a social movement, in which activists are important. These are activists that are more expressively racist, active especially through social media web blogs and journals (Hellström 2016), but also through manifestations. In this sense, Sweden Democrats may be seen as the central organization in a wider social movement in which racism is the key issue. On the other hand, the leadership is attempting to break the cordon sanitaire with the aim of becoming a potential governmental coalition partner to the right-wing parties. This entails a lower racist profile, targeting "only" Muslims and Roma, but also subscribing to a substantial realignment of economic policy towards a more traditional neoliberal position. This economic realignment with the right has been facilitated through increasing ties with the Confederation of Swedish Enterprise (*Svensk Näringsliv*) and affiliated organizations. The Swedish publicist, Mathisen (2016), concludes that, "The economic elite in Sweden obviously has interlocking interests with that of parliamentarian fascism." Informal consultations of the confederation with the Sweden Democrats represent, seen in this perspective, the mediating interface of a covert political agreement in becoming. It forges the grounds for an unholy marriage between the exclusionary racism championed by the Sweden Democrats and increasingly permeating most of the right-wing parties, with the exploitative racism of neoliberal capitalism. It guarantees employers long-term access to an abundant cheap and readily disposable global labour force, yet in the same fell swoop, it appeases the extreme right with guarantees that only a chosen minority among these new helots (Cohen 1987) of a globalized apartheid will ever gain access to privileges of citizenship and membership of the nation. However, this repositioning of the Swedish political right is still instable, as exemplified in the increasing support for the neoliberal *Centerpartiet*, which – while proposing to lower wages for entrants to the labour market, likely to especially target migrants – at the same time refuse to join the bandwagon of the Sweden Democrats' racist discourse.

Reclaiming democracy and citizenship from the ground up

Another manifestation of today's countermovement comes as urban uprisings. It is, using the term of Chatterjee (2002), a "politics of the governed", in the form of riots of precaritized youth in racialized and socially disadvantaged city regions – in Sweden referred to as "suburbia" (*förorten*), a term and spatio-social milieu corresponding to the French "*banlieus*". Extensive riots took place in the Swedish cities of Malmö, Gothenburg and Uppsala in 2009, and again in Stockholm, and several other cities, in 2013. We see these so-called riots (Swedish: *kravaller*) as a *rebellion* of what has been called an "uncivil society" (Bayat 1997) out of the reach of neoliberal governance. The term signifies a distance to a so-called civil society tamed and disciplined through techniques of governmentality (Neocosmos 2011). In the context, the idiom, "policing the crisis" (Hall et al. 1978) holds as substantial a meaning as ever. A permanent tension between the police and young people, building up across a disadvantaged Swedish suburbia has produced urban hotbeds for rebellion.

In these disadvantaged spaces, mostly populated by migrants and post-migrant generations, the police are the most visible targets for resentment in their function of guarding a regime of financialization, commodification of welfare provision, a grabbing of the commons and extensive gentrification propelling new urban geographies of racialized inequality. These are rambling processes of precarization, which have undermined trust in political institutions and agencies of the state. A widespread frustration among youth of, in particular, migrant background, racialized through systemically embedded stigmatization and discrimination, has, combined with a lack of spaces for democratic participation and decision-making relating to programmes for urban planning (Léon-Rosales and Ålund 2017), generated feelings of powerlessness and became a driving force for their uprising (Schierup, Ålund, and Kings 2014).

The contemporary city constitutes a strategic terrain for conflict and contestation, with "advanced marginality" – a term introduced by Loïc Wacquant (1996) – as point of departure for exploring causes and implications of contemporary urban geographies of poverty and precarization. It highlights processes of institutional transformation, whereby "organizations presumed to provide civic goods and services – physical safety, legal protection, welfare, education, housing and health care – have turned into instruments of surveillance, suspicion and exclusion rather than vehicles of social integration and trust-building". Dikeç (2007) critically deepens the meaning of "advanced marginality", highlighting that deprived neighbourhoods may be actually sprawling with collective grassroots activism. Reflecting on French urban policy, Dikeç emphasizes that space and place cannot be considered as given, but are produced by multiple practices and discourses. Suburban multiethnic districts are, on the one hand, increasingly constituted as "badlands" in public discourse and, on the other hand, exposed to repressive forms of state intervention. But they are also potential or actual sites for political mobilization driven by democratic ideals. Beyond the smokescreen of conspicuous violence, the contemporary Swedish scene also makes visible the emergence of an autonomous, focused and organizationally embedded justice movement contesting urban degradation and reclaiming Sweden in terms of inclusive citizenship, social welfare and democracy (Sernhede, Thörn, and Thörn 2016). Out of the boiling cauldron of burning cities, we have thus seen the birth of a new justice movement, with an array of networks, and more or less temporary organizations spearheaded by young people from marginalized urban neighbourhoods with a high proportion of citizens of migrant background, especially from Africa and the Middle East. These are visible minorities stigmatized in terms of "race", "national origin" and "migrant background".

We illustrate in the following how one, among many, local activist organization, The Megaphone (*Megafonen*), founded and driven by youth, developed counter politics as their answer to police violence, racism, segregation and the lack of democratic participation, in order to bring forward their own voices (cf. Hall 1992a) and claims for deepened democracy onto a wider public-political arena. The Megaphone started in Husby 2008 a neighbourhood in the area of Järvafältet belonging to Metropolitan Stockholm. Activists in the Megaphone present themselves as a Swedish suburban movement (*förortsrörelse*). The notion of "the suburban movement" was coined in a press release in 26 January 2012 announcing the end of the occupation of *Husby träff*, a meeting point of local inhabitants. The occupation was a reaction to a series of closures of welfare service institutions, such as schools, health centres, the post office, the municipal office, the social insurance office, etc. (Megafonen 2012).

However, the name of The Megaphone – aiming at becoming the voice of suburbia in response to negative fame inhibiting stigmatizing representation of suburban areas in the mainstream public (Idagsidan 2012) – was disseminated worldwide in connection with the dramatic youth riots in Stockholm in 2013 (Schierup, Ålund, and Kings 2014). Then the Megaphone became known for its sharp critique of the Swedish police and for making public an understanding of the institutional violence, social marginalization, the discrimination and racial stigmatization that led to the Stockholm uprising in the first place. "The Megaphone does not start fires", they stated and continued:

> We believe that this is not the right method for long-term change. But we know that it is a reaction to the shortcomings of this society. Unemployment, inadequate schools and structural racism are the underlying causes of what is happening today.[5] (Megafonen 2013)

Claiming that they represent those whose voices are silenced and excluded from the public arena (Léon-Rosales and Ålund 2017), Al-Khamisi (2015a), one of the founders of The Megaphone, sums up the forward development of the suburban movement as follows: "We understood the need to create our own platforms, structures and activities which allowed us to develop intellectually, socially, mentally as equal citizens." He refers, among other, to the network

"United Suburbs": a digital platform for organization of "suburban people" making an impact on the Swedish cultural scene. It is one example of becoming a public voice among numerous appearances on conferences, seminars, workshops, festivals and a regular contribution of articles in Swedish mass media.

Still, in its initial formative period, the main impact of the organization, as of the suburban movement in general, has been in organising local communities, the creation of a collective identity related to *place* (the neighbourhood) and a multifaceted engagement in what is called "place struggle". We see it as a particular contemporary Swedish version of what Sivanandan (1989), with reference to the U.K., calls "organic communities of resistance", presaged in "the black struggles of the 1960s and 1970s", which have also served as ideal models inspiring the young racialized urban Swedes, their organization, their community work, and their national and international networking. The notion of "place struggle" revolves around the shared collective-identity work of the inhabitants of marginalized neighbourhoods and comes to be expressed in a composite political agenda addressing problems of segregation, welfare retrenchment and deepening racialized class inequality (León-Rosales and Ålund 2017; Sernhede, Thörn, and Thörn 2016). In what was phrased in terms of a long-term principled political programme, The Megaphone states that they organize suburban youth in a struggle for social justice: "By mobilizing forces that repression breeds in the suburb we want to create a society free of racism, sexism and class oppression", they write on the homepage.[6] Through a seven-point programme, they demand opportunities for people in the disadvantaged urban neighbourhoods to influence politics which affects the everyday lives of their inhabitants. They demand development and investment in public services and investments to stimulate social activities in the suburbs, a fair educational system and full secondary competence in all schools, work for everyone in the suburbs; the replacement of racialized securitization by sustainable social programmes and a housing policy that recognizes the right to decent housing for all.

"Place struggle", civil society and the state

We understand the Swedish suburban movement as a "Learning from the Ground up" (Choudry and Kapoor 2010) in which knowledge production and practice/action are interconnected; an interconnection that can bring forward a voice of the subaltern, carrying a critical perspective forward to the wider national context and addressing "tensions over whose knowledge and voice(s) are heard". Related to this, the systematic training of "organic intellectuals" in the art of rhetoric became a key strategy of the urban justice movement to enable participation in public-political discourse. Frustrated by the lack of participation and possibilities to influence local renewal programmes they have boosted a more sturdy "public voice" through which the perception of disadvantaged Swedish suburbs and their inhabitants is being anchored in the wider public space (Léon-Rosales and Ålund 2017).

But it is in particular in the new urban justice movement's relation to established Swedish civil-society organizations that we may see an opening towards anti-racist democracy. Discussing experiences of the Swedish urban justice movement with activists from U.S.A., South Africa and France, Al-Khamisi, who is a student of law, presented a report (Al-Khamisi 2015b), based on a study visit to the U.S.A., which discusses potentials of social movement lawyering as an instrument in the service of grassroots organizations in promoting social justice. The report, commissioned by Arena Idé, a leading Swedish think tank of the labour movement, illustrates one of several examples of connections between new and old, established, popular movements in Sweden. Another example was a major public event: a conference in Stockholm (6–7 May 2015), organized by a number of civil-society organizations around the issue of "The crisis of Democracy". The aim of the conference reads as follows (Rädda Barnen 2015):

> The Swedish social model has grown out of engagement in civil society. Swedish citizens created organizations that have contributed to the development of society, socially, culturally and politically. These popular movements have formed the backbone of Swedish democracy by being the voice of the people in relation to public institutions and private interests. In recent decades, Sweden has undergone major changes. One of the clearest changes is that the composition of the population has changed fundamentally due to migration of people from other parts of the world. The traditional Swedish civil society has in far too small extent managed to incorporate this part of the population in the democratic process. It weakens civil society and the Swedish democracy. This we want to change.

The established civil-society organizations (Save the Children, The Workers Educational Association [ABF], People's Parks and Community Centers, Study Promotion, The National Council of Swedish Youth Organisations [LSU]), hosted the conference. The idea was to bring together new movements from suburbia and, as it was announced by hosts, to "create pathways into our organizations for those who are outside, and we want to support the emergence of new organizations that can meet new needs of our society" (Barnen 2015). Obviously, these "new needs" are rooted in the lack of representation of new movements and their voices within the established civil-society organizations, and beyond.

In this gathering, "voice" was the dominant theme. The focus was on two issues – representation and identity. It underlined that "voice" is pivotal for strategies of representation (Hall 1992a) – in established civil-society organizations, in cultural politics and social practice – as the expression of citizen participation through deliberative engagement in local and national political and institutional contexts. The conference on the crisis of democracy enhanced possibilities for collaboration which are already in the process of being realized.

Members of the new urban justice organizations have presently become employed within several established civil-society organizations. We see today an increasing representation of formerly vilified youthful rebels across established and institutionalized civil-society organizations and NGOs, and in influential positions in *public* services. Many embark on careers within education and the media. This presents us with another challenge in terms of theory and empirical research. What is in the making: co-optation and disciplinary governmentality, or a renaissance for participatory democracy realized through a more mature stage in the short history of the new justice movements?

Potentially this involvement can result in a renaissance of what was once known as "people's movements" being a cradle of Swedish democracy. Today, most of these established movements are rather "tamed", institutionalized and professionalized service organizations making truth of Kaldor's (2003, 589) argument that "[b]ecoming 'tamed' means that you become the respectable opposition – the partner in negotiations". But we may alternatively, in a Gramscian perspective, see the current transformation as a more mature face of an innovative anti-racist project transmuted from a strategy for influencing the state from "the outside" towards an "outside–inside" strategy; a war of position, which, through integration with and simultaneous renewal of a multifaceted and contestative Swedish civil society, could increasingly traverse the institutions of the state. And here, returning to Fraser, we can trace the position of emancipatory movements within the wider context of civil society. While interconnecting with parts of established organizations, integrated in state–market "partnerships", urban justice movements have so far, albeit in an ambiguous position, not lost their significance as "parallel discursive arenas where members of subordinated social groups invent and circulate counter discourses to formulate oppositional interpretations of their identities, interests, and needs" (Fraser 1990, 67). They still strive to combine resistance against oppressive norms of racializing stigmatization with claims for inclusionary social protection, as a basis in struggles for emancipation.

Ambiguous fault lines in a precarious present

Returning to the Polanyian perspective that we have introduced at the beginning of this paper, we argue that the success of neoliberalism has proceeded so far as to almost annihilate all other political projects presenting economic and social alternatives. It pertains in particular to the social democratic project, which in its different forms has almost totally succumbed to and internalized the neoliberal agenda. Left parties did or could not muster much of a counter-movement to the entrenchment of neoliberalism. It is thus either on the margins that the seeds of a countermovement began to develop, or in the shape of distorted nativist constellations of populist protest, carrying forth fascist and racist movements, and parties.

Similar to other anti-immigration populist movements across Europe, with France's *Front National* as the exemplary case, a pivotal ideological tenet of the discourse of the extreme-right Sweden Democrats has been a convoluted critique of *immigration* as political programme and practice. The extremist right has become an increasingly respectable partner for mainstream political parties, for whom social citizenship and universal welfare policies have progressively dried up as sources for legitimacy. The ideologies and discourses of racism are gaining terrain in the EU pertaining, in effect, to a dead end "declassified" (Maré 2014) conception of race; that is with a signification of "race" void of reference to "class" and void of a critique of the political economy on which processes of racialization are contingent (cf. Kyriakides and Torres 2012).

In the second part of our paper, we have discussed the rise of a new urban justice movement among disadvantaged and racially stigmatized youth in terms of an antagonistic opposite to the Sweden Democrats reclaiming Sweden in terms of an inclusive citizenship, social welfare and democracy from the ground up. They present a vision of society that articulates a re-imagination of the nation as a future in making; as a multifaceted community of culturally sundry but equal citizens. This brings the matter of race to a head. While the discourse of "the suburb" represents the interpellation of a struggling subject, it is also a contribution to a particular form of applying "race" as a floating signifier? "Place struggle" is at the same time an adumbration alluding to a junction where "race" and "class struggle" coalesce. Reference to the "people of the suburb" is evidently a thin veiling of a call for an open class-conscious pan-racial/ethnic/migrant and post-migrant mobilization of Sweden's racialized. It represents alternative ways of framing a "We" that is constructed through race and class as an anti-racist project. The urban justice movement is a race critical project initiated and chiefly driven by Sweden's most disadvantaged. It mobilizes Swedes of colour and stigmatized descent. But it frames, at the same time, an open project that does not preclude the inclusion of precaritized white folks, under a common umbrella of "We are the Poors";[7] a movement from the margin addressing a need for recognition of the excluded as a political voice against the re-emergence of the spectre of totalitarianism in a present turmoil and transformation of democratic frameworks of rights, welfare and nation.

Notes

1. Alluding to Hall (1992b).
2. http://www.youtube.com/watch?v=5UiUdpYVubY.
3. http://www.aftonbladet.se/nyheter/article21386442.ab (9 September 2015).
4. http://www.expressen.se/debatt/antisemitismen-lever-inom-sd/ (7 October 2016).
5. Compare, e.g. the analysis by *Comité invisible* (2007) discussing similar issues in France.
6. http://megafonen.com/om/politiskt-program/.
7. Alluding to Desai's (2002) seminal account of the South African poor people's movement.

Disclosure statement

No potential conflict of interest was reported by the authors.

Funding

This work was supported by Forte [2006-1524], Svenska Forskningsrådet Formas [250-2013-1547] and Vetenskapsrådet [2007–7269, 721-2013-885].

References

Al-Khamisi, Rami. 2015a. "Förortsrörelsen existerar mer än någonsin." In *ETC*. ETC.
Al-Khamisi, Rami. 2015b. *Rörelsejurister. Vägen mot en samhällsförändrande juridik – om makt, civilsamhälle och behovet av nya jurister*. Stockholm: Arena.
Ålund, Aleksandra, Carl-Ulrik Schierup, and Anders. Neergaard, eds. 2017. *Reimagineering the Nation. Essays on Twenty First Century Sweden*. Frankfurt am Main: Peter Lang.
Bayat, Asef. 1997. "Un-civil Society: The Politics of the 'Informal People'." *Third World Quarterly* 18 (1): 53–72.
Block, Fred. 2001. *Introduction. The Great Transformation*. Boston: Beacon Press.
Chatterjee, Partha. 2002. *The Politics of the Governed*. New York: Columbia University Press.
Choudry, Aziz, and Dip Kapoor. 2010. *Learning from the Ground Up: Global Perspectives on Social Movements and Knowledge Production*. New York: Palgrave Macmillan.
Cohen, Robin. 1987. *The New Helots: Migrants in the International Division of Labour*. Aldershot: Avebury.
Comité invisible. 2007. "L'insurrection qui vient." In *La fabrique éditions*. Paris: La fabrique.
Desai, Ashwin. 2002. *We Are the Poors. Community Struggles in Post-apartheid South Africa*. New York: Monthly Review Press.
Dikeç, Mustafa. 2007. *Badlands of the Republic. Space, Politics and Urban Policy*. Oxford: Blackwell.
Du Bois, W. E. B. 1903. *The Souls of Black Folk*. Chicago: A.C. Mcurg.
Fennema, Meindert. 1997. "Some Conceptual Issues and Problems in the Comparison of Anti-immigrant Parties in Western Europe." *Party Politics* 3 (4): 473–492.

Fennema, Meindert. 2005. "Populist Parties of the Right." In *Movements of Exclusion: Radical Right-Wing Populism in the Western World*, edited by J. Rydgren, 1–24. New York: Nova Science.

Fraser, Nancy. 1990. "Rethinking the Public Sphere: A Contribution to the Critique of Actually Existing Democracy." *Social Text* 25 (26): 56–80.

Fraser, Nancy. 2013. "A Triple Movement? Parsing the Politics of Crisis after Polanyi?" *New Left Review* 81 (May): 119–132.

Hall, Stuart. 1992a. "New Ethnicities." In *"Race", Culture and Difference*, edited by Donald James and Ali Rattansi, 252–260. London: Sage.

Hall, Stuart. 1992b. "The West and the Rest: Discourse and Power." In *Formations of Modernity*, edited by Stuart Hall and Bram Gieben. London: Polity Press in Association with The Open University.

Hall, Stuart. 1997. "Race, the Floating Signifier: Transcript of Lecturee Delivered at Goldsmiths College in London." Northampton: MEDIA EDUCATION FOUNDATION. 1–17. http://www.mediaed.org/transcripts/Stuart-Hall-Race-the-Floating-Signifier-Transcript.pdf.

Hall, Stuart, Chas Critcher, Tony Jefferson, John N. Clarke, and Brian Roberts. 1978. *Policing the Crisis: Mugging, the State and Law and Order*. London: Macmillan.

Hellström, Anders. 2016. *Trust Us: Reproducing the Nation and the Scandinavian Nationalist Populist Parties*. New York: Berghahn Books.

Holmes, Douglas R. 2000. *Integral Europe: Fast-Capitalism, Multiculturalism, Neofascism*. Princeton, NJ and Oxford: Princeton University Press.

Idagsidan. 2012. "Inte bara snack i Megafonen." In *Svenska Dagbladet*. Svenska Dagbladet.

Kaldor, Mary. 2003. *Global Civil Society. An Answer to War*. Cambridge: Polity Press.

Kyriakides, Christopher, and Rodolfo D. Torres. 2012. *Race Defaced: Paradigms of Pessimism, Politics of Possibility*. Stanford, CA: Stanford University Press.

Laclau, Ernesto. 2005. *On Populist Reason*. London and New York (NY): Verso.

León-Rosales, René and Aleksandra Ålund. 2017. "Renaissance from the Margins – Urban Youth Activism in Sweden." In *Reimagineering the Nation. Essays on Swedish Society*, edited by B. Author, 353–376. Frankfurt: Peter Lang.

Maré, Gerhand. 2014. *Declassified. Moving Beyond the Dead End of Race in South Africa*. Auckland Park: Jacana Media.

Mathisen, Daniel. 2016. *Svenskt Näringsliv – SD:s maskhål till makten*. Stockholm: Dagens Arena.

Megafonen. 2012. "Megafonen kräver respekt." Megafonen. http://megafonen.com/husby-kraver-respekt/.

Megafonen. 2013. "Uttalande om Megafonens roll under förortsrevolterna." Megafonen. http://megafonen.com/uttalande-om-megafonens-roll-under-forortervolterna/.

Mudde, Cas. 2010. "The Populist Radical Right: A Pathological Normalcy." *West European Politics* 33 (6): 1167–1186.

Mulinari, Diana, and Anders Neergaard. 2017. "From Racial to Racist State? The Sweden Democrats Reimagining the Nation." In *Reimagineering the Nation. Essays on Twenty First Century Sweden*, edited by Aleksandra Ålund, Carl-Ulrik Schierup, and Anders Neergaard, 257–284. Frankfurt am Main: Peter Lang.

Neergaard, A. 2017. "The Swedish Model in Transition: Trade Unions and Racialised Workers." In *Reimagineering the Nation. Essays on Twenty First Century Sweden*, edited by Aleksandra Ålund, Carl-Ulrik Schierup, and Anders Neergaard, 85–118. Frankfurt am Main: Peter Lang.

Neocosmos, Michael. 2011. "Transition, Human Rights and Violence: Rethinking a Liberal Political Relationship in the African Neo-colony." *Interface: A Journal for and about Social Movements* 3 (2): 359–399.

Norocel, Ov Cristian. 2016. "Populist Radical Right Protectors of the Folkhem: Welfare Chauvinism in Sweden." *Critical Social Policy* 36 (3): 371–390.

Piore, J. Michael. 2008. *Presidential Address. Second Thoughts: On Economics, Sociology, Neoliberalism, Polanyi's Double Movement and Intellectual Vacuums. SASE Meeting 2008.* Economic Flexibility and Social Stability in the Age of Globalization. SASE: San Juan, Costa Rica.

Polanyi, Karl. (1944) 2001. *The Great Transformation: The Political and Economic Origins of Our Time.* Boston, MA: Beacon Press.

Pred, Allan. 2000. *Even in Sweden. Racisms, Racialized Spaces, and the Popular Geographical Imagination.* Los Angeles: University of California.

Rädda Barnen. 2015. "Demokratins kris är vår – vad gör vi åt den?" *Save the Children.* Accessed January 25, 2016. http://www.mynewsdesk.com/se/radda_barnen/documents/demokratins-kris-aer-vaar-vad-goer-vi-aat-den-45358.

Rydgren, Jens. 2002. "Radical Right Populism in Sweden: Still a Failure, But for How Long?" *Scandinavian Political Studies* 25: 27–56.

Schierup, Carl-Ulrik, and Aleksandra Ålund. 2011. "The End of Swedish Exceptionalism? Citizenship, Neoliberalism and the Politics of Exclusion." *Race & Class* 53 (1): 45–64.

Schierup, Carl-Ulrik, Aleksandra Ålund, and Lisa Kings. 2014. "Reading the Stockholm Riots – a Moment for Social Justice?" *Race & Class* 55 (3): 1–21.

Schierup, Carl-Ulrik, and Simone Scarpa. 2017. "How the Swedish Model Was (Almost) Lost. Migration, Welfare and the Politics of Solidarity." In *Reimagineering the Nation. Essays on Twenty First Century Sweden,* edited by Aleksandra Ålund, Carl-Ulrik Schierup, and Anders Neergaard. Frankfurt am Main: Peter Lang.

Sernhede, Ove, Catharina Thörn, and Håkan Thörn. 2016. "The Stockholm Uprising in Context: Urban Social Movements and the Rise and Demise of the Swedish Welfare State City." In *Urban Uprisings: Challenging Neoliberal Urbanism in Europe,* edited by M. Mayer, C. Thörn, and H. Thörn, 353–376. Basingstoke: Palgrave Macmillan.

Sivanandan, Ambalavaner. 1989. "All That Melts into Air Is Solid: The Hokum of New Times." *Race & Class* 31 (3): 1–30.

Wacquant, Loïc. 1996. "The Rise of Advanced Marginality: Notes on its Nature and Implications". *Acta Sociologica* 39 (2): 121–139.

Wingborg, Mats. 2016. *Den blåbruna röran: SD:s flirt med Alliansen och högerns vägval.* Stockholm: Leopard.

Racialization and counter-racialization in times of crisis: taking migrant struggles in Italy as a critical standpoint on race

Federico Oliveri

ABSTRACT

Migrant struggles in contemporary Italy offer a critical standpoint for understanding the uses of race in times of crisis. This paper analyses racialization first as a structural feature of neoliberalism in Italian society, and then as a crisis management strategy in the transition to late neoliberalism. Against this background, migrant struggles – for freedom of movement and the right to life, for equality at work, for the right to housing – will be interpreted as examples of counter-racialization. Through the development of counter-discourses on the crisis and austerity, in terms of causes, responsibilities and alternatives policies, and through practices of solidarity those struggles deconstruct the dominant frame of "ethnic competition for scarce resources" and try to reunite "those below" against "those above" across national and other racializing lines.

Introduction

There is an enduring denial of racism as a structural trait of Italian society. Tellingly, after the murder in July 2016 of a Nigerian asylum seeker who was defending his wife from a verbal assault, the General Director of the National Anti-Discrimination Office declared:

> If one asked me if Italy were a racist country, I would answer that *racism is a beast* which can never be considered defeated. (…). Nevertheless, it would be an error to say that Italy is a racist nation. Talking like this does not help us in fighting racism. (Sappino 2016)

I see two major weak points in such a vision: racism appears as the expression of a backward culture, restricted to individual actions and fuelled by largely irrational ideas and feelings; accordingly, anti-racism should be grounded on better information and education, and eventually on law enforcement, instead of focusing on the hegemonic power relations in our society.

This denial of racism leads to insufficient or misleading understanding of the race-crisis nexus. For instance, racist incidents have been reported as growing in Italy during the crisis (Lunaria 2014); yet, they have often been presented as the main evidence of a causal link between economic downturn, widespread social insecurity and rising xenophobia among popular classes. There is a consensus among human rights agencies that recession has played a key role in the rise of racist attitudes and episodes across Europe (FRA 2010; ENAR 2015). "Ethnic competition" provides the main frame for this interpretation: "less well-off sections of the majority population perceive minorities and foreigners as unwelcome competitors for scarce resources. People show their resentment of this by using violence" (Björgo and Witte 1993, 8) or by blaming immigrants for their worsening status.

In this paper I will develop the following alternative hypotheses. Shortcomings in the interpretation of the race-crisis nexus – such as presenting xenophobia of popular classes as almost natural and competition for scarce resources as a given – should be overcome by focusing on the racialization of (and counter-racialization by) people with a migration background. Racialization should be seen as a structural feature of neoliberalism, which became dominant in Italy during the 1990s. In times of recession, racialization functions as a crisis management strategy facilitating the enforcement of austerity measures and the establishment of late neoliberalism. Migrant struggles claiming freedom of movement and right to life, equality at work and right to housing, may be seen in this juncture as examples of counter-racialization. Through their discourses on the crisis and austerity, in terms of causes, responsibilities and alternatives policies, and their practices of solidarity those struggles try to reunite "those below" against "those above" across national and other racializing lines.

Theoretical and methodological issues on racialization

If "crisis racism" (Balibar and Wallerstein 1991) cannot be reduced to a natural reaction of ordinary people menaced by social regression and manipulated by right wing movements, how can we make sense of it? I argue that moving from biological and essentialized concepts of race to socially constructed processes of racialization (Murji and Solomos 2005) provides an ideal framework for grasping the race-crisis nexus. Focusing on race-making processes allows me to explore three points which are crucial for my argument: how racial meanings assigned to border controls, labour and housing have been used to manage the crisis; how this racialization of the crisis, especially in terms of ethnic competition, reproduces social hierarchies; how these uses of race are made almost unintelligible to people, who still represent themselves as non-racist and institutions as race-blind.

In order to function as an analytical tool, racialization should be first defined at a high level of abstraction and then articulated in its basic elements. Thanks to this theoretical move I hope to avoid the lack of clarity in the concept, caused by the fact that some authors tend to conflate different aspects of racialization, such as the subjects involved, the mechanisms, the functions and the effects of the process. My effort is to provide a systematic reading of racialization, broadly defined as the conflictual production of racial subjects, accompanied by a racial sense making of any aspect of social life to which those subjects participate. This definition will be further specified by four inter-related processes of racialization, and by the idea of counter-racialization.

First, dominant groups develop norms, practices and discourses that categorize other groups by unilaterally assigning to them a set of real or imaginary fixed markers, such as colour, class, gender, nationality (Anthias and Yuval-Davis 1992), immigration status (Fekete 2001), age, culture, language and religion (Lentin and Titley 2011). Through the interaction of the media, public intellectuals and politicians, those markers become common sense, often reactivating colonial legacies (Mellino 2012) and nation-building mechanisms. They also produce racializing frames specific to class, gender and education level within the dominant group.

Second, racializing markers produce essentially differentiated, inferior and/ or non-assimilable categories of people, through a wide range of mechanisms including criminalization, commodification and victimization. The placement of people in those categories frames social relations in hierarchical terms, articulating race with class and gender (Sudbury 1998). Law and the state play a key role in racialization (Haney López 1996): they legitimize differences of treatment no longer perceived as discriminatory; they rationalize social arrangements of inequality and injustice, violence and exploitation; they permit the public expression of generally concealed feelings of hate and disgust against those who are considered out of place.

Third, critical social trends such as today's rising precarious work and unemployment, declining incomes, shrinking access to public goods and services, rising criminality, lacking sense of community, become problematized in connection with race (Balibar and Wallerstein 1991), migrants and migration (Sayad 1991). Racialization thus functions as a powerful mechanism for displacing social responsibility and containing social anxieties.

Fourth, racialization deploys effects on the organization of society as a whole. It isolates and disempowers racialized groups, which are forced to accept domination and interiorize it as legitimate. It splits them internally through mechanisms of "differential racialization" (Brah 1996) and opposes them to the rest of the population, especially to other subaltern groups who see themselves as members of the dominant group. It inhibits solidarity between equally oppressed but racially differentiated communities, by dividing the working class between natives and migrants, different nationalities and generations, qualified and unqualified workers, men and women. It reinforces the identity of in-groups against out-groups. As a result, racialization perpetuates the material and symbolic privileges of the insiders, as much as subordination of the outsiders.

Despite its structural effects, racialization should be seen as historical and reversible. This is also why, in analogy with notions such as counter-hegemony or counter-power, I introduce here the concept of counter-racialization broadly defined as the processes through which "racialized outsiders" (Virdee 2015) affirm their political subjectivity, contest the place assigned to them in society and engage in struggles for a radical change. Like other forms of anti-racism, which historically provided the standpoint for questioning racism (Lentin 2004), counter-racialization is crucial for de-constructing racialization and its four basic elements. Against categorization enforced through fixed markers, racialized outsiders may organize themselves in order to disrupt the given political scene, speaking and acting autonomously. Against otherization and inferiorization, they may claim their right to have equal rights. Against the racialization of social problems as a strategy for displacing responsibilities, they may provide critical accounts of the hidden interests which reproduce power structures. Against inter- and intra-ethnic hierarchies and oppositions functional to the *status quo*, they may produce solidarity and coalitions among different oppressed groups.

To the specific scope of this paper, I will concentrate on the racialization of people with a migrant background and counter-racialization enacted by struggling migrants during the crisis in Italy (Oliveri 2015). Taking the race-crisis nexus as the main focus, I will analyse only those migrant struggles which have developed a counter-discourse on the economic and border crises, in terms of causes, responsibilities and alternatives. In my view, this applies to struggles for freedom of movement and the right to life, for equality at work and for the right to housing. Mobilizations will be analysed by taking account of their critical understanding of the crisis-race nexus. To do this, I will intersect multiple sources: public petitions, banners and other documents produced by struggling migrants and militants acting in solidarity with them; press articles published by national and local Italian newspapers; interviews to activists conducted by other scholars or by myself. The background of each struggle will be briefly reconstructed with the support of official statistics, NGOs reports and a selection of the available literature.

From neoliberalism to late neoliberalism: the race-crisis nexus in Italy

The global economic recession has often been explained as the outcome of failures in the neoliberal strategy of global capitalism. Nevertheless, this strategy has never been radically questioned in order to find a way out of the crisis. On the contrary, it has been enhanced and made more flexible, in order to cope with a permanent economic state of emergency and the risks of social unrest. The outcome of this reloaded neoliberal strategy is what some authors call "late neoliberalism" (Della Porta 2016). This notion allows us to grasp the paradox of austerity measures meant to address a crisis which was the result of the same neoliberal logic.

Against this background, I will first reconstruct how neoliberalism produced migrants as racialized outsiders, then how race has been used as a crisis management strategy in the transition to late neoliberalism, and finally how migrant struggles have contested this strategy. For many reasons, Italy provides a significant case study: it became a country of immigration in parallel with neoliberalization (Ferrero and Perocco 2011); it has been one of the European countries most hit by crisis and austerity measures (Fana, Guarascio, and Cirillo 2015); it is one of the countries most involved in managing the refugee crisis through the so-called hotspot approach.

During the 1990s, under pressure of increasingly competitive global markets, the Italian economic and institutional system entered a phase of deep restructuring. Reforms enforced with few variations by governments of different colours tried to apply a neoliberal agenda: less regulation and taxation, privatization of State owned firms and public services, tertiarization and delocalization of industrial production, shrinking public expenditure, welfare provision and employment protection, segmentation and hierarchization of the labour market, taming trade unions' power (Gallino 2012). In the same years, Italy was also required to make macroeconomic adjustments in order to participate in the European monetary union, which implied the end of competitive devaluation of the lira as the main strategy for supporting export.

Between 1991 and 2015, the share of foreigners in the working population rose from 0.3 per cent to 10.4 per cent (Ministero del Lavoro 2016), becoming a structural component of the Italian labour market. Racialization has been crucial in managing this steep growth of immigration during the transition to neoliberalism. On the one hand, migrants have been employed in low-paid, hazardous, insecure jobs, confined in increasingly ethnicized sectors such as agriculture, domestic and care work, small and medium-sized manufacturing enterprises, construction, cleaning, hotels, sex work. On the other hand, despite migrants having generally been complementary to native workers rather than substitutes, their high precariousness has been often perceived as menacing a general downgrading of working conditions.

Border controls are crucial for producing this racialized, disposable and stratified labour force (Mezzadra and Neilson 2013). In Italy the increasingly strict link between visa, permit to stay and regular labour contract has become one of the key legal mechanisms enforcing racialization.[1] Like in other Mediterranean countries, irregularity has not been a failure but a systemic outcome. The majority of migrants in Italy entered with some kind of temporary visa, overstayed and went through a time of irregularity, including possible reclusion in administrative detention centres. Only those who accepted to live with no or few rights would be admitted to the rank of regulars, after employers decided to regularize them through the annual flow decree or periodic amnesties (Ferrero and Perocco 2011). Italy has thus become a model neoliberal migration regime: on the one hand, migrants' rights are strictly linked to their usefulness for the market; on the other hand, criminalization and deportability (Palidda 2011) function as powerful disciplining mechanisms which expose both regular and irregular migrants to exploitation. Against this background, there is only an apparent contradiction between strong internal and external fencing policies and weak internal gate-keeping policies (Triandafyllidou and Ambrosini 2011).

The neoliberal turn in Italy induced a decline of real incomes and consumption, and the increase of inequalities and precariousness: it prepared the conditions for the global crisis hitting hard and becoming endemic. European institutions played a crucial role in the transition to late neoliberalism, as they imposed austerity measures pretending to face recession while promoting a further restructuring of socio-economic and institutional arrangements. Italian governments, again with slight variations according to different political orientations, enforced cuts in educational and health systems, pensions and local public services, introduced a constitutional provision on balancing the state budget, curtailed the remaining protection on the labour market, such as the right to reinstatement in case of illegitimate firing. The alleged goal was to boost competitiveness while reducing the public debt. The result was the country sliding to the semi-periphery of the EU in terms of economic capacity, with more than two million jobs destroyed between 2008 and 2015, accompanied by the rise of the undeclared economy (ISTAT 2016b). This situation is mirrored by new strong emigration to Northern Europe, especially of young skilled workers reacting to disqualification and downgrading in life perspectives: for the first time in four decades, the balance between Italian emigration and immigration has been reversed (ISTAT 2016a).

In transition to late neoliberalism racialization has been enhanced for at least two reasons. First, the frame of ethnic competition for scarce resources had to be reinforced while presenting austerity as a given. Asylum seekers, rescued in the Mediterranean and accommodated by the national reception system, have thus become the target of populist campaigns exaggerating the costs of welcoming and asking the government to support instead the Italian poor (Mangano 2016). Second, migrants should accept the generalized downgrading provoked by the crisis, including higher levels of unemployment, exploitation and labour market segregation.

As a matter of fact, recession reversed what many migrant workers achieved during the previous decade in terms of social mobility from irregular to regular status, from underground to formal economy, from insecure to relatively stable jobs, from agriculture to manufacture and services, from Southern to Northern Italy (Pugliese 2014). For instance, between 2007 and 2012 the official unemployment rate of migrants rose more than that of native workers, from 5.3 per cent to 12.7 per cent for men, and from 12.7 per cent to 15.7 per cent for women and reached 17.2 per cent in 2013 and 16.9 per cent in 2014: a significant share of those people probably slid into irregularity, as official departures were comparatively low. Especially male migrants became unemployed because they were over-represented in manufacture and construction, and in small-medium firms, more hard-hit by the crisis. Losses of jobs in industry and construction were partially compensated by gains in services, especially domestic and care work largely reserved to women, and in agriculture (Ministero del Lavoro 2016).

Freedom of movement and right to life against the racialization through border controls

Since the 1990s, internal freedom of circulation for citizens of the Schengen area has been compensated by tighter controls on non-citizens at the European external frontiers (Walters 2002), especially through visa obligations, sanctions on vectors and the externalization of border enforcement to neighbour countries, and by the proliferation of internal controls on mobility, especially through centres for identification, reception, administrative detention and deportation (Guild 2005). This border regime has been crucial in the racialization of migrants in Italy, and became very soon the target of resistance and struggles, including the refusal to provide fingerprints and personal identity, revolts in detention centres, escapes from camps, occupation of public sites.

The first racializing marker contested by struggling migrants is the control of their mobility across borders and their hierarchization along national/non-national and legal/illegal distinctions. Freedom of movement represents for everyone a vital source of emancipation, yet the right to migrate is today a privilege for people living in the global North. The "others", because of their peripheral position in the world system of production and consumption, want to move to improve their life opportunities but are locked in the lowest strata of the "global hierarchy of mobility" (Bauman 1998): they are generally prevented from entering Western countries as a result of prohibitive visa requirements. Even asylum seekers have to reach in an irregular way the European border before being allowed to claim international protection, and after their arrival they are forced to stay in the country of first entry.[2]

During the refugee crisis, in connection with the enduring enforcement of austerity, border controls have re-articulated the legal/illegal distinction in terms of selection between "economic migrants" or "illegal aliens" and "true refugees". In times of allegedly scarce resources, this kind of differential racialization allows the government to reduce numbers and rights of asylum seekers to the minimum.[3] A very narrow concept of the right to asylum, linked to displacement from recognized zones of conflict, provides the main basis for this distinction, with some countries such as Syria, Iraq and Eritrea being presumptively qualified as sending people in "clear need of international protection".[4] In the case of internal controls within the Schengen area, such as the French-Italian border, checks become overtly race-based: "our African appearance is the main criterion police uses for stopping and searching us, and pushing us back. They are wrong if they believe that this will stop us from trying again to cross the border and *be free*".[5] As for fingerprinting, many asylum seekers across Italy refuse to be identified through this system, as they know this will prevent them from claiming asylum in other European countries. As a reaction, there is an increasing use and abuse of force in taking fingerprints (Amnesty International 2016).

The second racializing marker, rejected in particular by the families of missing migrants, is exposure to the risk of anonymous mass deaths, as a sign of less worthy or unworthy lives. An imaginary divide arises, accordingly, between a surplus humanity which can be put in danger and a legitimate humanity whose life is protected. Non-insured lives have the only alternative of either being let die or being rescued by military ferry-boats. As search and rescue operations are in the end arbitrary practices, states have the "power to make life and let die" (Foucault 2003). This power not only allows to control immigration through death (Squire 2016), but also to manage world population as a whole. A new legalized eugenics assigns the value of lives, distinguishing between those who could make a contribution to societies of destination and those who would be only a "burden". This approach has been exacerbated in times of austerity: search and rescue operations, especially by NGOs, are accused to encourage more sea crossings.

Against this racializing banalization of death, families of missing migrants affirm that the lives of their relatives matter: they claim the right to know what happened to them at sea, the right to identify bodies, and the right to mourn. They also question the representation of shipwrecks as natural accidents, with no responsibilities except that of other racialized subjects such as the "smugglers". Contesting this approach, families of missing migrants keep asking "where are our sons?" in order to make institutions accountable for border deaths (Oliveri 2016).

Equality at work against the racialization of labour

As shortly explained above, the racialization of the labour force has been a powerful tool for producing cheap and disposable migrant workers to sustain neoliberal socio-economic reforms in Italy. In the crisis, this mechanism has been enhanced, in order to relaunch rates of profit and support consumption despite low salaries and austerity, especially for necessary goods (food) and services (care). The racialization of the crisis supported the transition to late neoliberalism in many ways: by making social downgrading acceptable to migrants; by strengthening competition within the working class and undermining resistance; by using the crisis as an alibi for worsening working conditions in general while blaming migrants, or by making only racialized gang-masters or social cooperatives accountable for exploitation. Elements of counter-racialization have emerged in those struggles where migrants have tackled the roots of their vulnerability by claiming "residence permits for all", decoupled from top-down regularizations and from the working contract; where they have raised claims to "equal rights for equal work" and better working conditions for all; where they have re-framed causes and responsibilities for the crisis; where they have promoted class solidarity across migrants of different status and nationality, and with Italian workers.

Public authorities played a significant role in this juncture. As unemployment started increasing, the Italian government wanted to show the will to defend "Italian jobs" against migrant workers. In 2008 new entries of non-seasonal workers were allowed only up to 150,000, mostly in domestic and care services, and afterwards new entries of this kind were further reduced. Moreover, between 2008 and 2011, the government enforced several emergency measures known as "Security Packages" intended to "fight illegality linked to irregular migration and organized crime", in reality aimed at disciplining the migrant labour force.[6] In particular, it qualified in 2009 the "illegal entry and stay in the country" as a penal offence and it increased the maximum detention time in centres for to-be-expelled migrants from 90 to 180 days, further extended from 6 to 18 months in 2011. At the same time, it opened in 2009 an amnesty limited to domestic and care workers, followed in 2012 by another general regularization with high selective criteria.

According to the Migrant Strike Collective [*Coordinamento per lo sciopero migrante*], which supported the first Italian "Day without migrants" on 1st March 2010 (Cobbe and Grappi 2011), "through the so called Security Packages [...] the government is forcing workers to pay for the crisis. The institutional racism expressed by these measures and the illegality it creates makes migrants much more exposed to every kind of blackmail" (Coordinamento per lo sciopero 2010). These provisions were intended to reduce the stock of irregular migrant workers in times of recession by encouraging return to country of origin; yet, they enhance subordination and exploitation through criminalization: "most expulsions are not enacted, but they are an instrument to blackmail migrants" (Coordinamento per lo sciopero 2010). Moreover, identification and detention centres for migrants are seen here as "a safety valve for the labour market. When demand is lower, the excess migrant labour force is illegalized" (Coordinamento per lo sciopero 2010).[7]

To be sure, securitized and market-based immigration laws, in connection with exploitation, have been the target of migrant struggles in Italy since the late 1980s. Under the pressure of rising unemployment these struggles received new impulse, as those fired would lose their residence permit after six months of unemployment.[8] Claiming the right to stay without conditions, such as the work contract, or to be regularized without undergoing through selective and employer-driven amnesties (Montagna 2012), migrants rejected the racialization of labour enforced through their irregularization and production as disposable commodities. Moreover, as affirmed by the promoters of the first Migrant Strike, "immigration controls weaken labour as a whole, starting from the weakest and most defenceless workers, and imposing precariousness as a general condition".[9]

In this legal background, employers have used the crisis as an alibi in order to strengthen exploitation and segregation, enforce labour substitution and minimize resistance. As a reaction, migrants struggled to be recognized as workers entitled to equal rights: since 2008, a cycle of mobilizations has developed across Italy, mostly in agriculture and logistics, taking the form of self-organized sit-ins and strikes. Eventually supported by grassroots organizations, they were often met with indifference or even hostility by traditional trade unions and left-wing parties (Cappiali 2017).

In Rosarno (Calabria), in January 2010, hundreds of seasonal African orange pickers revolted against everyday racist violence used by local Mafia as a tool for managing the labour force in the citrus fruit harvest. At a certain point, migrants were perceived as being "in excess" in relation to employability. In the crisis, many migrants fired from companies in Northern Italy were coming to the town in search for jobs, without any public planning of reception; at the same time, cuts in European agricultural subsidies and a drop in farm prices induced many small farmers to leave fruit on the trees (Pugliese 2012). The riot exploded after two workers were injured by local youngsters in a drive-by shooting, and it was followed by a "black man hunt" unleashed by the resident population and by the eviction of about 2000 Africans.

> To all those who blame us [for the riot], we would say that oranges do not fall from the sky. Ours are the hands that picked them. We were tired of being invisible. We struggled, in the end, for *dignity as workers and human beings*. And to change this *system* which pit us one against the other.[10]

In Nardò (Apulia), in Summer 2011, hundreds of seasonal African farmworkers went on strike for about two weeks, claiming to be regularly hired by land-owners instead of going through "black gang-masters", to be paid 6 euros instead of 3.50 for each crate of big tomatoes and 10 euros instead of 7 for each crate of small tomatoes, to stop working 10–12 hours per day. As in many parts of the Italian countryside, gang-masters in Nardò provide workers with transportation, food, water and accommodation, deducing a broker's fee from the daily salary. "We are workers like the others" was the main argument raised by the strikers against the racialization of labour ending in slavery-like conditions. As stated by the leader of the strike:

> To those who ask you to come back to work at any price, and continue suffering from this dirty job and being part of this dirty system, you must answer that [...] *you are human beings*. [...]. That the *time of slavery is over*. That you want a true contract, as other workers have. (Perrotta and Sacchetto 2012, 37–38)

In Latina (Latium), in April 2016 about 2,000 Indian Sikh farmworkers went on strike for a whole day and marched across the city, with the support of the main local trade union and a grassroots pro-migrant association (Omizzolo 2016). Under the banner "Same blood, same rights", they protested against severe exploitation: this included, among other things, arbitrary deductions from the pay, which amounted in the end to 3 euro per hour for a 12-hour working-day, against a legal pay of 8.3 euro per hour for a 6.5-hour working-day. Moreover, in order to keep up the inhumane work-rhythm imposed by the "masters" many workers took pain killers (In Migrazione 2014). "Our strike is not only about fair salary, it's also about stopping being humiliated".[11] In fact, some Sikhs have also been forced to trim their beards because it annoyed the employer, who sometimes even made them walk at a certain distance from him (Sciarra 2014).

Struggling migrants tried to subvert racialization not only as a mechanism which subordinates them to employers and sets them against Italian workers, but also as a tool which produces hierarchies among migrants themselves. The most interesting mobilizations of this kind have taken place in the logistic sector since 2011, especially in Piacenza and Bologna (Emilia-Romagna) (Massarelli 2014). According to a striker,

> in warehouses the gang-master used to say to Moroccans that they are better than Tunisians, to Tunisians that they are better than Egyptians or Romanians. The objective is to split up workers, putting one group against the other: "if you behave well, I'll pay you more; do not join the struggles". (Curcio 2013)

Under the slogan against "racist logistics [which] provides slavery-like jobs", migrant workers of different nationalities came together with the aim of enhancing their working conditions, opposing unjustified wage cuts and dismissals, and contesting retaliation against the most active militants. These struggles developed with the support of grassroots trade unions, within a large coalition involving students and precarious workers, political collectives and social centres. Strong forms of protest were tried out, such as boycotts of companies involved in exploitation and blockades at the retail logistic warehouses. During one of those actions, on 15 September 2016, an Egyptian worker died when he was hit by a truck driven by an Italian colleague who wasn't on strike (Ciccarelli 2016).

Finally, these struggles offered an alternative frame for understanding the crisis and rejected the idea of recession as implying sacrifices for workers alone. They made employers, particularly in big companies, traders and retail chains, the main people responsible for declining wages and working conditions; not the migrants, nor racialized gang-masters and subcontracting cooperatives, which are only intermediaries of the most powerful agents in the market.

Right to housing against the racialization of space

The neoliberalization of many Italian cities, driven by deregulation of the housing market, gentrification, privatization of public space and cuts in local public expenditure, in connection with the increasing presence of migrants in everyday life spaces (Cancellieri and Ostanel 2015), provided since the 1990s the context for campaigns on urban security and priority in accessing social housing for Italians.

The racialization of urban and rural space has been a key feature in these processes. Housing discrimination, in particular, has played a crucial role in reproducing segregation and vulnerability to exploitation along racial divides, while further alimenting conflicts with natives. Lacking access to dwellings, migrants are often forced to accept below standard accommodation. In the case of seasonal workers, housing is provided by gang-masters or employers; yet, living in the working place exposes people to the risk of excessive working hours, abuses and even sexual violence. A significant share of migrants, including refugees, live in informal shelters. The largest of these settlements are in Southern Italy near the main harvest sites and are commonly called "ghettos": workers who live in these areas are not prevented from moving away, but they are effectively trapped there because they have no viable alternatives (Sagnet and Palmisano 2015).

In the crisis these mechanisms have been enhanced, not only to keep the costs of migrants' social reproduction as low as possible, and normalize the failures of the asylum reception system, but also to manage tensions relating to a nationwide housing emergency, especially in suburbs characterized by the presence of working poor and unemployed people. For instance, being far more dependent on the private housing market than Italians, migrant families have also been proportionally more hit by evictions for involuntary rent arrears during the recession, representing twenty-two per cent of all the cases in 2009, twenty-four per cent in 2010, twenty-six per cent in 2011 and 2012 (Sunia-CGIL 2012). As a result, they are currently far more exposed than Italians to severe housing deprivation, with a rate of 14.5 per cent compared to 4.7 per cent. About 10,000 refugees and asylum seekers including women and children are living outside the official reception system in appalling conditions (Doctors Without Borders 2016).

To be sure, migrant struggles for the right to housing developed in the country since the late 1980s. They experienced a significant revival in times of austerity, with migrants currently playing a significant role in many housing movements, in terms of both numbers and organizational capacity (Nur and Sethman 2017). Besides the occupation of empty buildings, as an immediate solution to the emergency, mobilizations include anti-eviction pickets and rallies with more explicit political aims, also in terms of counter-racialization. This has happened in many ways: by contesting measures of institutional racism (illegal occupation of a property as grounds for refusing legal residence; legal residence as a condition for renewing the permit to stay; length of residence as a requirement for social housing); by creating solidarity between nationals and non-nationals facing evictions; by reframing housing issues beyond ethnic competition in terms of structural problems, failures and deliberate choices of national and local housing policies.

In 2014, in order to repress squatting by migrants and other groups, the government passed a Decree stating among other things that "anybody who illegally occupies a property without any title cannot ask for municipal residence registration, nor be connected to public services in relation to that property".[12] This was just the last of many provisions passed in recent years for limiting the right to housing of migrants, justified as a way to defend Italian working class. As a result, despite the enduring rhetoric of migrants unfairly competing with nationals for social housing, only a minority of non-nationals in need have access to public facilities. As a general rule, only migrants with a two-year permit to stay or with a long-term residence permit, who are regularly employed, qualify for social housing.[13] Since 2000 many municipalities have introduced tougher eligibility conditions, such as a lengthy period of residence in the municipality, which usually has a greater impact on non-citizens. In 2008, as the government adopted the first austerity measures,[14] the new National Housing Plan set up restrictive criteria for accessing social housing and benefits, such as a ten-year legal residence in the country or a five-year legal residence in the same region.

Against the racialization of housing emergency, social movements have promoted in many Italian cities anti-eviction pickets including low-income migrants and Italians as well. As an activist told me,

this is the only effective way of being anti-racist today, by enforcing active solidarity among people with different national and ethnic backgrounds. Through
the mutual defence of *our common right to housing*, Italians and migrants recognize themselves "on the same side of the barricade", against greedy landlords
and hostile or ineffective municipalities.[15]

Similar examples of counter-racialization involving multi-ethnic solidarity can be
seen in many other Italian cities, where resistance to evictions, sit-ins for the right
to housing, collective occupations, *pro bono* legal aid, protests against living
conditions of asylum seekers, have taken place over recent years.[16]

Counter-racialization rests in this case on the critical assessment of Italian
housing and wage policies as the material cause for a racialized competition
for scarce resources. Under neoliberal deregulation of the housing and labour
markets, and growing real estate speculation, the gap between incomes and
rents has dramatically increased: between 1991 and 2009 incomes grew
around eighteen per cent while rents grew around 105 per cent (Cittalia-Anci
2010). During the recession, this gap increased and produced a rise in evictions:
in 2013, 68,000 families were ordered to leave their homes because they had not
paid their rent in time, while in 2007 the number of families in the same situation
was 33,500. Against this background, the failure of the national housing welfare
system became apparent. With around seventy per cent of available houses
being owner occupied, social housing has not been a political priority in Italy
for decades. In 2010 only about four per cent of the national housing stock
was made up of social dwellings, declining by around twenty per cent
between 1991 and 2007 (Cittalia-Anci 2010). Moreover, throughout Italy
between 30,000 and 40,000 council houses are currently vacant even though
there are 650,000 people who requested to live in them.

The new cycle of struggles in times of austerity has tried to develop this
counter-discourse of the crisis, claiming radically alternative housing and
economic policies. The large rally which took place in Rome on 19
October 2013 was opened by a banner that read "Only one big project:
income and houses for everyone!" contesting the government choice to
support high-speed railways and other costly infrastructures, instead of
addressing urgent social needs. This agenda was set up and promoted by
the Living in the Crisis Network, a coalition of Italian housing movements,
along with many autonomous groups such as student movements, grassroots trade unions, precarious workers and migrants. The urgency of this
critical approach to the crisis became apparent a year later, when a
working-class neighbourhood in Southern Rome experienced protests
against the opening of a reception centre for asylum seekers. A protester
said the demonstration had nothing to do with racism or xenophobia: "I
have always voted for left-wing parties and have nothing against anyone.
What I am tired of is the state of neglect the whole area has been left in
by the municipality" (Mucci 2015).

Conclusion

Racial fractures are essential to the Italian social and economic system, which needs low-cost and disposable labour, and to a political system which denies any responsibility for the enduring crisis, by letting migrants and their descendants be blamed instead. Moreover, these fractures are dramatic because they disempower working and popular classes.

To develop a new anti-racist agenda, I have suggested here to explore the making and unmaking of migrants as racialized outsiders in Italy, first under neoliberalism and then under late neoliberalism. I have recommended in particular to take migrant struggles within and against the crisis as a critical standpoint on race and on its peculiar uses during the enforcement of austerity measures. In fact, those struggles have reacted to enhanced racialization processes, especially through new laws, practices and discourses targeting migrants as a menace for borders and security, and as unfair competitors for limited resources.

In the end, what migrant struggles mentioned above have in common is the ideological and practical deconstruction of ethnic competition as a fatal consequence of austerity, and the effort to reunite "those below" against "those above" across racializing lines. Counter-discourses focusing on the real causes and responsibilities of the crisis and on alternatives to austerity, associated with practices of inter-ethnic solidarity, constitute the key elements which allowed me to see these struggles as examples of counter-racialization. These examples should be taken seriously as a key contribution towards a structural anti-racist strategy. This strategy should include, among other things, legally recognized freedom of movement and residence, an exploitation-free system of production and consumption, public investment in social housing and welfare. In Italy and elsewhere, it would be extremely beneficial for anti-racist and anti-austerity movements to converge: they should both embrace racialization for understanding the race-crisis nexus, counter-racialization as a key strategy against social injustice, and struggling migrants as a fundamental force for a change. Without such a turn in the political approach, there will be very little room for a real alternative to the *status quo*.

Notes

1. This regime has been institutionalized by Law No. 189/2002, which is still in force.
2. EU Regulation No 604/2013 establishing the criteria and mechanisms for determining the Member State responsible for examining an application for international protection (so-called Dublin III Regulation).
3. Decree law on asylum procedures and irregular immigration No 13/2017 exemplifies this logic. In the name of speeding up judicial procedures and lightening

the "burden" on the reception system, asylum seekers will no longer have the chance to appeal the rejection of their claims. There will be no hearing, as the judge will be provided with a video recording of the interview. Asylum seekers are required to perform "socially useful work" on a voluntary basis.

4. Ministry of Interiors, Circular letter on the Hotspot approach and the relocation procedures, No. 14106/2015.
5. Interview with a migrant activist, Ventimiglia, 11 August 2016.
6. Law No. 125/2008; Law No.94/2009; Law No. 129/2011.
7. In recent years, there is growing evidence that in many sectors a substitution of irregular with regular migrant workers is taking place: newcomers with limited intention of settling, such as EU citizens especially from Romania, or asylum seekers wanting to move to Northern Europe, are often easier to exploit than other non-EU migrants who became established in the country. This may eventually change again, as many asylum seekers will be rejected but will remain in Italy, feeding the undeclared economy.
8. The term of six months, introduced by Law No. 189/2002, was extended to twelve months by Law No. 92/2012.
9. Primo Marzo. 2009. "Chi siamo". See http://primomarzo2010.blogspot.it/2009/10/chi-siamo.html.
10. Interview with a migrant activist, Rome, 17 February 2010.
11. Interview with a migrant activist, Bella Farnia, June 2016.
12. Law No. 80/2014.
13. Legislative Decree No. 286/1998.
14. Law No. 133/2008.
15. Interview with a housing rights activist, Pisa, April 2014.
16. For updates on the mobilizations for the right to housing, with a special focus on the participation of migrants, see the "Living in the crisis" network: http://www.abitarenellacrisi.org/.

Disclosure statement

No potential conflict of interest was reported by the author.

References

Amnesty International. 2016. *Hotspot Italy. How EU's Flagship Approach Leads to Violations of Refugee and Migrant Rights*. London: Amnesty International.

Anthias, F., and N. Yuval-Davis. 1992. *Racialized Boundaries: Race, Nation, Gender, Colour and Class and the Anti-Racist Struggle*. London: Routledge.

Balibar, É., and I. Wallerstein. 1991. *Race, Nation, Class: Ambiguous Identities*. London: Verso.

Bauman, Z. 1998. *Globalization: The Human Consequences*. New York: Columbia University Press.

Björgo, T., and R. Witte. 1993. "Introduction." In *Racist Violence in Europe*, edited by T. Björgo, and R. Witte, 1–16. London: Macmillan.

Brah, A. 1996. *Cartographies of Diaspora: Contesting Identities*. London: Routledge.

Cancellieri, A., and E. Ostanel. 2015. "The Struggle for Public Space: The Hypervisibility of Migrants in the Italian Urban Landscape." *City* 19 (4): 499–509. doi:10.1080/13604813.2015.1051740.

Cappiali, T. M. 2017. "'Whoever Decides for You Without You, S/he Is Against You!': Immigrant Activism and the Role of the Left in Political Racialization." *Ethnic and Racial Studies* 40 (6): 969–987. doi:10.1080/01419870.2016.1229487.

Ciccarelli, R. 2016. "Logistica, la ribellione dei migranti contro lo sfruttamento. Intervista a Giorgio Grappi." *il manifesto*, September 16

Cittalia-Anci. 2010. *I Comuni e la questione abitativa. Le nuove domande sociali, gli attori e gli strumenti operativi*. Rome: Cittalia-Anci.

Cobbe, L., and G. Grappi. 2011. "Primo marzo, percorsi di uno sciopero inatteso." In *La normale eccezione. Lotte migranti in Italia*, edited by F. Mometti, and M. Ricciardi, 55–90. Rome: Alegre.

Coordinamento per lo sciopero. 2010. *10 tesi sul lavoro migrante*.

Curcio, A. 2013. "The Revolution in Logistics." *Effimera*, November, 27.

Della Porta, D. 2016. "Late Neoliberalism and Its Discontents: An Introduction." In *Late Neoliberalism and Its Discontents in the Economic Crisis: Comparing Social Movements in the European Periphery*, edited by D. Della Porta, M. Andretta, T. Fernandes, F. O'Connor, E. Romanos, and M. Vogiatzoglou, 1–38. Cham: Springer.

Doctors Without Borders. 2016. *Out of Sight. Asylum Seekers and Refugees in Italy: Informal Settlements and Social Marginalization*. Rome: Medici Senza Frontiere Italia.

ENAR. 2015. *Racist Crime in Europe. ENAR Shadow Report 2013–2014*. Brussels: European Network Against Racism.

Fana, M., D. Guarascio, and V. Cirillo. 2015. "Labour Market Reforms in Italy: Evaluating the Effects of the Jobs Act." *ISI Growth Working Paper*, 5. http://www.isigrowth.eu/2015/12/08/labour-market-reforms-in-italy-evaluating-the-effects-of-the-jobs-act/.

Fekete, L. 2001. "The Emergence of Xeno-Racism." *Race and Class* 43 (2): 23–40.

Ferrero, M., and F. Perocco. 2011. *Razzismo al lavoro. Il sistema della discriminazione sul lavoro, la cornice giuridica e gli strumenti di tutela*. Milan: Franco Angeli.

Foucault, M. 2003. *"Society Must Be Defended." Lectures at the Collège de France, 1975–1976*. New York: Picador.

FRA. 2010. *Protecting Fundamental Rights During the Economic Crisis*. Vienna: European Union Agency for Fundamental Rights.

Gallino, L. 2012. *La lotta di classe dopo la lotta di classe*. Rome: Laterza.

Guild, E. 2005. *A Typology of Different Types of Centres in Europe*. Brussels: European Parliament.

Haney López, I. 1996. *White by Law: The Legal Construction of Race*. New York: New York University Press.

In Migrazione. 2014. *Sfruttati a tempo indeterminato*. Rome: In Migrazione.

ISTAT. 2016a. *Bilancio demografico nazionale*. Rome: Istituto Nazionale di Statistica.

ISTAT. 2016b. *Rapporto Annuale. La situazione del paese*. Rome: Istituto Nazionale di Statistica.

Lentin, A. 2004. *Racism and Anti-Racism in Europe*. London: Pluto Press.

Lentin, A., and G. Titley. 2011. *The Crises of Multiculturalism: Racism in a Neoliberal Age*. London: Zed Books.

Lunaria. 2014. *Chronicles of Ordinary Racism. Third White Paper on Racism in Italy*. Rome: Lunaria.

Mangano, A. 2016. *Ruspe o biberon. Migranti. Oltre i luoghi comuni dei buoni e dei cattivi*. Roma: Terrelibere.

Massarelli, F. 2014. *Scarichiamo i padroni. Lo sciopero dei facchini a Bologna*. Milan: Agenzia X.

Mellino, M. 2012. "De-Provincializing Italy. Notes on Race, Racialization, and Italy's Coloniality." In *Postcolonial Italy. Challenging National Homogeneity*, edited by C. Lombardi-Diop, and C. Romeo, 83–99. New York: Palgrave Macmillan.

Mezzadra, S., and B. Neilson. 2013. *Border as Method, or, the Multiplication of Labor.* Durham: Duke University Press.

Ministero del Lavoro. 2016. *I migranti nel mercato del lavoro in Italia. Quinto Rapporto Annuale.* Rome: Ministero del Lavoro e delle Politiche Sociali.

Montagna, N. 2012. "Labor, Citizenship, and Subjectivity: Migrants' Struggles Within the Italian Crisis." *Social Justice* 39 (1): 37–51.

Mucci, A. 2015. "Italy's Immigration Tensions Explode." *Al Jazeera*, January 12.

Murji, K., and J. Solomos. 2005. "Introduction. Racialization in Theory and Practice." In *Racialization: Studies in Theory and Practice*, edited by K. Murji, and J. Solomos, 1–28. Oxford: Oxford University Press.

Nur, N., and A. Sethman. 2017. "Migration and Mobilization for the Right to Housing in Rome: New Urban Frontiers?" In *Migration, Squatting and Radical Autonomy: Resistance and Destabilization of Racist Regulatory Policies and B/Ordering Mechanisms*, edited by P. Mudu, and S. Chattopadhyay, 78–92. London: Routledge.

Oliveri, F. 2015. "Migrant Struggles in Italy Within and Against the Economic Crisis." In *Exploring the Crisis: Theoretical Perspectives and Empirical Investigations*, edited by A. Borghini, and E. Campo, 113–128. Pisa: Pisa University Press.

Oliveri, F. 2016. "'Where Are Our Sons?' Tunisian Families and the Repoliticization of Deadly Migration Across the Mediterranean Sea." In *Migration by Boat. Discourses of Trauma, Exclusion and Survival*, edited by L. Mannik, 154–177. New York: Berghahn.

Omizzolo, M. 2016. "Caporalato nel Pontino, così vivono (e scioperano) i braccianti sikh." *Left*, May 24.

Palidda, S. 2011. "The Italian Crime Deal." In *Racial Criminalization of Migrants in the 21st Century*, edited by S. Palidda, 164–175. Milan: Agenzia X.

Perrotta, M., and D. Sacchetto. 2012. "Un piccolo sentimento di vittoria. Note sullo sciopero di Nardò." In *Sulla pelle viva. Nardò: la lotta autorganizzata dei braccianti immigrati*, edited by Brigate di solidarietà attiva, G. Nigro, M. Perrotta, D. Sacchetto, and Y. Sagnet, 9–55. Rome: Derive Approdi.

Pugliese, E. 2012. "Il lavoro agricolo immigrato nel Mezzogiorno e il caso di Rosarno." *Mondi Migranti*, 3: 7–28. doi:10.3280/MM2012-003001.

Pugliese, E. 2014. "The Crisis, Immigrants and the Labour Market." In *Chronicles of Ordinary Racism. Third White Paper on Racism in Italy*, edited by Lunaria, 34–41. Rome: Lunaria.

Sagnet, Y., and L. Palmisano. 2015. *Ghetto Italia. I braccianti stranieri tra capolarato e sfruttamento.* Rome: Fandango.

Sappino, L. 2016. "Dire che l'Italia è un Paese razzista non aiuta." *L'Espresso*, July 7.

Sayad, A. 1991. *L'immigration ou les paradoxes de l'altérité.* Brussels: De Boeck.

Sciarra, E. 2014. "Modern Slavery in Italian Rural Areas: Sikh Community at Risk." *The Global Oyster*, July 10.

Squire, V. 2016. "Governing Migration Through Death in Europe and the US: Identification, Burial and the Crisis of Modern Humanism." *European Journal of International Relations*, September16: 1–20. doi:10.1177/1354066116668662.

Sudbury, J. 1998. *'Other Kinds of Dreams'. Black women's Organization and the Politics of Transformation.* London: Routledge.

Sunia-CGIL. 2012. *Crisi e sfratti, i numeri del disagio abitativo.* Rome: Sunia-CGIL.

Triandafyllidou, A., and M. Ambrosini. 2011. "Irregular Immigration Control in Italy and Greece: Strong Fencing and Weak Gate-Keeping Serving the Labour Market." *European Journal of Migration and Law,* 13 (3): 251–273. doi:10.1163/157181611X587847.

Virdee, S. 2015. *Racism, Class and the Racialized Outsider.* Basingstok: Palgrave Macmillan.

Walters, W. 2002. "Mapping Schengenland: Denaturalizing the Border." *Environment & Planning D: Society & Space* 20 (5): 561–580. doi:10.1068/d274t.

Migration, crisis, liberalism: the cultural and racial politics of Islamophobia and "radical alterity" in modern Greece

Elisabeth Kirtsoglou and Giorgos Tsimouris

ABSTRACT
This paper attempts a critical and ethnographically informed reading of the complex assemblage of linkages between migration, racialization and liberal values in modern Greece as a symptomatic case of European attitudes to migration. In line with recent scholarship on racialization and Islamophobia, we discuss novel forms of racism, that support the construction of hierarchies and geographies of entitlement, going beyond notions of biological difference. Processes of inclusion and exclusion, we argue, rest on a meshwork of seemingly disparate identification markers that form the basis of universalist, hegemonic visions of citizenship. Migrants are ultimately expected by considerable sections of the Greek public to demonstrate their acceptance of an array of values regarded as "European", and to manifest their support to (neo)liberal regimes of subjectification. We conclude by arguing that racialization can be traced back to an imagined "orient", and just as well, to contemporary cultural and political imperialist projects.

Introduction

The present paper focuses on a critical analysis of the culture–race–migration kaleidoscope found in public attitudes and state policies in modern Greece. We take Greece as a symptomatic case of the racialized character of national and EU immigration policies and discourses. By examining a variety of settings in a period that ranges from the early 1990s to the present, we argue in favour of a unified analysis of the culturalist, racialist and historically *cum* economically produced conditions of the alterity of the migrant other. We suggest that migrants and displaced persons are caught in hierarchies of entitlement and often reduced to a perpetual status of *allochthony* (foreignness) (cf. Silverstein 2005). The complexity and shiftiness of contemporary forms of racism (cf. Balibar 2007, 21) led us to consider the shared philosophical roots of conservative, right wing and liberal political projects (cf. Choudhury 2015). The focus on the economies of desirability and undesirability, exclusion and inclusion of migrant others, reveals the need to reflect on (neo)liberal visions of "modernity", "progress" and "integration" as decisive factors in the conceptualisation of (supra)state policies and public attitudes to migrants. In order to develop and substantiate this argument, our paper is organized in three distinct sections. The first section touches upon the rise of ultra-nationalism and the far right in Greece and discusses the intimate connections between racial and cultural politics of "radical alterity" (cf. Kirtsoglou and Tsimouris 2016). The second section proceeds to examine Islamophobia as a variation of the racialized attitudes to migrant populations. We examine the spatial politics of the production of the Muslim "other" as a partial and potentially dangerous presence and we explain the tensions between religious and secular configurations of the Greek state. Taking our cue from recent attempts to establish a "Euro-Islam" (cf. Ramadan 2004), we examine the distinctions between "good" and "bad" Muslims and their relation to (neo)liberal values of self-transformation. The manner in which (neo) liberal governmentalities are implicated in the illegality and deportability of migrants in contexts of new labour relations is further discussed in the third and final section of the paper. Taking the Albanian migrant as the most "successful" case of incorporation in modern Greek society, we problematize the concept of "integration" and its association with universalist visions of European superiority. The paper concludes by stressing the role of hegemonic narratives of cosmopolitanism prevalent in Greek and European discourses on migration.

The coloured people

While conducting fieldwork with diaspora communities in Athens, in 2014,[1] we found ourselves in a taxi on Patision street. Patision – a central Athenian avenue – connects densely populated, currently impoverished neighbourhoods, once inhabited by the middle-classes and now home to various migrant communities.

> *Look Madame! Look!* – the taxi driver exclaimed, pointing to pedestrians – *the place is full of coloured people (gemisame eghromous). The once superb neighbourhoods of central Athens are now full of immigrants (metanastes). People are afraid to go out at night. Most residents [i.e. Greeks] (katoikoi) have left. It is only the poor and the elderly that have nowhere else to go, who continue living here. Black, white, yellow (mavroi, asproi, kitrinoi), they all gather here. They drink, they steal, they kill*

each other, fight, prostitute themselves; they show no respect. They occupy every bit of space, sometimes sleep on the streets and use the pavements as toilets. Awful mess! Central Athens has turned into an awful mess.

Focusing on the period between 2009 and 2015, the present section will establish that widespread xenophobia is symptomatic of deep-seated, negative attitudes towards particular categories of people perceived as "foreign" and by consequence regarded as threatening to the Greek nation. Original ethnographic data will be discussed against analytical approaches on the production of migrants as a problem of cultural and racial difference (cf. Vertovec 2011, 242). By examining literature on cultural politics and racialization, we wish to argue that the Greek case is better explained through a combined emphasis on cultural and racial essentialism, rather than a single-handed focus on any one of the two aspects.

In May 2013, a cultural group called "Atenistas" organized an open tour in Kypseli, one of the most densely populated neighbourhoods off-Patision street. The tour was scheduled to end in the premises of a primary school where three "famous Kypseliots" (a poet *cum* writer, a director and an architect) would deliver speeches about their neighbourhood. Parts of the speech of the established poet and writer Kiki Dimoula became the subject of a bitter public debate due to their xenophobic depictions of the current demography of the neighbourhood and its effects to the lives of "original" Kypseliots. We will hereby translate the most contentious parts of the talk[2] and invite the reader to compare their spirit with that of the taxi-driver's comment quoted in the very beginning of this section.

I live in Kypseli for 76 years; on the very same street. I have lived through the nice years of Kypseli (ta oraia hronia tis Kypselis) ... Pythias' street, where I lived, was full of beautiful detached houses with gardens, the inhabitants all knew each other. It was very picturesque ... I still live here, not entirely reconciled with the changes ... Let us not forget that the foreigners, who found themselves here, did so because of the poverty of their countries ... But we must state, as well, that they are a constant danger. The locals are in danger of being mugged on the street ... 42 Pythias' street, where my sister lives. She was hospitalised twice. Twice she was beaten by someone outside her door because she could not find her key house quickly enough ... Limited cases, yes, but the fear is unlimited. I do not mean to say that the foreigners of Kypseli are burglars. But if one goes to the square, there is no space to walk. Foreign people sit on the benches –naturally, they want to pass the time – and they play some strange card games of their own and the whole place becomes full of little cards. Of course, the Kypseliots have been displaced; this is a fact. Of course we love the foreigners, since they left their countries to come and live here, to work, but the spaces need to be somehow distributed[3] ... I have become accustomed to foreigners; accustomed to waking up and seeing them. I have come across many blacks pushing supermarket trolleys ... I wish hunger did not exist, I wish all the races of the world were mixed, but here there is a problem now. How are these people [referring to "foreigners"] *supposed to sustain themselves? I am really pleased today that I found myself among other Kypseliots. Really pleased.*

Dimoula's speech metonymically stands for the dominant narrative, prevalent among Greek people who reside or visit frequently the impoverished parts of the urban centres of Athens where most diaspora communities live. With the striking exception of politicised members of pro-migrant activist groups, associated mainly with the radical left and/or anarchist circles, the majority of respondents articulated stereotypically negative discourses about the "migrants". Foreigners, *xenoi*[4] were almost indiscriminately portrayed as a cultural and physical threat to local communities and the nation in general (cf. Silverstein 2005, 376; Vertovec 2011, 243). The organizing themes of this dominant narrative, the convenient "story seeds" (Knight 2013, 153) relate to perceptions of migrants as dangerous, potentially prone to criminal activity, as unhealthy and possibly contagious, and as religious and cultural misfits that will never "assimilate" (*den afomoionontai*) in Greek society. Their countries of origin are imagined as "poor" and "destitute", while their "cultures" are frequently judged as "backwards", "inferior" or lagging modernisation.

Such narratives about the "Other" do not limit themselves to supporters of the far right (cf. Virdee 2014). Different respondents, according to their political affiliation, general knowledge and level of religiosity were elaborating on some or all of the aforementioned themes. Anti-migrant discourses reflect therefore a whole spectrum of positions and often assume the form of "dogmas of cultural difference" (cf. Strathern 1995, 16; Vertovec 2011, 244). Virdee's study of race and English working class explains eloquently the manner in which socialist "arguments and struggles to secure economic and social justice for the excluded came to be ideologically located in the terrain of the nation" that "operated as a power container limiting the political imagination ... of the representatives of the exploited and the oppressed" (2014, 5). Regarding the liberal side of the political spectrum, in a discussion of the shared philosophical roots of right wing and liberal political theory, Choudhury argues that both strands converge on ideas about civilizational superiority that ultimately produce new kinds of racism (2015, 48). The co-constructed character of "culturalist" and "racist" discourses against immigrants has been first noted by Barker who saw the emergence of a "new racism", hidden "inside apparently innocent language about culture" (1981, 3). The seemingly "incommensurable racial difference" of immigrant populations forms the basis of new "racist paradigms" in Europe, whereby biological differences between races, that once formed the backbone of racism, are now increasingly expressed in terms of cultural incompatibility (Grillo 2003; cf. Silverstein 2005, 364, 365).

Such culturalist discourses – based on perceptions of cultures as static, essentialised, biologised and inherited (Baumann 1996; cf. Vertovec 2011) – need not divert our attention from the processes through which migration has become a "racialised category" (Silverstein 2005, 367). The manner in which "race" is implicated with migration issues reminds one of Ingold's concept of the "meshwork", namely of a network of interacting concepts, entangled lines of discourse and co-constructed ideas about seemingly disparate notions such as "culture", "civilisation", "progress", "modernisation", "descent", religion, gender and "biology" (to name some, but not all) (cf. Ingold 2011, 63). This meshwork of interdependent concepts is not static. On the contrary, in line with Ingold's original idea, it is in a constant state of flux, growth and movement (Ingold 2011). In this sense, we are in complete agreement with the analytical conviction of Kibria, Bowman and O'Leary that the race–migration kaleidoscope is a "fluid and intertwined bundle of linkages" (2013, 5), a highly complex and complicated political project "rooted in colonialism and imperialism" (Erel, Murji, and Nahaboo 2016, 1343). The transformation of biological racism into cultural, and/or religious racism enabled scholars to realise that "race moves" (Erel, Murji, and Nahaboo 2016; cf. also Mishra Tarc 2013, 373) and transforms itself independently of "the old certainties of colour" (Lazaridis and Koumandraki 2001, 279–301) taking on multiple guises.

Race has been sharply critiqued in analytical and scientific terms. It remains nonetheless an organising theme of public discourses and perceptions of the "other" in Greece and elsewhere (also Balibar and Wallerstein 1991; cf. Silverstein 2005, 364–365). When problematizing race, we follow Silverstein's definition of a

> cultural category of difference that is contextually constructed as essential and natural – as residing within the very body of the individual – [being] thus generally tied, in scientific theory and popular understanding to a set of somatic, physiognomic, and even genetic and other traits. (2005, 364)

These traits may be corresponding to a person's phenotype, or inferred and imagined in ways that render categories such as "whiteness", "blackness" and everything else "in-between" – so to speak – fluid and unstable. The fluidity of race refers not only to cases recorded in the literature, namely Eastern European people, Jews or Roma (cf. Malkki 1992; Barrett and Roediger 1997), but also to the everyday politics of banal racial "identification" that prove to be highly dependent on other factors, like linguistic fluency, birthplace or descent. Modern Greeks, for instance, would easily joke about how a darker member of the family "looks like a gypsy" (cf. also Panourgia 1995), but they would never question that person's rightful belonging to the "white race" (with which they readily identify themselves). Similarly, a lighter-skinned Roma, or Asian would still be cast as "other", "foreign" or person of colour on the basis of their origin, or Greek language skills (compare with Vargas-Ramos 2014). A closer look at the ethnographic data suggests that rather than race itself (cf. Anthias 1990), it is *perceptions of race* that matter. Ultimately, the manner in which race as a political category is imagined, socially, historically and economically constructed, points to the pertinence of the concept of *racialization* that we have employed in our discussion (cf. Gilroy 1987, 38). Racialization refers precisely to those "dynamic and dialectical processes of categorisation and meaning construction in which specific meanings are ascribed to real or fictitious somatic features" (Wodak and Reisigl 1999, 180; cf. Silverstein 2005, 364). The "racial system" according to which immigrants and various "others" are taxonomically categorized largely corresponds to the hierarchy of entitlements imposed onto them in everyday social situations, and in their relations to the state, the law and supranational formations.

Researchers have long pointed out the racialized character of national and EU policies in relation to immigration (cf. Cabot 2014; Erel, Murji, and Nahaboo 2016). Racialized perceptions of migrants are produced both within every day banal contexts of cultural racism, and through policy narratives and categories such as illegality and deportability (cf. De Genova 2002, 2010; Hiemstra 2010, 75). The current complex European border regime (Green 2013) reveals the role of the EU as a "racial supra-state" (Garner 2007, 14; Cole 2009; cf. Erel, Murji, and Nahaboo 2016, 1344). State and policy-conceived racialized taxonomies appear to be congruent with racialized *geographies*, establishing a firm connection between racialization and colonial histories of the past, as well as, between racialization and current asymmetrical structures of extractive economic relations between national and supranational entities (cf. Virdee 2014). The meshwork of culture, race, civilisation, progress, modernity, religion, gender and ethnicity is – we claim – a (post)colonial technology that permeates state-citizen relations, policy narratives and casual sociality. It is a technology that aims at managing difference; sometimes by transforming difference into forms of "radical and incommensurable alterity" (cf. Kirtsoglou and Tsimouris 2016), and at other times by hegemonically commanding the conditions of the "Other's" integration.

Islamophobia and the politics of space

One of the most shocking ideas in Dimoula's speech cited in the previous section regards the division of public space (*na moirastoun oi horoi*). Currently, in Greece and elsewhere, the politics of distribution of migrants, asylum-seekers and refugees is a field where state policies both produce (cf. Shore and Wright 1997) and are inspired by various xenophobic and segregationist narratives that coagulate chiefly around Islamophobia as yet another expression of the racialization of certain populations (Fulcher and Scott

2003; Levey and Modood 2009, 241). The present section builds on ethno-graphic data gathered jointly by the co-authors in 2015 and 2016 in Athens.[5] Our primary aim is to comment on the effects of racialized Islamo-phobia as a form of "radical alterity" following the thought of scholars who argue that "religion is raced" (Sayyid and Vakil 2010; Vakil 2010, 276; cf. also Mandel et al. 2015). We also wish to touch upon the gendered aspects of these racialized perceptions of Islam (cf. Triandafyllidou 2001) and to discuss the importance of spatial politics in the development of Islamophobic discourses and attitudes in the public sphere. We will introduce the impor-tance of neo-liberal understandings of personhood in the construction of interconnected false dichotomies between "good" and "bad" Islam, and between "good" and "bad" migrants. The role of neo-liberal ideologies as dis-ciplining technologies productive of further hierarchies of entitlement will be further explored in the third and final section of this paper.

In December 2015, we found ourselves conducting fieldwork in Victoria square, located not very far away from Patision street. Due to its direct public transport connection with the port of Piraeus, where most refugees who crossed from Turkey[6] eventually arrived, Victoria square was a transit point of mainly Afghan refugees, but also a few Moroccans and Tunisians. Large families with children as young as a few months old remained in the square through the day trying to arrange their transportation to Greece's northern border.

Local communities (encouraged by the positive attitude of the Greek state) demonstrated high levels of empathy towards displaced persons in 2015–2016 (cf. Kirtsoglou and Tsimouris 2016; Kirtsoglou 2018). Despite the gener-alized positive attitude of the Greek public towards the refugees, a number of interlocutors in the square expressed their concern and reservations especially towards young "foreign" men who did not appear to be part of larger families. *Can't you see?* (a local small-business owner commented, pointing towards the direction of a company of young Afghan men) *they are all of conscription age.*[7] *These are not refugees. They are an invading army.* Amidst a strong spirit of solidarity exhibited towards the 2015–2016 refugees, xenophobic voices (admittedly, usually belonging to the conserva-tives or the far right) insisted that on the back of the "refugee crisis", a number of "radical Muslims" (*skliropyrinikoi Mousoulmanoi*) were entering Europe with the specific intention to "corrupt the values of European civilis-ation" (*na alloiosoun tis aksies tou Europaikou politismou*). The widely circulat-ing (in Greece and generally in Europe) xenophobic narrative of "Muslim cultural invasion" is, of course, another version of the official discourse, upheld by high-level policy figures, which transforms refugees to a security risk[8] by claiming that Muslim terrorists, radicalised individuals, or terrorist sympathizers regularly infiltrate refugee populations.

Following September 11 and the War on Terror, the young (single) Muslim man, imagined as culturally and racially different in ways that are incompatible with the imagined community of W.E.I.R.D.[9] nationals has become an iconic figure of radical alterity. The young Muslim man –similarly to the covered Muslim woman– is a synecdochical[10] representation (Bowen 2007, 246; cf. Vertovec 2011, 249) of Islamophobia. The alleged incompatibility of Islam with "Western liberal values" (*dytikes dimokratikes aksies*) has been repeatedly summarised by our Greek informants in the phrase "these people cannot be assimilated" (*autoi oi anthropoi den afomoionontai*). The neo-colonial expectation that Muslims need to be "assimilated" arises from widespread, orientalist understandings of Islam as generally inferior to Western cultural superiority (cf. Choudhury 2015). Anti-Muslim prejudice that leads to fully developed forms of racialised Islamophobia has been a prominent feature of colonial and post-colonial histories (Choudhury 2015). The production of the Orient as a distinct and different entity (cf. Said 1979), inferior to the Occident (cf. Mandel et al. 2015), rests on the systematic "coupling of modernity and civilisation with liberal Western law" – among other institutions – and the spirit of secularism (Choudhury 2015, 51). As Mahmood (2006) rightly observes, however, when it comes to Islam, liberal politics do not actually promote secularisation, but rather attempt to control and transform religious expression in a fashion that is closer to liberal values.

In the case of Greece – similarly to other European countries (Choudhury 2015, 55) – the state controls meticulously religious affairs. Unlike other European countries, the Greek state is far from secular in the liberal sense of the term (cf. Kravva [2003] 2004). Apart from the fact that the ministry of education is also the ministry of "religious affairs" (*ypourgeio paideias kai thriskeumaton*), the Greek Orthodox Church is energetically engaged in the regulation of the religious landscape. For the last twenty years or so, Athens (that has, mostly as a result of immigration, a sizeable population of Muslims of different denominations) does not have an official mosque. The attempts of different centre-left governments to build one have been vehemently opposed by the Orthodox Church. Supported by conservatives and the far right, Christian Orthodox religious leaders mobilized the general public against the erection of a mosque. It is only in spring 2017 that relevant legislation finally gained parliamentary approval and it remains to be seen whether and when the mosque will be actually built. Until then, the Muslims of Athens are forced to pray in impromptu unofficial mosques hidden from the public eye. These literally separate and separated spaces of religious expression are only symptomatic of the general desire (echoed in the public speech of Dimoula) of many ordinary Greeks to remain – as much as possible – physically and certainly socially apart from migrant populations.

The politics of space affect much more than everyday sociality. The impoverished "migrant neighbourhoods" of central Athens are being slowly transformed into unsafe spaces for all kinds of residents (cf. Veikou 2016, 156), introducing new asymmetries between the rich (who have the economic power to desert them) and the poor who have no other choice but to remain in them. Migrants of first, and often second generation, are condemned to a "perpetual status of *allochthony* (foreigness)" and remain "marginalised along class [and] racial lines" (Silverstein 2005, 366).

Racialized Islamophobia is certainly one of the decisive factors of the partial presence and the persisting abjection of certain migrant populations. Images of the "radical" Islam as politically threatening, culturally inferior and incompatible with "modern values", were first introduced to Greece by the media as a result of September 11 and the War on Terror (cf. Kirtsoglou 2013). Gradually, Islamophobic attitudes expanded and became dominant in public discourse. The literature does not provide a unified definition of Islamophobia (cf. Klug 2012). Most authors follow Bleich's description of the phenomenon as "indiscriminate negative attitudes and emotions directed at Islam or Muslims" (2012; cf. also Helbling 2012, 6; Borell 2015, 411). There is, however, considerable debate over whether the term is analytically useful, or supportive of further simplifications and essentialist assumptions about the existence of an undifferentiated Islam (cf. Halliday 1999). Other authors insist on the usefulness of the term in special relation to the racialization of Muslims (cf. Rana 2007; Meer and Modood 2011). "The figure of the Muslim", Klug argues,

> is essentially a figment of fiction; any resemblance to real Muslims, living or dead is purely incidental. But when this fantasy figure is projected onto the screen of reality, Muslims as Muslims morph into the "other" essentially different from "us". (2012; 678 cf. also Allen 2010; Esposito and Kalin 2011; Morey and Yaqin 2011)

The political and historical construction of the radical alterity of the Muslim 'Other', is not unrelated to political and historical processes of the past (colonialism) and the present (American imperialism) (cf. Sheehi 2011). The alleged incommensurability of Islamic and Christian or secular traditions is also intimately connected to neo-liberal understandings and figurations of subjectivity. Echoing Zizek (2010), Veikou pointedly observes that "in today's liberal multiculturalism the experience of the other must be deprived of its otherness" (2016, 163). Commenting on the effects of liberal political philosophy and cultural agenda, Zizek claims that we are prepared to tolerate immigrants insofar as they become "detoxified from their dangerous qualities" (2010; Veikou 2016, 163). This "lighter" version of Islam takes the form of what Ramadan calls "Euro-Islam", represented in the figure of a "Muslim personality, faithful to the principles of Islam, dressed in European and Americal cultures, and definitely rooted in Western societies" (2004, 4; cf. Mandel et al. 2015, 366). Separating Muslims into followers of a "good" or a "bad" Islam (cf. Kumar 2013) is characteristic of discourses prevalent in Greece (similarly to the rest of Europe) and representative of a wider tendency of distinguishing "good" from "bad" migrants. Reminiscent of financial tools[11] this (neo)liberal vision of other religious and cultural communities rests on specific conceptualisations of agency and the autonomous subject (cf. Mahmood 2005) who is capable – and indeed expected – to transform oneself in order to fit in wider societal structures (cf. Pedwell 2012). Just as "becoming a good Muslim" relates to reconfiguring one's religious subjectivity in ways that are culturally congruent with liberal values, becoming "a good migrant" is connected to the neo-liberal vision of upward mobility through hard work (cf. Erel, Murji, and Nahaboo 2016, 1348). In the third and final section that follows, we will concisely discuss the passage from "Albanophobia" to representations of Albanians as "integrated" migrants in Greece, in an attempt to further decipher the hegemonic character of the concept of migrant "integration" and its intimate connection to liberal perceptions of what constitutes "migrant success".

From Albanophobia to becoming (like a) Greek: constructing the "good" and the "bad" migrant

Greece, classified for most of its history as a predominantly migrant-sending state, started receiving significant numbers of migrants and asylum-seekers since the late eighties. Since then, approximately one million immigrants arrived in Greece, at first mostly from Balkan countries. Around 56 per cent of the newcomers were of Albanian origin.[12]

The Greek state was legislatively ill-prepared to receive considerable numbers of migrants (Pratsinakis 2014, 1298). The immigration law of 1991 was conceived as part of a "zero immigration" policy aim (Pratsinakis 2014). Successive legislative frameworks (as late as 2010) remained organised around the principle of *jus sanguinis* and directly or indirectly supported a "silent policy of tolerance towards the entry of cheap foreign labour due to pressures from employers of small-labour intensive units, trying to survive the competition through numerical flexibilisation, or from farmers who needed extra seasonal labour" (Lazaridis and Koumandraki 2001, 287).

The case of Albanian migrants, as the iconic representatives of economic immigration to Greece, showcases the elaborate connections between migration and neo-liberal governmentality. It reveals the manner in which state policies and public perceptions of racialized cultural differentialism aided by liberal visions of subjectivity coalesce in the creation of hierarchies of entitlement and asymmetrical political, social and economic relations. The different permutations of racism, we argue, are inspired by historical relations of exploitation and firmly established in the present socio-economic and ideological context that fosters racialized structures of exploitation specific to migrant populations (cf. Anderson, Gibney, and Paoletti 2011). Labour relations, irregularity and deportability (De Genova 2002, 2010), as well as notions of the "self-made", upwardly mobile, hard-working migrant form the complex pattern of (neo)liberal governmentality of immigration.

Irregularity and deportability were established in Greece through bordering practices, "sweep" police operations frequently launched in major city-centres, cumbersome naturalisation procedures and the absence of a long-term sensible reception and integration plan on behalf of the Greek state (cf. Papailias 2003; Christopoulos 2006; Cabot 2014). Successive Greek governments (socialist and conservative) succumbed to the domestic demands of employees and dealt with immigrants as cheap labour regulated by the needs of the parallel economy and the black labour market (Cholezas and Tsakloglou 2009; Triandafyllidou and Ambrosini 2011). The absence of appropriate legislative frameworks resulted in the legal limbo of as many as 700,000 immigrants (cf. Pratsinakis 2014, 1298) creating the space for the proliferation of illegal and exploitative labour relations (Lazaridis and Poyago-Theotoki 1999).

The relationship between "configurations of illegality" promoted by migration regimes (cf. De Genova 2002, 424), and the manner in which "policies do not only impose conditions … but [also] influence people's indigenous norms of conduct" (Shore and Wright 1997, 6) has been long established in migration studies' literature (cf. Andreas 2009; Vertovec 2011, 246–248). In the case of Greece, state-led irregularity, illegality and the reduction of Albanian immigrants to non-citizens promoted a generalised condition of moral panic in public discourse and the media (Papastergiou and Takou 2013). Immigrants were constructed as either (and both) a *class dangereuse* (cf. Lazaridis and Wickens 1999, 646) and as the precarious proletariat of a society that was becoming increasingly fascinated with consumption. Albanian immigrants were tolerated in as much as they provided cheap labour, performing the difficult tasks that local people gradually avoided. In this context, any discussion about human or legal rights of the immigrants was deflected, or dismissed as "unpatriotic". So much so, that on one occasion, representatives of farmer associations in Macedonia, North Greece, protested against deportations of Albanian migrants on the account of being deprived of manual workers to cover for their seasonal needs and demanded that foreign workers were deported only after the end of the agricultural season.

Perhaps the most telling example of exclusion, however, was the issue of the "flag" in the early 2000s. Twice a year, during national celebration days Greek students participate in parades held throughout Greece. The best student of the school (the one with the highest GPA) holds the flag and leads the rest of the group. In 2000 the best student was of Albanian origin. Parents and the community in a small suburb of Thessaloniki (Northern Greece) demanded that the "Albanian" boy was not allowed to hold the Greek flag. Despite the fact that the relevant law and the ministry of education were clear that the student could parade holding the flag, since he had the highest GPA, the hostility of parents and the local community forced him to withdraw (Tzanelli 2006). Apart from the ultra-nationalist rhetoric which proclaimed that the flag is a national symbol and thus should not be carried by a non-national person, what is important to note here is that immigrants (even those born or raised in Greece) were not allowed to participate in the heritage and history of the ethnos, while at the same time they were also disallowed from celebrating their own history and heritage. Characteristic of the latter is the case of a reception teacher reported to the relevant authorities by the parents' association because she encouraged Albanian students to draw the flags of their own countries and pinned them on the wall next to the Greek ones.

Denying immigrants the right to exist as cultural and historical subjects, or to even partake in the national culture and history is a form of existential violence, paradigmatic of modern Greek resistance to cosmopolitanism both as an ethical and as a political project (cf. Kirtsoglou and Theodossopoulos 2010). The status and notion of the *economic* migrant, further reduces persons, and eventually entire populations, to the status or precarious proletarians. Being a "worker" (cf. Arendt [1958] 1998) becomes the defining feature that determines one's conditions of personhood (cf. Veikou 2016, 159) in the context of an unequal "immigrant-native power struggle", that shapes dominant "perceptions about how immigrants should behave and what their position should be" in a given society (Pratsinakis 2014, 1297). As Virdee has demonstrated, in the English context, racialization of the "other" was mediated by the state and the hegemonic narratives of the elite and became a constituent force in the development of "white" working-class identity, which coalesced around colour and religion (2014) In the case of Albanians and other migrant subjects in Greece, this unequal power struggle is explicated in the ambivalent feelings of the state and Greek society as a whole towards migrant populations that are regarded – on the one hand – as a desirable labour force and – simultaneously – as a class of undesirable citizens. Caught in this paradox, whole generations of immigrants, since the late eighties adopted different "integration" strategies compatible with (neo)liberal values and the demands of "local" societies that "foreigners" are only partially present in Greek social life. That is, unless they are/become rich or famous.

Before proceeding to explain how upward mobility and the subjectivity of the "hard-working person" became the major integration avenues for different generations of immigrants in Greece, we would like to clarify our use of the term neoliberalism in this section. As Hall (2011) argues, neoliberalism is not a singular force restricted to the financial sector. As a vehicle of liberal values, it becomes the organising principle of different spectrums of society and culture (Hall 2011). Neo-liberal governmentality as "a set of actions" (Foucault 1997, 92–93) affects in diverse ways different subjects, countries and regions modifying previous hierarchies, forms of governance and modes of subjectification.

In the case of Albanian immigrants, upward mobility facilitated their acceptance by Greek society, to the point that a number of our respondents would refer to second-generation Albanians as "having become (like) Greeks" (*ehoun ginei (san) Ellines*). Pratsinakis (2014) discusses the integration of Albanian migrants in Greece comparing it to the case of Former Soviet Union (FSU) subjects who immigrated to the country approximately in the same period. Pratsinakis reports how his Northern Greek respondents appeared to prefer Albanian immigrants from FSU Pontian Greeks (2014, 1303). Despite the fact that both groups were mostly employed in physically demanding, low-skilled and underpaid jobs, Pontian Greeks were reproached for maintaining their linguistic and cultural distinctiveness, asking for "rights" (*dikaiomata*) and making use of state resources (2014, 1299–1303; cf. also Voutira 2004). Albanian immigrants, on the other hand, were portrayed as "peaceful, hardworking" individuals "who caused no problems" in the community (2014, 1303).

Despite being still victimised and vilified, Albanian migrants – left on their own devices – managed to adapt to an array of cultural, religious and (neo)liberal expectations. Through mass baptisms, by concealing or underplaying their religious affiliation, by presenting themselves as "soft" Muslims who participate in instances of drinking conviviality in rural coffee-shops, through exhibiting a hard-working ethos, and linguistic competence, Albanian immigrants attested to what Hage (2000) calls "practical nationality". By "practical cultural nationality" Hage refers to styles and practices that assume the form of cultural capital and afford the bearer certain degrees of national inclusion (2000, 51–62).

The case of first- and second-generation Albanian "good" migrants is indicative of the kaleidoscopic relationship between culturalist, nationalist, racialized, neo-liberal and neo-colonial understandings of the place and "ideal" trajectory of the migrant in Greece and Europe, in general. Modern Greek phobic and ambivalent attitudes towards migrant populations are not, of course, unrelated to the hegemonic dogma of Greek political elites that Greece – culturally, economically and historically – belongs to the West (cf. Kirtsoglou 2006). The Western, liberal orientation of Greek national culture crystallised in popular ideology in a fashion that supported ambivalent and often hostile attitudes towards "oriental others" (compare with Virdee 2014). In this sense, our research attests to the validity of Ong's call for "a broader conception of race and [cultural] citizenship shaped by the history of European imperialism" (Ong 1996, 738).

Concluding remarks

The present paper attempted a critical and ethnographically informed reading of contemporary literature on the complex assemblage of linkages between migration, racialization and liberal values in modern Greece as a symptomatic case of European attitudes to migration. Our main argument supports the idea that we need a holistic, intersectional and unified framework for the analysis of contemporary migration, reception and integration conditions. Echoing the approach of Vertovec (2011), we offered ethnographic evidence of how migrants are routinely produced as racially, religiously and culturally differen- tiated subjects supposedly threatening to the cohesion of particular nations and of "western" liberal values. In line with recent scholarship on racialization and Islamophobia, the paper discussed novel forms of racism that go beyond notions of biological difference and support the construction of hierarchies and geographies of entitlement. Processes of inclusion and exclusion, we argued, rest on a meshwork (cf. Ingold 2011) of seemingly disparate notions and identification markers such as culture, religion, gender, descent, modernisation and progress (to name some), which form a fluid and shifting reservoir of convenient story seeds (cf. Knight 2013) about the self and the other. In the absence of a definable organising principle of inclusion and exclusion, we proposed that citizenship and membership to national and supranational bodies ultimately rests on the hegemonic acceptance of (neo)- liberal regimes of subjectification and of an array of "European" values that form the basis of a universalist hegemonic vision of the world. We traced racia- lization back to an imagined "orient" (cf. Said 1979), but also to contemporary cultural and political imperialist projects. Ultimately, this paper traced the limits of cosmopolitanism and multiculturalism to the requisites for mobility and difference established in the ambiguities of state policies, legal frame- works, everyday sociality and the spaces in-between desirable and undesir- able migrants.

Notes

1. Fieldwork with Pakistani, Bangladeshi and Syrian diaspora in Athens, in 2014, was generously funded by Durham University, Seedcorn Fund. The funding was awarded to Dr Elisabeth Kirtsoglou, Dr Stephen Lyon. Dr G. Tsimouris, Dr Daniel Knight and Dr Maria Kastrinou.
2. The entire speech can be found in Greek here: http://www.tanea.gr/news/ greece/article/5016105/ti-akribws-eipe-h-kikh-dhmoyla-gia-thn-kypselh-kai-toys- metanastes/.
3. Dimoula has a perfect command of the language. Her choice of words, grammar and syntax here cannot be possibly misunderstood. She does not refer to the "sharing" of space (na moirastoume to horo), but to the division, separation or assigning of different spaces to "locals" and "foreigners" (na moirastoun oi horoi).
4. For a discussion of the term xenos (foreigner, outsider) versus dhikos (insider, one of our own) see Kirtsoglou (2018); Herzfeld (2003, 142); and Panourgia (1995, 16–17).

5. This research was part of the ESRC/DFID-funded project *Transitory Lives* (October 2015–July 2017).
6. Between the summer of 2015 and the spring of 2016, approximately one million refugees crossed the Aegean from Turkey and Greece, before they eventually continued their journeys to Northern Europe through an unofficial humanitarian corridor which was closed in late February 2016. The majority of them were Syrians who fled the war, closely followed by Afghans, Iraqis and Kurds.
7. In Greece conscription is compulsory.
8. See, for instance, the 2016 Risk Analysis of FRONTEX http://frontex.europa.eu/assets/Publications/Risk_Analysis/Annula_Risk_Analysis_2016.pdf
9. W.E.I.R.D. stands for Western, Educated, Industrialised, Rich, Democratic. It is an especially popular acronym amongst various social scientists, especially experimental psychologists, that refers to biases arising from the demography of their samples.
10. Vertovec employs the term synecdoche, a figure of speech whereby the part stands for the whole (*pars for toto*) to explain "the extraordinary symbolic weight" that certain images and symbols (like the head scarf) carry in public perception (2011, 249).
11. We refer here to strategies like the dissolving of financial institutions into their "good" and "bad" constituents on the basis of "good debt" (regularly served) and "bad debt" (non-regularly served, or not served at all).
12. http://www.immigrantwomen.gr/portal/images/ektheseis/statistika_dedomena.metanaston.pdf (6.)

Disclosure statement

No potential conflict of interest was reported by the authors.

Funding

This work was supported by Economic and Social Research Council (ES/N013727/1) and Leverhulme Trust (Framing Financial Crisis and Protest: North-West a).

References

Allen, C. 2010. *Islamophobia*. Farnham: Ashgate.
Anderson, B., M. J. Gibney, and E. Paoletti. 2011. Citizenship, Deportation and the Boundaries of Belonging. *Citizenship Studies* 15 (5): 547–563.
Andreas, P. 2009. *Border Games: Policing the U.S.-Mexico Divide*. 2nd ed. Ithaca, NY: Cornell University Press.
Anthias, F. 1990. "Race and Class Revisited – Conceptualising Race and Racisms." *The Sociological Review* 38 (1): 19–42. doi:10.1111/j.1467-954X.1990.tb00846.x.
Arendt, Hannah. (1958) 1998. *The Human Condition*. Chicago: Chicago University Press.
Balibar, É. 2007. "Is There a "Neo-racism"?" In *Race and Racialization: Essential Readings*, edited by T. Das Gupta, C. E. James, R. C. A. Maaka, G. Galabuzi, and C. Andersen, 83–88. Toronto: Canadian Scholars' Press.
Balibar, É., and I. Wallerstein. 1991. *Race, Nation, Class: Ambiguous Identities*. London: Verso.
Barker, M. 1981. *The New Racism*. London: Junction.

Barrett, J., and D. Roediger. 1997. "In Between Peoples: Race, Nationality, and the 'New Immigrant' Working Class." *Journal of American Ethnological History* 16 (3): 3–44.

Baumann, G. 1996. *Contesting Culture: Discourses of Identity in Multi-Ethnic London*. Cambridge: Cambridge University Press.

Borell, K. 2015. "When is the Time to Hate? A Research Review of the Impact of Dramatic Events on Islamophobia and Islamophobic Hate Crimes in Europe." *Islam and Christian-Muslim Relations* 26 (4): 409–421. doi:10.1080/09596410.2015.1067063.

Bowen, J. 2007. *Why the French Don't Like Headscarves: Islam, the State and Public Space*. Princeton, NJ: Princeton University Press.

Cabot, H. 2014. *On the Doorstep of Europe: Asylum and Citizenship in Greece*. Philadelphia: University of Pennsylvania Press.

Cholezas, I., and P. Tsakloglou. 2009. "The Economic Impact of Immigration in Greece: Taking Stock of the Existing Evidence." *Journal of Southeast European and Black Sea Studies* 9 (1–2): 77–104.

Choudhury, C. A. 2015. "Ideology, Identity and Law in the Production of Islamophobia." *Dialectical Anthropology* 39: 47–61. doi:10.1007/s10624-014-9357-y.

Christopoulos, Dimitris. 2006. "Greece." In *Acquisition and Loss of Nationality: Policies and Trends in 15 European Countries*, edited by R. Bauböck, E. Ersbøll, K. Groenendijk, and H. Waldrauch, 253–287. Amsterdam: Amsterdam University Press.

Cole, M. 2009. "A Plethora of 'Suitable Enemies': British Racism at the Dawn of the Twenty-first Century." *Ethnic and Racial Studies* 32 (9): 1671–1685. doi:10.1080/01419870903205556.

De Genova, N. P. 2002. "Migrant 'Illegality' and Deportability in Everyday Life." *Annual Review of Anthropology* 31: 419–447. doi:10.1146/annurev.anthro.31.040402.085432.

De Genova, N. 2010. "The Deportation Regime: Sovereignty, Space and the Freedom of Movement." In *The Deportation Regime: Sovereignty, Space and Freedom of Movement*, edited by N. De Genova and N. Peutz, 33–68. Durham, NC: Duke University Press.

Erel, U., K. Murji, and Z. Nahaboo. 2016. "Understanding the Contemporary Race–Migration Nexus." *Ethnic and Racial Studies* 39 (8): 1339–1360.

Esposito, J. L., and I. Kalin. 2011. *Islamophobia: The Challenge of Pluralism in the 21st Century*. Oxford: Oxford University Press.

Foucault, M. 1997. *I Mikrofisiki tis exousias (The Micro-physics of Power)* (in Greek). Athens: Ypsilon.

Fulcher, J., and J. Scott. 2003. *Sociology*. Oxford: Oxford University Press.

Garner, S. 2007. "The European Union and the Racialization of Immigration, 1985–2006." *Race/Ethnicity: Multidisciplinary Global Perspectives* 1 (1): 61–87.

Gilroy, P. 1987. *'There Ain't No Black in the Union Jack': The Cultural Politics of Race and Nation*. Chicago: University of Chicago Press.

Green, S. 2013. "Borders and the Relocation of Europe." *Annual Review of Anthropology* 42: 345–361. doi:10.1146/annurev-anthro-092412-155457.

Grillo, R. D. 2003. "Cultural Essentialism and Cultural Anxiety." *Anthropological Theory* 3 (2): 157–173.

Hage, G. 2000. *White Nation: Fantasies of White Supremacy in a Multicultural Society*. New York: Routledge.

Hall, S. 2011. "The Neoliberal Revolution." *Cultural Studies* 25 (6): 705–728.

Halliday, F. 1999. "'Islamophobia' Reconsidered." *Ethnic and Racial Studies* 22: 892–902. doi:10.1080/014198799329305.

Helbling, M. 2012. "Islamophobia in the West: An Introduction." In *Islamophobia in the West: Measuring and Explaining Individual Attitudes*, edited by M. Helbling, 1–18. London: Routledge.

Herzfeld, M. 2003. "It Takes One to Know One: Cultural Resentment and Mutual Recognition Among Greeks in Local and Global Contexts." In *Counterworks: Managing the Diversity of Knowledge*, edited by R. Fardon. London: Routledge.

Hiemstra, N. 2010. "Immigrant 'Illegality' as Neoliberal Governmentality in Leadville, Colorado." *Antipode*, 42 (1) (online version). doi:10.1111/j.1467-8330.2009.00732.x.

Ingold, T. 2011. *Being Alive*. New York: Routledge.

Kibria, N., C. Bowman, and M. O'Leary. 2013. *Race and Immigration*. Cambridge: Polity.

Kirtsoglou, E. 2006. "Unspeakable Crimes: Athenian Greek Perceptions of Local and International Terrorism." In *Terror and Violence: Imagination and the Unimaginable*, edited by A. Strathern, P. Stewart, and N. L. Whitehead, 61–88. London: Pluto Press.

Kirtsoglou, E. 2013. "The Dark Ages of the Golden Dawn Anthropological Analysis and Responsibility in the Twilight Zone of the Greek Crisis." *Suomen Antropologi Journal of the Finnish Anthropological Society* 38 (1): 104–108.

Kirtsoglou, E. 2018. "We Are Human: Cosmopolitanism as a Radically Political, Moral Project." In *An Anthropology of the Enlightenment: Moral Social Relations Then and Today*, edited by N. Rapport and H. Wardle. Bloomsbury: ASA Monograph Series.

Kirtsoglou, Elisabeth, and Dimitrios Theodossopoulos. 2010. "The Poetics of Anti-Americanism in Greece: Rhetoric, Agency and Local Meaning." *Social Analysis* 54 (1): 106–124.

Kirtsoglou, E., and G. Tsimouris. 2016. "'*Il était un petit navire*': The 'Refugee Crisis', Neo-orientalism, and the Production of Radical Alterity." *Journal of Modern Greek Studies, Occasional Paper Series* 9: 1–14.

Klug, B. 2012. "Islamophobia: A Concept Comes of Age." *Ethnicities* 12 (5): 665–681. doi:10.1177/1468796812450363.

Knight, Daniel M. 2013. "The Greek Economic Crisis as Trope." *Focaal: Journal of Global and Historical Anthropology* 65: 147–149.

Kravva, V. (2003) 2004. "The Construction of Otherness in Modern Greece: The State, the Church and the Study of a Religious Minority." In *The Ethics of Anthropology: Debates and Dilemmas*, edited by P. Caplan, 155–171. London: Routledge.

Kumar, D. 2013. *Islamophobia and the Politics of Empire*. Chicago: Haymarket Books.

Lazaridis, G., and M. Koumandraki. 2001. "Deconstructing Naturalism: The Racialization of Ethnic Minorities in Greece." In *The Mediterranean Passage: Migration and New Cultural Encounters in Southern Europe*, edited by R. King, 279–301. Liverpool: Liverpool University Press.

Lazaridis, G., and J. Poyago-Theotoki. 1999. "Undocumented Migrants in Greece: Issues of Regularization." *International Migration* 37 (4): 715–740. doi:10.1111/1468-2435. 00091.

Lazaridis, G., and E. Wickens. 1999. "'Us' and the 'Others': Ethnic Minorities in Greece." *Annales of Tourism Research* 26 (3): 632–655. doi:10.1016/S0160-7383(99)00008-0.

Levey, G. B., and T. Modood. 2009. "Liberal Democracy, Multicultural Citizenship and the Danish Cartoon Affair." In *Secularism, Religion and Multicultural Citizenship*, edited by G. B. Levey and T. Modood, 216–242. Cambridge: Cambridge University Press.

Mahmood, S. 2005. *Politics of Piety: The Islamic Revival of the Feminist Subject*. Princeton, NJ: Princeton University Press.

Mahmood, S. 2006. "Secularism, Hermeneutics, and Empire: The Politics of Islamic Reformation." *Public Culture* 18 (3): 323–347. doi:10.1215/08992363-2006-006.

Malkki, L. 1992. "National Geographic: The Rooting of Peoples and the Territorialization of National Identity among Scholars and Refugees." *Cultural Anthropology* 7 (1): 24–44. doi:10.1525/can.1992.7.1.02a00030.

Mandel, R., N. Meer, P. A. Silverstein, J. Robbins, and E. Özyürek. 2015. "Islamophobia, Religious Conversion, and Belonging in Europe." *History and Anthropology* 26 (3): 362–379.

Meer, N., and T. Modood. 2011. "The Racialisation of Muslims." In *Thinking Through Islamophobia: Global Perspectives*, edited by S. Sayyid and A. Vakil, 69–84. London: Hurst Chicago, University of Chicago.

Mishra Tarc, A. 2013. "Race Moves: Following Global Manifestations of New Racisms in Intimate Space." *Race, Ethnicity & Education* 16 (3): 365–385. doi:10.1080/13613324.2011.645564.

Morey, P., and A. Yaqin. 2011. *Framing Muslims: Stereotyping and Representation After 9/11*. Cambridge, MA: Harvard University Press.

Ong, A. 1996. "Cultural Citizenship as Subject-making: Immigrants Negotiate Racial and Cultural Boundaries in the United States." *Current Anthropology* 37 (5): 737–762. doi:10.1086/204560.

Panourgia, N. 1995. *Fragments of Death, Fables of Identity: An Athenian Anthropography*. Madison: Wisconsin University Press.

Papailias, P. 2003. "'Money of Kurbet is Money of Blood': The Making of a 'Hero' of Migration at the Greek-Albanian Border." *Journal of Ethnic and Migration Studies* 29 (6): 1059–1078. doi:10.1080/1369183032000171366.

Papastergiou, V., and E. Takou. 2013. *I metanastefsi stin Ellada: enteka mythoi kai mia alitheia* [Migration in Greece: Eleven Myths and One Truth]. Athens: Foundation Rosa Luxempbourg (Greek Branch). http://rosalux.gr/publications.

Pedwell, C. 2012. "Affective (Self-)transformations: Empathy, Neoliberalism and International Development." *Feminist Theory* 13 (2): 163–179. doi:10.1177/1464700112442644.

Pratsinakis, M. 2014. "Resistance and Compliance in Immigrant–Native Figurations: Albanian and Soviet Greek Immigrants and Their Interaction with Greek Society." *Journal of Ethnic and Migration Studies* 40 (8): 1295–1313. doi:10.1080/1369183X.2013.859071.

Ramadan, T. 2004. *Western Muslims and the Future of Islam*. New York: Oxford University Press.

Rana, J. 2007. "The Story of Islamophobia." *Souls* 9 (2): 148–161. doi:10.1080/10999940701382607.

Said, E. 1979. *Orientalism*. New York: Vintage Books.

Sayyid, S., and A. Vakil. 2010. *Thinking Through Islamophobia: Global Perspectives*. London: Hurst.

Sheehi, S. 2011. *Islamophobia: The Ideological Campaign Against Muslims*. Atlanta, GA: Clarity Press.

Shore, C., and S. Wright. 1997. "Policy: A New Field of Anthropology." In *Anthropology of Policy*, edited by C. Shore and S. Wright, 3–39. London: Routledge.

Silverstein, P. A. 2005. "Immigrant Racialization and the New Savage Slot: Race, Migration and Immigration in the New Europe." *Annual Review of Anthropology* 34: 363–384. doi:10.1146/annurev.anthro.34.081804.120338.

Strathern, M. 1995. "Comments: Talking Culture." *Current Anthropology* 36 (1): 16.

Triandafyllidou, A. 2001. *Immigrants and National Identity in Europe*. London: Routledge.

Triandafyllidou, A., and M. Ambrosini. 2011. "Irregular Immigration Control in Italy and Greece: Strong Fencing and Weak Gate-keeping Serving the Labour Market." *European Journal of Migration and Law* 13: 251–273.

Tzanelli, R. 2006. "'Not My Flag!' Citizenship and Nationhood in the Margins of Europe (Greece, October 2000/2003)." *Ethnic and Racial Studies* 29 (1): 27–49.

Vakil, A. 2010. "Who's Afraid of Islamophobia?" In *Thinking Through Islamophobia: Global Perspectives*, edited by S. Sayyid and A. Vakil, 271–278. London: Hurst.

Vargas-Ramos, C. 2014. "Migrating Race: Migration and Racial Identification among Puerto Ricans." *Ethnic and Racial Studies* 37 (3): 383–404. doi:10.1080/01419870.2012.672759.

Veikou, M. 2016. "Economic Crisis and Migration: Visual Representations of Difference in Greece." *Cultural Studies* 30 (1): 147–172. doi:10.1080/09502386.2014.974641.

Vertovec, S. 2011. The CulturalPolitics of Nation and Migration. *Annual Review of Anthropology* 40: 241–256.

Virdee, S. 2014. *Racism, Class and the Racialized Outsider*. Palgrave: Macmillan.

Voutira, E. 2004. "Ethnic Greeks from the Former Soviet Union as 'Privileged Return Migrants'." *Espace Populations Sociétés* 3: 533–544.

Wodak, R., and M. Reisigl. 1999. "Discourse and Racism: European Perspectives." *Annual Review of Anthropology* 28: 175–199. doi:10.1146/annurev.anthro.28.1.175.

Zizek, S. 2010. "Liberal Multiculturalism Masks an Old Barbarism with a Human Face." *Guardian*, October 3. https://www.theguardian.com/commentisfree/2010/oct/03/immigration-policy-roma-rightwing-europe.

Blackboard as separation wall: classrooms, race and the contemporary crisis in Germany

Russell West-Pavlov

ABSTRACT

This article suggests that racism, construed as a reified and artificial dichotomization of social bodies into acutely hypostatized and opposed identities, can best be understood by placing it within a larger global context of exploitative hierarchies which racism retrospectively legitimizes. The loss of the global perspective and the obscured knowledge of global networks of toxic causalities allow the broader context of racism to remain invisible, thus condemning local anti-racist activism to mitigated success. The article suggests that the classroom as a vital site of education of citizens tends to be isolated from the world; racism can be combatted in the classroom by opening its walls up to the larger global context in which education is a significant factor. A pedagogical practice of interrogative critical assemblages may facilitate the reconstruction of invisible global networks, which in turn may enable us to better understand the workings of micro-racisms within a larger context of global macro-racism.

Like theatres, classrooms have a fourth wall. Where the classical proscenium stage has a transparent boundary between the audience and the actors, which allows spectatorship but imposes a reality/fiction demarcation vital to the theatrical illusion, the classroom has a blackboard (or perhaps more frequently today, a whiteboard, or a smartboard). That surface of pedagogical inscription is where much teaching actually happens, rendering tangible the classroom's functioning as a space of modelling: in the classroom, learners practice at a safe distance from the real-world skills that they will need later in real professional scenarios; the classroom, like the theatre, is a protected space of "modelling" play (that is, its activities have the structure of real-world activities, say, maths or writing, but can be practised without real-world consequences; Bateson 1974, 177–193). Curiously enough, however, the blackboard that enables pedagogical "modelling" or educational "play" by separating the classroom from the world may also hinder that pedagogical practice. The blackboard can have a "segregative" effect, rendering the very real connections between pedagogy and the world so opaque as to reduce that teaching to a reified inculcation of mere "skills". This paradoxical mixture of connection and separation, I would suggest, is analogical to, as a bad black/white pun might intimate, and perhaps structurally related to that of racism.

Racism can be defined as an artificially imposed differentiation, based on arbitrary but easily identifiable (or imaginable) markers of difference, which occludes deeper socio-political connections. Racism is a rhetoric of difference that separates out populations that share the same spaces – populations that are all too often closely linked to each other by manifold connections: history, intermarriage, migration and competition for scarce resources. Discrimination seeks to occlude these connections, thereby aiding and at the same time obfuscating the complex functioning of contemporary global capitalism (Mbembe 2017).

In this article, I wish to explore the ways in which, by reconnecting the often lost links between the classroom and the world, we may be able to contribute, at least indirectly, to laying bare the deeper global connections that are obfuscated by the speciously differentiating structures of racism. My thesis is that a direct opposition to or contradiction of racism, while remaining a moral imperative and civil duty, will probably not do much to change the underlying structures of racism. What is needed instead, I suggest, not in lieu of but alongside an oppositional condemnation, is a practice of connections – in the first place cognitive, then existential and finally, what I will be calling "affective". In addition to a sturdy condemnation of racism in all its forms, a positive strategy, one that resists racism's own separative impulses by operating a dynamic reconnection of causes and effects, of identities and practices may be the apposite epistemological or educational response to the current multi-crisis the racist backlash that goes hand in hand with it. The increasingly acute nature of what is becoming evident as a contemporary global multi-crisis makes it imperative to pose such questions.

Like most of us writing in his issue, and probably many of you who are reading it, I am a teacher (in the university sector), and more specifically, a teacher who trains teachers. For that reason, I will be considering ways this tactic of diagnostic reconnection may be carried out in the most immediate context I am familiar with, that of the university classroom where future high school teachers of English are trained. I suggest that the classroom should become a forum in which "racism" as a local phenomenon (manifest in the current German system by an increasing level of racist-motivated violence and arson) should be put in a larger network of global crises. To that extent, it would become a performative act of self-inclusion that would equip students for locating themselves and their own practices within those networked practices. The purpose of such a diagnostic pedagogy would not be to dictate the stance(s) that students should take, but to lay bare the simultaneously destructive dynamic of racism and the increasingly dichotomized economic structures that make up racism on a global scale. Once students have located themselves in the broader context, it may become possible for them to decide how their own activist or future professional practices within clearly circumscribed but networked contexts might constitute a reaction and a riposte to racism. The very fact of making connections is not merely a cognitive exercise, but one that establishes lines of "affective" connection – that is not merely an emotional "tie", but also a linkage that empowers engagement (Massumi 2015).

My argument runs as follows: (1) I begin by suggesting that racism is a symptom of larger structures of disconnectivity: it separate causes and effects, thereby making it easy to blame outsiders rather than to identify systemic factors; (2) a solution to this obfuscation of connections is to reintroduce the making of connections at the systemic level; this is all the more important in an environment where racism is on the rise because the scope of global multi-crises are increasing and scapegoats must be found; (3) connectivity thus restores connection between opaque global complexes, between students and the world, and between the educational process and the world; exercises in connection, alongside frontal confrontation with racism, may enable students to gain a sense of connectivity and agency that presents possibilities of engagement that also allow one to "tinker", at a micro-level, with single aspects of those relationships; (4) one site where this important work can be done is the classroom (whether high school or university) – usually, in the German context, a highly reified location that can, however, be opened up to the outside world via processes of interrogative critical assemblage and cognitive mapping.

Racism as a global phenomenon

This article posits that racism depends upon a polarization and a freezing of essentially fluid identities, provoked or legitimized by excessively mercurial and unpredictable political and economic events. Racism itself is not only a corrosive power to reduce identities to a differentiated essence but also a divisive view that needs to be replaced by a sense of all that connects people; it also needs to be reconnected, as a phenomenon, to a multitude of other phenomena that do not excuse it, nor explain it away, but rather explicate it and render explicit the causal networks within which it functions.

In the closing pages of *Society Must be Defended*, Foucault (2003, 257–259) suggests that the origin of racism lies in colonial genocide. Racism, he posited, was not the driving force of genocide, but its retrospective legitimization, the fabricated rationale that justified and legalized a biopolitical regime of lawlessness that could unleash itself far from the juridical limitations imposed by the European nation-state (2003, 375); it was from the genocide in the colonies that the racist war on European territory would subsequently develop.[1] Recent German commentators have suggested, very much in parallel to Foucault, that colonialism and the slave trade were the global projects of primitive accumulation and predatory labour/resource extraction that needed retrospective legitimization via racism (Arndt 2017). This means, then, that racism is not a phenomenon which should be examined and confronted only in its own right, but rather an reflexive epiphenomenon that refracts a large number of other broader phenomena that could be gathered up under a meta-category biopolitics and its close connection to war (Mbembe 2016), which produces, when fully fledged, what Mbembe (2003) terms "necropolitics". Within this larger framework of exploitative bio/necropolitics, Mbembe (2017) identifies the phenomenon "becoming black" as a global process of *longue durée* racist dehumanization. But as Mbembe's notion of a creeping, ever-more-encompassing global category of racist "thingification" suggests, such reification is part of a long-term global politics of planetary destruction whose effects are slowly catching up on us (Mbembe 2012).

In other words, when we speak about racism, we should place it within a global network of other political issues that may have to do with employment (and/or) labour exploitation, slavery (ancient and modern), immigration, landgrabbing, access to water, food and mineral resources, social unrest, violence, terrorism and the war on terrorism, and so on. This is no easy task, but I posit that it is a vital undertaking for the contemporary humanities, and a central plank in a new university- and school-based pedagogy of planetary awareness and citizenship education that, at least within the German context in which I work, is currently largely absent.

To establish an initial framework for starting this process of contextualizing diagnosis, I suggest that the North-South divide is the meta-racism within which all other localized racisms of today (from those afflicting the reviled asylum seekers of Europe, or the Muslim targets of European Islamophobia (Fassin 2016), to the threatened "black lives" of the contemporary US crisis (Denby 2016), or the "intra-African" racism that bedevils the post-apartheid democracy of South Africa) have their overdetermined, often indirect, but ultimate causality; recent research on the history of international relations (Vitalis 2015) suggests that in the first half of the twentieth-century, this notion was widely recognized by conservative political theorists. The question of racism is a global one, and connectivity is central to understanding and combating it. In general, resource extraction under inhuman conditions, or commodity production without social protection, occurs in the Global South, because those populations are seen as not needing or deserving dignity or protection. Racism as we usually consider it in the European context, that is as a domestic phenomenon, is the Northern tip of the iceberg. That is not to say that it is not worthy of attention, nor that it needs to be combatted less, but simply that it can only be genuinely understood when it is placed within a global perspective. This is not to say that local interventions against racism, especially in an educational context, have lost their relevance. There are many excellent approaches to anti-racism and anti-discrimination training in schools (e.g. for the German context, Liebscher and Fritzsche 2010; for the UK context, Epstein 1992). This article does not suggest that this sort of pedagogical work is irrelevant, overhauled or out of date; on the contrary, such work would appear even more acutely necessary than ever before. Rather, however, the article suggests that alongside such direct pedagogical practices, a structural approach to racism and its broader systemic logic is necessary to complement – and finally link up with and reinforce – punctual and local interventions.

Patently, racism itself reposes upon a chimera, the notion of a substantial difference between social groups – usually reposing upon easily visible, or easily imagined, but generally superficial differences. It is absolutely necessary but also absolutely inadequate to deconstruct this chimera, as the critical social sciences have been doing for a good half-century (see Latour 2004; Paulson 2001). The reason for this is that quite apart from the self-confirming nature of racist stereotypes (Taguieff 1987), and the deep embedding of racism in habitus and affective structures, the driving rationale of racism in fact lies in a multiplicity of other factors. What must be reconstructed, then, are the networks within which racism is one highly visible, even spectacular phenomenon that plays various ideological roles within wider and more complex networks of causalities.

But how are we to seize this moment of reconnection and transform it into an opportunity to combat racism, that is to reconnect, on an equal basis, hierarchically differentiated groups within the society where the principle of discrimination (in the sense of both differentiation and exclusion) is delineated according to some form of racism? I would suggest that the moment is apposite for developing a stronger sense of the multiple causal entanglements of "a world that is as interconnected as it is divided" (García Canclini 2014, xii). The current multi-crises besetting the planetary community make it imperative to address these issues; but they also make it easier to do so, because the issues are becoming more and more flagrantly salient.

Systemic connections

A solution to this obfuscation of connections is to reintroduce the making of connections at a systemic level. In mid-2016, the German left-liberal *Die Zeit* registered a sense of an "epochal shift" in world politics in the "week of madness" in which the Brexit referendum, reciprocal black–white violence in the US and several IS-sponsored attacks in Nice and Würzburg took place (Ulrich 2016). Doubtless, such rhetoric was overblown. And of course it was parochial: what registers as crisis for populations in the Global North may be crisis-as-norm for peoples elsewhere, as Benjamin (1999, 248–249) knew: "[t]he tradition of the oppressed teaches us that the 'state of emergency' in which we live is not the exception but the rule". We here in Europe have been largely protected from the sustained havoc wreaked, for instance, by the 1970s debt crisis and 1980s–90s structural adjustment programmes upon many countries in the Global South. As Morton (2013, 14) notes, "from the standpoint of the oppressed, the state of emergency is a permanent historical condition, rather than an aberration in a liberal narrative of historical progress". Nonetheless, there are many symptoms of an increasingly strong sense of what can be identified as a complex of interrelated and increasingly acute multi-crises that currently beset the global population. It may be objected that the notion of a multi-crisis is too imprecise and too broad to serve a rigorously analytical purpose. That, however, is precisely my point: we are confronted by a bewildering concatenation of looming catastrophes of global proportions whose dimensions make them what Morton (2013) calls "hyper-objects" that defy comprehension, let alone the formulation of solutions. Listing them is a first step, however, towards beginning to tease out connections, and with that, our own precise location and opportunities for agential intervention.

First and foremost is of course the increasingly evident global climate crisis, whose results are overdetermined, thus driving an accelerating upwards spiral of interlocking causes and effects (for instance, global warming causes the ice-caps to melt, which reduces the area of heat-reflecting ice and increases the area of dark, heat-absorbing water, which propels global warming, which causes the ice-caps to melt even faster ...) (Friedrich et al. 2016; Scheffers et al. 2016). The effects of global warming include rising water levels (Goodell 2017) and concomitant land scarcity; desertification, drought, food scarcity (FSIN 2017), with famine also being used as a weapon of war (de Waal 2017), resource conflicts (Herders against Farmers 2017) and forced migration (Missirian and Schlenker 2017; UNCHR 2016); increased fire danger (Davis 2017); and increased seismic activity (Jones 2017), with the risk of tsunamis, resulting in catastrophes such as Fukushima (Crist 2018, 12). Other global crises include the widening gap between rich and poor driven by the neoliberal economy (Milanovic 2016; Sassen 2014; Streeck 2017), with evidence of poverty in many bastions of social-democratic Euro-America (for the UK see Armstrong 2017; for Germany see Paritätischer Gesamtverband 2017); the prevalence of widespread forms of modern slavery (Kara 2017); looming food scarcity (Ambler-Edwards et al. 2009) and the rise of land-grabbing as a predatory response (Allan et al. 2013; Engelert and Gärber 2014); the imposition of Structural Adjustment Policies and regimes of austerity even within Europe, in the wake of the Greek debt crisis (Flassbeck and Lapavistas 2015; Varoufakis 2017); the looming threat of further global financial crises (Richards 2017); a rise of populism, with a concomitant victimization of immigrants and asylum seekers; the retreat of democracy evinced everywhere, even in Euro-American heartlands of parliamentary democracy, especially in the UK and the US (Crouch 2004; Kurlantzick 2013; Streeck 2013), and the disturbing rise of autocracy in Hungary, Poland and Turkey; the rise of conflicts, with long-running wars in Ukraine, Syria, and so on (Münkler 2004), with the real danger of nuclear conflicts in Asia, and concomitant catastrophic results for world food supplies (Toon, Robock, and Turco 2008); and so on.

Some German commentators suggest that the currently acute sense of crisis is endemic to modernity: a basic characteristic of modernity is the formation of autonomous social systems, each of which has its own logic and language and way of looking at the world; each system (the economy, academia, the law) offers a perspective which is consistent and coherent from its own point of view, but incompatible with that of the others (Luhmann 1984). The absence of any form of synthesis, and thus of a narrative which would give subjects the sense of mastery of an ungovernable world, is the cause of a sense of "crisis" which, according to this systems theory account, bests modernity from the outset (Nassehi 2015). This sociological account is neat and doubtless not without an element of diagnostic accuracy, but harbours a number of problems when it comes to therapy.

The first is its tendency simply to reinscribe in the analysis precisely the problem we are trying to address here. Systems theory accepts the reciprocal opacity of societal systems to one another, thus replicating the essentially monadic, isolating processes of modernity identified for instance by Adorno (1971, 88–104) or Rosa and Endres (2016, 36–48) at the level of sociological theory, without being able to offer any riposte to it. Despite the "system of systems" that systems theory aims to offer (Luhmann 1997), there are no resources within systems theory for escaping a fundamental systemic solipsism and for making larger connections between systems.

Thus, and this is the second problem, this sort of diagnosis ignores several other central factors. On the one hand, by suggesting that crisis is endemic to modernity, this theory works in a deflationary direction. Certainly, in some cases, this may be salutary, especially where "end times" or "catastrophe" rhetoric serves obviously manipulative political purposes (e.g. Titlestad 2013). The current global circumstances are however a different case. The current overdetermined multi-crises are becoming genuinely more acutely measured, for instance by the increasingly evident effects of global warming, which is impacting climate unpredictability (e.g. more severe

storms, fires, seismic activity, etc.), food scarcity, land loss, resource-based conflicts and increasing flows of forced migration in empirically measurable ways.
Relegating the ambient sense of crisis to an epistemological effect of reciprocal sub-systemic opacity merely reveals the poverty in the fact of genuinely
accelerating and escalating chains of economic, climate-driven and geopolitical causes/effects.

This increasing acuteness of global multi-crisis culminates in an imperative
to map the current complex and overdetermined situation. Though the
systems theory approach suggests that the respective languages of the sub-
systems are mutually incompatible but resist any construction of a master narrative capable of synthesizing them, I would object that this, though
appealing in intellectual terms, is empirically unfounded. It is true that the
number of systemic crises to be understood is daunting and that the connections between them are extremely complex. However, though these systems
manifestly function according to distinct logics, it is entirely possible, by dint
of hard work, to gradually establish the connections between the different
phenomena. This practice of "diagnostic" mapping (Nealon 2016, 121)
would create chains of connections that I can only present here in a very schematic linear fashion: Climate change → desertification across the Sahel band
(Weizman and Sheikh 2015) → food scarcity, resource-based conflicts (e.g.
herders, Fulani conflicts) → rising levels of forced migration on the South–
South axis and on the South–North axis (McAdam 2014; McLeman 2013; Wennersten and Robbins 2017) → part of the growing pressure on the Mediterranean migrant route→ increasing closure of borders in Europe and so on →
moral obligation upon Germany to keep its borders open in 2015 in order
to compensate for its bad press over the imposition of SAPs on Greece (Varoufakis) → global dynamic of capital transfer towards a small elite and away
from the larger population of any given state (Milanovic 2016; Piketty 2014) →
in Germany, a drop in employees' real wages since the 1990s, a rise in precarious employment and arise in poverty (Bosch and Kalina 2016; Böckler-
Impulse 2017; Hagelüken 2017), which fuel the increasing influence of populist discourses of "homeland" (Heimat) (Schüle 2017) at one end of the spectrum, via a retreat from politics (Streeck 2014) or the rise of populist parties
such as the AfD and an alarming rise in anti-immigrant violence (Amnesty
2016), through to the mobilization of *ressentiment* that result, in extreme
forms, in terrorist activities (Mishra 2017), and so on. These are rudimentary
chains of connection (not always of direct causality), but they can be extended
ad infinitum, because the globe is a single interconnected whole, and its crises
are interconnected. Such framings of interconnected can be staged, with a bit
of work. One exemplary gesture of such connective contextualization might
be Klein's (2016) avowedly polemical article where she connects carbon
fuels, global warming, American wars in the Middle East, the emergence of
"Orientalist" stereotypes and their morphing into contemporary Islamophobic

racism, and Europe's willingness to condone the tens of thousands of ongoing refugee deaths in the Mediterranean.

Connections: Performatives, Affect and Agency

With my trainee-teacher students, I have tried to construct visual concept maps of such networks of causality so as to militate against the "segregation" of the classroom. This is a tried-and-tested method of visualization of complex contents, often used under the rubric of "mind mapping" as a brainstorming technique, or as a means of organizing material (Novak 2012; Wittkower 2011). My implementation of such techniques aims less to organize student-produced material as to reconstruct in schematic form multiple and overlapping connections between global issues. The exact content or nature of those connections (e.g. what is the relationship between desertification and forced migration) is itself complex and defies squeezing into such schematic network-like diagrams: at this point, the classroom activity needs to transit to discussion and must refer to scholarly sources. The benefit of the visual networking technique is quite simply to create a framework where connections become evident, even if their precise nature needs to be elaborated separately. Given the multiply overdetermined natures of these global causalities, the pedagogical results of such conceptual maps are predictably messy and of course open-ended and contingent.

The connective, networking pedagogy I am proposing here means that knowledge must be constructed precisely by making connections, across disciplines, across "subjects" and above all across the restrictive frontiers of the classroom, and indeed of the nation and of "Fortress Europe". Rabinow (2007, 5) suggests that the contemporary moment itself may appear to us as a mode of "assemblage", constructed in ways that are not definitive or closed off. It is perceived as a collage of events and sites that do not immediately form a whole, but rather, reach us as a fluid, shifting configuration that includes our own place of participatory observation (see Barad 2007). A networking mode of learning would accept the disparate and fragmented nature of the contemporary world as it presents itself to us, and would set about trying to put together the pieces of the puzzle. It would be a constructivist work of assembly. Unsurprisingly, a provisional "bricolage"-mode of learning, or what the Canadian performance artist and theoretician Kapwani Kiwanga (2016, 93) calls a practice of "critical assemblage" – connecting things with one another – may then be the most apposite way of structuring the business of making sense of the contemporary in the classroom.

The pedagogical gain of such "acts of cognition, not transferrals of information" (Friere 1972, 53) is clear. Students acquire a sense of the bewildering complexity of global interconnections that is perhaps initially discouraging; at the same time, however, they glimpse the possibility of ascertaining that there *are* connections; this is a distinct cognitive/affective/agential advance on the visceral sense of excessive complexity and resultant opacity and the concomitant loss of agency that is experienced. The usage of conceptual maps offers the potential to locate oneself on the map. This provides a sense of locatedness within a world that is otherwise opaque and resists any sense of synthesis or overview: here I am, in a classroom that is part of a network of complex webs of causality. Such a recognition of connectedness finally offers a fabric for agency, however limited or local that may be (there is no scale of effectiveness or of responsibility or of relevance for political action: this is something that must be decided by the individual; of more importance is to recognize oneself as a political agent within a network of interconnections).

The history of scientific progress over the last century or so has been that of the successive rediscovery of the unsuspected connectedness and entanglement of things that the Enlightenment assumed were unconnected with each other: time and space, gravity and light (relativity), body and mind (psychosomatic medicine) and the entirety of planetary processes (radioactivity, pollution, global warming). The global system is an interconnected whole (Capra and Luisi 2014). Affect theory (Clough and Halley 2007; Gregg and Seigworth 2010; Massumi 2002) explores the multiple connections that enable entities to exert agency and to take effect upon one another, to make something happen. Affect theory is far more than a theory of the "emotions", although the ways in which subjects are connected to each other by non-cognitive processes (whence the double meaning of "feeling") (Damasio [1994] 2000, 2003) is one part of that theory. The connections identified by affect theory extend well beyond humans and their cognates (e.g. domestic animals), enveloping all beings, thus producing a theory of interlinked agency in which non-human and non-sentient entities feel, think, speak and act in social networks (Cruikshank 2005; Ingold 2011; Latour 1986; 2005). Affect theory restores connections between entities and acknowledges that these connections are vital to distributed agency (Hodder 2012). What I am suggesting here is that the classroom is also a place of such connectedness and agency. The classroom is connected to the outside world, not separated from it. Learning takes place in ways that are driven by affect (e.g. "classroom atmosphere or climate"), but in a much broader sense than is currently acknowledged (e.g. Arnold 1999). Recently, Hartmut Rosa and Wolfgang Endres (Rosa 2017; Rosa and Endres 2016) have used the device of "resonance" to describe an enhanced sense of connectedness within the classroom. What I am proposing here would integrate such "pedagogy of resonance", but would extend it to go beyond the classroom walls into the world of the natural environment and the world of politics and crisis. Rosa's (2017) sociology of "Weltbeziehungen" ("relations to the world") tends to privatize such resonances, rather than politicizing and globalizing them.

Making connections in a pedagogical context is a speech act: it does not merely describe those connections (as a locutionary speech act); it situates the self (via an illocutive speech act) within those connections, and by making them, it makes something else happen (thus making it a perlocution-ary speech act) (Austin 1962). The making of pedagogical connections is not merely cognitive, but has real effects, partly at the emotional level, but more significantly to the extent that a connection recognized is a connection endowed with an enhanced form of multidirectional and multi-actantial agency (Hickey-Moody and Page 2016; Sedgwick 2003). Serres (2008, 124) claims: "To perceive beings fills them with being. Simply by their perceptions, human beings – living things –in this case, women, fabricate negentropy, produce information, and thereby oppose the irreversible degradation of things". Perception is an active process that is always already intentional, interventionist and interactive (Bohm and David Peat 2011, 53–96).

The making of cognitive connections thus has two interrelated effects: it opens up connections in places where separation was previously assumed to be the governing factor, and it introduces new co-actors where agency was presumed to be absent; in this way, it extends the scope and form of pol-itical agency (Massumi 2015). It thus inherently militates against the under-lying structures of racism, both in re-establishing connectivity where racism imposes putatively essentialist divisions and in acknowledging personhood of all beings (Viveiros de Castro 2014, 2016) where racism reduces the other to the status of non-person, in the most extreme version to the status of animal (Mbembe 2001) or to that of thing (Mbembe 2017).

The Classroom in the World

Having sketched the way a connective practice might work, and what effects it might have, I now return to the classrooms where I currently work. I am a trainer of future teachers within a German university English department: my students qualify as high school teachers who will mainly work in the upper secondary division, where they will be teaching adolescents with a reasonably well-developed palette of academic literacies and a fair grasp of contemporary socio-political (perhaps less economic) issues. Paradoxically, however, there is little sense, within German schools seen as institutions (indi-vidual teachers are always a different case) that a number of basic givens upon which educational philosophies and practices are built have fundamen-tally shifted. The world outside has changed, but the institution is so discon-nected from it that these changes have not registered within educational policy and institutional practice. Several interconnected examples will suffice.

For instance, the seismic effects of transformations of the nature of work as a result of computerization (Frey and Osborne 2013; Job-Futuromat 2016), and the massive effects of global warming on human population displacement (Nealon 2016, 121; NIC 2017, 21, 32–33, 39), are still off the horizon for the German "Gymnasium" system (i.e. the sector of a streamed, stratified education system that qualifies students for university entrance), whose frames of reference, it would seem, are those of the 1970s and 1980s, with close to full employment in classical middle-class professions in a sector of an employment market closed to immigrants. With regard to migration, the German school system across the board remains predomi-nantly monolingual in approach (Gogolin 1994), disavowing the multilingual learner in every three pupils in its classrooms (Chlosta, Ostermann, and Schroeder 2003; Fürstenau, Gogolin, and Yagmur 2003; Schroeder 2007), using textbooks that present children with a "migrant background" in discri-minatory terms (Niehaus et al. 2015), and streaming pupils with such a "migration background" away from university entrance towards manual pro-fessions (e.g. Agarwala, Schenk, and Spiewak 2016, 61; Freidooni 2016; OECD/ EU 2015). Despite long-standing calls for a "pedagogy of diversity" ("Pädago-gik der Vielfalt"; Prengel 1993), the German school system remains persistently inured to its own social complexity. In this way, the German school system stubbornly ignores the realities of world outside its walls – and de facto inside: in many cases, refugee children now sit alongside permanent residents and citizens in German primary or secondary schools, if they are not kept at arm's length in specially segregated classes (Mehr als … 2016), not to mention children with a first- or second-generation "migration background" (now roughly a third of the school population and rising; Statistisches Bunde-samt 2016, 37). The systemic "racism" that is endemic all across the German school system and enforced by its stratified structures is thus closely linked to the educational system's hermetic isolation from broader social realities – even when those realities have long since invaded the school at the level of the "real existing" classroom. The school system itself, an integral part of German bourgeois society, is thus structurally moulded by what Adorno (1971, 100–102), once called "bourgeois indifference" ("bürgerliche Kälte"). Such "coldness" is evinced, for instance, in a lack of empathetic imagination on the part of youth workers that prevents them from appreciating the effects of trauma and the long-term psychic stress imposed by the constantly looming threat of deportation on their young refugee and asylum-seeker clients (Terkessidis 2017, 62). The school system is fundamentally disconnec-tive and negatively reproductive – of reified knowledge and of exclusionary white middle-class social structures.

How would such a practice of (re)connective pedagogy look concretely? Let me imagine, in what follows, how such a cognitive mapping or networking in the classroom might be inaugurated. Once again, my proposals repose upon experimental discussions with my own teacher-trainee students. Rather than taking on the raft of global issues that were addressed in section 2 above, it might be worth beginning with a more local problem, namely, the reification of the classroom itself. The construction of the absent networks could be launched by asking a number of questions about the connections customarily elided by discourses subtending classroom practices. Let me reimagine my opening blackboard/fourth wall as a site upon which incessant question marks are inscribed, each one demanding that the learner-questioner traverse the blackboard barrier to see what lies on the other side. In the English-teacher-trainee (or German-teacher-trainee) classroom, these questions might include the following: What language is studied in this classroom, and what language is the medium of study? Is that language a medium of exclusion or inclusion? What languages are spoken by the learners in the classroom, in particular when they are outside the classroom? Do those languages have *droit de cité* in the classroom? How do those language zones (those of the classroom, those of the street or the home, those of the languages themselves) interact? What histories of migration or interculturality are indexed by those languages? What sort of material (epoch, topic, genre, complexity) is studied in the classroom, in which language and what sort of language? What context does it emerge from? What does it presuppose about us as the learners themselves? Why is it being taught? Is it felt to be relevant to the learners' life-worlds? Which contemporary issues does it address, however tangentially, or not address? Is this question asked, explicitly, in the classroom? If not, why? How is the material relevant to the learners' possible professional fields? What might those fields be? Do those possible fields assume about the (class, gender, ethnic, religious) identity? What can we say about the broader economic conditions they index (security, precarity, mobility, etc.)? What do they assume about the identity of the audiences that will be the recipients of those professional practices? Do they exclude some audiences? What mechanisms of exclusion may be at work beyond the classroom that are already implicit in the material and how it is learnt? Who selects or assigns the material, who has the right to change it? Who has the power to make decisions at the other interfaces discussed, and why? And so on …

It will be clear that this set of questions works by successive apposition, starting from any one of many possible points and following routes of possible inquiry, "making connections, drawing lines, mapping articulations, between different domains, discourses and practices" to quote Grossberg (1994, 18) again. Such questions follow the rhizomatic pattern of networked cognitive diagnosis. There is no ultimate point of arrival or arrest, for each connection provokes further questions. Indeed, in such an exercise, the question *is* the mode of connection. The question questions the specious segregation of the classroom. Such networks of question constitute "critical assemblage" (Kiwanga 2016) because they link diverse domains by asking not about the "core" or "essence" of the domain (i.e. confirming and reinforcing its operative assumptions) but by asking about its "outside", the surfaces where it meets other domains. These questions do not merely interrogate, they provoke answer/questions by which the learners "assemble" knowledge, creating mosaics of interrelated understandings of interrelationships. Asking about the "outside" of a practice – its underlying but unsaid exclusive mechanisms, and the effects that flow productively from those unsaids – constitutes a critical "edge". "Edge" is meant literally as a frontier that apposes two zones to one another. The "black-" or "whiteboard" I spoke of above becomes just such an edge: a border that is visible as such precisely because it adjoins a world beyond. This is a "border pedagogy" (Giroux 1991). This form of "critical" thinking is not merely negative: conceptually at least, it brings populations back together by making explicit the lines of demarcation that in fact join them. Thus, for instance, the border "native speaker of German"/"non-native speaker of German" may be presupposed and enacted by the material taught in the classroom, the teacher's ethnic identity, the teacher training inscribed in her/his person, the systems of prohibition that bear upon languages other than German in the classroom and in society, the role of German as a gatekeeper in grading, in access to higher education, in access to jobs, in future professional trajectories, in citizenships rights and acquisition procedures ... and so on. Such a discussion is not merely conceptual, but has material effects, transforming the dynamics of a class group and its own multiple relationships to its respective life-worlds.

Thus, the nexus of the topography of the classroom and that of the world may present a way of entering into an engagement, both critical and constructive, with the immensely complex and overdetermined terrain of the contemporary crisis. Race is a domain of specious segregation that provides a site for humanities that is both critical and analytical, but also conducive to considerations of the nexus of identity and agency: this is so because race gathers together issues of nationalism, identity, employment, exploitation, immigration, economics, futurities, violence and terror. To that extent, race may allow the "blackboard" to become a desegregated "contact zone" (Pratt 1992, 6–7), thereby facilitating the incremental, never-final, never-assured, never-teleologically preordained transformation of the fabric of their immediate, always politicized, environments: what García Canclini (2014) names a process of "imminence" which makes itself "immanent" in the classroom. If not there, where? And if not now, when?

Note

1. Thanks to Andrew McCann for a discussion on this issue.

Disclosure statement

No potential conflict of interest was reported by the author.

References

Adorno, Theodor W. 1971. *Erziehung zur Mündigkeit: Vorträge und Gespräche mit Hellmut Becker 1959-1969*, edited by Gerd Knadelbach. Frankfurt am Main: Suhrkamp.

Agarwala, Anant, Arnfried Schenk, and Martin Spiewak. 2016. "Flüchtlinge im Schulalltag." *Die Zeit* 29: 61–62.

Allan, John Anthony, Martin Keulertz, Suvi Sojamo, and Jeroen Warner, eds. 2013. *Handbook of Land and Water Grabs in Africa*. London: Routledge.

Ambler-Edwards, Susan, Kate Bailey, Alexandra Kiff, Tim Lang, Robert Lee, Terry Marsden, David Simons, and Hardin Tibbs. 2009. *Food Futures: Rethinking UK Strategy: A Chatham House Report*. London: Royal Institute of International Affairs. Accessed 27 February 2018. http://orca.cf.ac.uk/20465/.

Amnesty International. 2016. *Leben in Unsicherheit: Wie Deutschland die Opfer rassistischer Gewalt im Stich lässt: Amnesty Bericht*. London: Amnesty International. Accessed 23 February 2018. https://www.amnesty.de/sites/default/files/2017-05/Amnesty-Bericht-Rassistische-Gewalt-in-Deutschland-Juni2016.pdf.

Armstrong, Stephen. 2017. *The New Poverty*. London: Verso.

Arndt, Susan. 2017. "Rassismus: Eine viel zu lange Geschichte." In *Rassismuskritik und Widerstandsformen*, edited by Karim Fereidooni and Meral El, 29–46. Wiesbaden: Springer.

Arnold, Jane. 1999. *Affect in Language Learning*. Cambridge: Cambridge University Press.

Austin, J. L. 1962. *How to Do Things with Words*. Oxford: Clarendon Press.

Barad, Karen. 2007. *Meeting the Universe Halfway: Quantum Physics and the Entanglement of Matter and Meaning*. Durham, NC: Duke University Press.

Bateson, Gregory. 1974. *Steps to an Ecology of Mind*. New York: Ballantine Books.

Böckler-Impulse. 2017. "Atypische Beschäftigung: Neuer Höchststand". *Böckler-Impulse September*. Accessed 26 February 2018. https://www.boeckler.de/Impuls_2017_09_3.pdf.

Benjamin, Walter. 1999. *Illuminations*. Translated by Harry Zohn. London: Pimlico.

Bohm, David, and F. David Peat. 2011. *Science, Order, Creativity*. London: Routledge.

Bosch, Gerhard, and Thorsten Kalina. 2016. "Einkommensentstehung als Verteilungsfaktor: Wachsende Ungleichheit in der Primärverteilung gefährdet Mittelschicht." *Wirtschaftsdienst* 96: 24–31. doi:10.1007/s10273-016-1947-7.

Capra, Fritjof, and Pier Luigi Luisi. 2014. *The Systems View of Life: A Unifying Vision*. Cambridge: Cambridge University Press.

Chlosta, Christoph, Torsten Ostermann, and Christoph Schroeder. 2003. "Die Durchschnittsschule und ihre Sprachen: Ergebnisse des Projekts *Sprachenerhebung Essener Grundschulen* (SPREEG)." *Elise* 3: 43–139.

Clough, Patricia Ticineto, and Jean Halley, eds. 2007. *The Affective Turn: Theorizing the Social*. Durham NC: Duke University Press.

Crist, Meehan. 2018. "Besides, I'll be dead." *London Review of Books* 40 (4): 12–13.

Crouch, Colin. 2004. *Post-Democracy*. Cambridge: Polity.

Cruikshank, Julie. 2005. *Do Glaciers Listen? Local Knowledge, Colonial Encounters, and Social Imagination*. Vancouver: University of British Columbia Press.

Damasio, Antonio. 2003. *Looking for Spinoza: Joy, Sorrow, and the Feeling Brain*. New York: Harcourt.

Damasio, Antonio R. [1994] 2000. *Descartes' Error: Emotion, Reason, and the Human Brain*. New York: HarperCollins Quill.

Davis, Mike. 2017. "El Diablo in Wine Country." *London Review of Books* 39 (21): 14. Accessed 20 November 2017. https://www.lrb.co.uk/v39/n21/mike-davis/el-diablo-in-wine-country.

Denby, David. 2016. "Diary." *London Review of Books* 38 (17): 34–35.

Engelert, Birgit, and Barbara Gärber. 2014. *Landgrabbing: Landnahmen in historischer und globaler Perspektive*. Vienna: New Academic Press.

Epstein, Debbie. 1992. *Changing Classroom Cultures: Anti-Racism, Politics and Schools*. Stoke-on-Trent: Trentham.

Fassin, Didier. 2016. "Short Cuts." *London Review of Books* 38 (5): 23.

Flassbeck, Heiner, and Costa Lapavitsas. 2015. *Against the Troika: Crisis and Austerity in the Eurozone*. London: Verso.

Foucault, Michel. 2003. *Society Must Be Defended: Lectures at the Collège de France 1975-76*, edited by Mauro Bertani, and Alessandro Fontana. Translated by David Macey. New York: Picador.

Freidooni, Karim. 2016. *Diskriminierungs- und Rassismuserfharungen im Schulwesen: Eine Studie zu Ungleichheitspraktiken im Berufskontext*. Wiesbaden: VS Verlag für Sozialwissenschaften/Springer.

Frey, Carl Benedikt, and Michael A. Osborne. 2013. *The Future of Employment: How Susceptible Are Jobs to Computerisation?* Working Paper. Oxford: Oxford Martin Programme on Technology and Employment. Accessed 26 September 2016. http://www.oxfordmartin.ox.ac.uk/downloads/academic/future-of-employment.pdf.

Friedrich, Tobias, Axel Timmermann, Michelle Tigchelaar, Oliver Elison Timm, and Andrey Ganopolski. 2016. "Nonlinear Climate Sensitivity and Its Implications for Future Greenhouse Warming." *Science Advances* 2: e1501923. doi:10.1126/sciadv.1501923.

Friere, Paulo. 1972. *Pedagogy of the Oppressed*. Translated by Myra Bergman Ramos. Harmondsworth: Penguin.

FSIN (Food Security Information Network). 2017. *Global Report on Food Crises 2017*. Rome: World Food Programme/FSIN. Accessed 27 February 2018. http://documents.wfp.org/stellent/groups/public/documents/ena/wfp291271.pdf?_ga=2.226239706.1707770705.1519717562-1921151378.1519717562.

Fürstenau, Sara, Ingrid Gogolin, and Kutlay Yagmur, eds. 2003. *Mehrsprachigkeit in Hamburg: Ergebnisse einer Sprachenerhebung an den Grundschulen in Hamburg*. Münster: Waxmann.

García Canclini, Néstor. 2014. *Art Beyond Itself: Anthropology for a Society Without a Story Line*. Translated by David Frye. Durham, NC: Duke University Press.

Giroux, Henry. 1991. "Border Pedagogy and the Politics of Postmodernism." *Social Text* 28: 51–67.

Gogolin, Ingrid. 1994. *Der monolinguale Habitus der multilingualen Schule*. Münster: Waxmann.

Goodell, Jeff. 2017. *The Water Will Come: Rising Seas, Sinking Cities and the Remaking of the Civilised World*. Melbourne: Black Inc.

Gregg, Melissa, and Gregory J. Seigworth, eds. 2010. *The Affect Theory Reader*. Durham, NC: Duke University Press.

Grossberg, Lawrence. 1994. "Introduction: Bringin' It All Back Home – Pedagogy and Cultural Studies." In *Between Borders: Pedagogy and the Politics of Cultural Studies*, edited by Henry A. Giroux and Peter McLaren, 1–25. New York: Routledge.

Hagelüken, Alexander. 2017. *Das gespaltene Land: Wie Ungleichheit unsere Gesellschaft zerstört—und was die Politik ändern muss*. Munich: Knaur.

Herders against Farmers. 2017. "Herders against Farmers: Nigeria's Expanding Deadly Conflict." International Crisis Group, 19 September. Accessed 9 Jan 2018.

https://www.crisisgroup.org/africa/west-africa/nigeria/252-herders-against-farmers-nigerias-expanding-deadly-conflict.

Hickey-Moody, Anna, and Tara Page. 2016. *Arts, Pedagogy and Cultural Resistance: New Materialisms*. London: Rowman & Littlefield.

Hodder, Ian. 2012. *Entangled: An Archaeology of the Relationships Between Humans and Things*. Oxford: Wiley Blackwell.

Ingold, Tim. 2011. *Being Alive: Essays on Movement, Knowledge and Description*. London: Routledge.

Job-Futoromat. 2016. Kann ein Roboter meinen Job machen? (App). Accessed 26 October 2016. http://job-futuromat.ard.de.

Jones, Thomas. 2017. "If on a Winter's Night a Cyclone." *London Review of Books* 39 (10): 29–31.

Kara, Siddarth. 2017. *Modern Slavery: A Global Perspective*. New York: Columbia University Press.

Kiwanga, Kapwani. 2016. "Archaeological Digging (Interview with Sean O'Toole)." In *African Futures: Thinking About the Future in Word and Image*, edited by Lien Heidenreich-Seleme and Sean O'Toole, 85–98. Bielefeld/Berlin: Kerber.

Klein, Naomi. 2016. "Let Them Drown: The Violence of Othering in a Warming World." *London Review of Books* 38 (11): 11–14.

Kurlantzick, Joshua. 2013. *Democracy in Retreat: The Revolt of the Middle Class and the Worldwide Decline of Representative Government*. New Haven: Yale University Press.

Latour, Bruno. 1986. "The Powers of Association." In *Power, Action and Belief: A New Sociology of Knowledge?*, edited by John Law, 264–280. London: Routledge and Kegan Paul.

Latour, Bruno. 2004. "Why Has Critique Run Out of Steam? From Matters of Fact to Matters of Concern." *Critical Inquiry* 30 (2): 225–248.

Latour, Bruno. 2005. *Reassembling the Social: An Introduction to Actor-Network-Theory*. Oxford: Oxford University Press.

Liebscher, Doris, and Heike Fritzsche. 2010. *Antidiskriminierungspädagogik – Konzepte und Methoden für die Bildungsarbeit mit Jugendlichen*, edited by Rebecca Pates, Daniel Schmidt, and Susanne Karawanskij. Wiesbaden: VS Verlag für Sozialwissenschaften/Springer.

Luhmann, Niklas. 1984. *Soziale Systeme: Grundriß einer allgemeinen Theorie*. Frankfurt am Main: Suhrkamp.

Luhmann, Niklas. 1997. *Die Gesellschaft der Gesellschaft*. 2 vols. Frankfurt am Main: Suhrkamp.

Massumi, Brian. 2002. *Parables for the Virtual: Movement, Affect, Sensation*. Durham, NC: Duke University Press.

Massumi, Brian. 2015. *Politics of Affect*. Cambridge: Polity.

Mbembe, Achille. 2001. *On the Postcolony*. Berkeley: University of California Press.

Mbembe, Achille. 2003 . "Necropolitics." *Public Culture* 15 (1): 11–40.

Mbembe, Achille. 2012. "At the Centre of the Knot." *Social Dynamics: A Journal of African Studies* 38 (1): 8–14.

Mbembe, Achille. 2016. *Politiques de l'inimité*. Paris: La Découverte.

Mbembe, Achille. 2017. *Critique of Black Reason*. Translated by Laurent Dubois. Durham, NC: Duke University Press.

McAdam, Jane. 2014. *Climate Change, Forced Migration, and International Law*. Oxford: Oxford University Press.

McLeman, Robert A. 2013. *Climate and Human Migration: Past Experiences, Future Challenges*. Cambridge: Cambridge University Press.

Mehr als …. 2016. "Mehr als 300 000 minderjährige Flüchtlinge". *ARD Tagesschau*. Accessed 28 September 2016. http://www.tagesschau.de/inland/minderjaehrige-fluechtlinge-119.html.

Milanovic, Branko. 2016. *Global Inequality: A New Approach for the Age of Globalization*. Cambridge, MA: Belknap Press of Harvard University Press.

Mishra, Pankaj. 2017. *Age of Anger: A History of the Present*. London: Allen Lane/Penguin.

Missirian, Anouch, and Wolfram Schlenker. 2017. "Asylum Applications Respond to Temperature Fluctuations." *Science* 358 (6370): 1610–1614. doi:10.1126/science.aao0432.

Morton, Stephen. 2013. *States of Emergency: Colonialism, Literature and the Law*. Liverpool: University of Liverpool Press.

Münkler, Herfried. 2004. *Die neuen Kriege*. Reinbek bei Hamburg: Rowohlt.

Nassehi, Armin. 2015. "Der Ausnahmezustand Als Normalfall." *Kursbuch* 170: 34–49.

Nealon, Jeffrey T. 2016. *Plant Theory: Biopower and Vegetable Life*. Stanford: Stanford University Press.

NIC (National Intelligence Council of USA). 2017. *Global Trends: Paradox of Progress*. Washington, DC: NIC. Accessed 26 February 2018, www.dni.gov/nic/globaltrends .

Niehaus, Inga, Rosa Hoppe, Marcus Otto, and Viola B. Georgi. 2015. *Schulbuchstudie Migration und Integration*. Berlin: Beauftragte der Bundesregierung für Migration, Flüchtlinge und Integration.

Novak, Joseph D. 2012. *Learning, Creating, and Using Knowledge: Concept Maps as Facilitaive Tools in Schools and Corporations*. 2nd ed. New York: Routledge.

OECD/EU (European Union). 2015. *Indicators of Immigrant Integration: Settling In*. Paris: OECD Publishing. doi:10.1787/9789264234024-en.

Paritätischer Gesamtverband. 2017. *Menschenwürde ist Menschenrecht: Bericht zur Armutsentwicklung in Deutschland 2017*. Berlin: Der Der Paritätische Gesamtverband.

Paulson, William. 2001. *Literary Culture in a World Transformed: A Future for the Humanities*. Ithaca, NY: Cornell University Press.

Piketty, Thomas. 2014. *Capital in the Twenty-First Century*. Translated by Arthur Goldhammer. Cambridge, MA: Belknap Press of Harvard University Press.

Pratt, Mary Louise. 1992. *Imperial Eyes: Travel Writing and Transculturation*. London: Routledge.

Prengel, Annedore. 1993. *Pädagogik der Vielfalt*. Opladen: Leske & Budrich.

Rabinow, Paul. 2007. *Marking Time: On the Anthropology of the Contemporary*. Princeton, NJ: Princeton University Press.

Richards, James. 2017. *The Road to Ruin: The Global Elites' Secret Plan for the Next Financial Crisis*. London: Penguin Portfolio.

Rosa, Hartmut. 2017. *Resonanz: Eine Soziologie der Weltbeziehung*. Berlin: Suhrkamp.

Rosa, Hartmut, and Wolfgang Endres. 2016. *Resonanzpädagogik: Wenn es im Klassenzimmer knistert*. Weinheim: Beltz.

Sassen, Saskia. 2014. *Expulsions: Brutality and Complexity in the Global Economy*. Cambridge, MA: Belknap Press of Harvard University Press.

Scheffers, Brett R., Luc De Meester, Tom C. L. Bridge, Ary A. Hoffmann, John M. Pandolfi, Richard T. Corlett, Stuart H. M. Butchart, et al. 2016. "The Broad Footprint of Climate Change from Genes to Biomes to People." *Science* 354 (6313): aaf7671. doi:10.1126/science.aaf7671.

Schroeder, Christoph. 2007. "Sprache und Integration", *Aus Politik und Zeitgeschichte* 22/23 (29 May): 6–12. http://www.bpb.de/apuz/30449/integration-und-sprache?p=all.

Schüle, Christian. 2017. *Heimat: Ein Phantomschmerz*. Munich: Droemer.

Sedgwick, Eve Kosofsky. 2003. *Touching Feeling: Affect, Pedagogy, Performativity.* Durham, NC: Duke University Press.

Serres, Michel. 2008. "Feux et Signaux de Brume: Virginia Woolf's Lighthouse." Translated by Judith Adler. *SubStance #116* 37 (2): 110–131.

Statistisches Bundesamt [German Federal Bureau of Statistics]. 2016. *Bevölkerung und Erwerbstätigkeit: Bevölkerung mit Migrationshintergrund – Ergebnisse des Mikrozensus 2015.* Wiesbaden: Statisches Bundesamt.

Streeck, Wolfgang. 2014. *Buying Time: The Delayed Crisis of Democratic Capitalism.* Translated by Patrick Camiller and David Fernbach. London: Verso.

Streeck, Wolfgang. 2017. *How Will Capitalism End?: Essays on a Failing System.* London: Verso.

Taguieff, Pierre-André. 1987. *La Force du préjugé: Essai sur le racisme et ses doubles.* Paris: La Découverte.

Terkessidis, Mark. 2017. *Nach der Flucht: Neue Ideen für die Einwanderungsgesellschaft.* Stuttgart: Reclam.

Titlestad, Michael. 2013. "The Logic of the Apocalypse: A Clerical Rejoinder." *Safundi: The Journal of South African and American Studies* 14 (1): 93–110.

Toon, Brian, Alan Robock, and Rich Turco. 2008. "Environmental Consequences of Nuclear war." *Physics Today* 61 (12): 37. http://physicstoday.scitation.org/doi/10.1063/1.3047679.

Ulrich, Bernd. 2016 . "Mutentbrannt." *Die Zeit* 31: 2–3.

UNCHR. 2016. *UNCHR Global Trends Report: Forced Displacement in 2016.* Geneva: UNCHR. http://www.unhcr.org/5943e8a34.

Varoufakis, Yanis. 2017. *Adults in the Room: My Battle with Europe's Deep Establishment.* London: Bodley Head.

Vitalis, Robert. 2015. *White World Order, Black Power Politics: The Birth of American International Relations.* Ithaca, NY: Cornell University Press.

Viveiros de Castro, Eduardo. 2014. *Cannibal Metaphysics: For a Post-Structural Anthropology.* Translated by Peter Skafish. Ann Arbor, MI: Univocal.

Viveiros de Castro, Eduardo. 2016. *The Relative Native: Essays on Indigenous Conceptual Worlds.* Chicago, IL: University of Chicago Press.

de Waal, Alex. 2017. "The Nazis Used It, We Use It: The Return of Famine as a Weapon of War." *London Review of Books* 39 (12): 9–12.

Weizman, Eyal, and Fazal Sheikh. 2015. *The Conflict Shoreline: Colonization as Climate Change in the Negev Desert.* Göttingen: Steidl.

Wennersten, John R., and Denise Robbins. 2017. *Rising Tides: Climate Refugees in the Twenty-First Century.* Bloomington: Indiana University Press.

Wittkower, Dylan E. 2011. "Mind-Mapping Inside and Outside of the Classroom." In *Learning Through Digital Media: Experiments in Technology and Pedagogy,* edited by R. Trebor Scholz, 221–229. New York: Institute for Distributed Creativity.

Index

coded racism 15–16
Colley, Linda 59
Cologne, sexual assaults in 27–9
colonialism 150; racism 63
coloured people 129–33
concentration camps: Theresienstadt 39,
47, 51, 52n2
connectedness and agency 156
Copenhagen criteria (1993) 41
Corbyn, Jeremy 69
cosmopolitanism 139
counter-racialization, concept of 112, 122
countermovement 93, 94, 97, 99, 105
Crenshaw, Kimberlé 48
criminals: control 13; expatriation of
citizens 13; and terrorists 10
crisis: of democracy, conference 103–4;
economic and political 93; endemic to
modernity 153; financial 3–4, 41, 84;
immigration 4; management strategy
113; multi-crises 151–5; politics of
74–88; of post-politics 82–6; of race
and policing 77–82; and racism/
political mainstream 66–8; refugee 6,
9, 40, 43, 93; see also migrant crisis
"critical assemblage", practice of 155
Čulík, Jan 39
culture 92
Czech Republic: Břeclav railway station
38–40, 51–2; immigration detention
centres in 49–50; and Visegrád states
40–3

The Daily Mail 47
Danish People's Party 6
Dansk Folkeparti (DF, Danish People's
Party) 6
De Genova, Nicholas 16, 19
Dean, Jodi 41
deaths (migrant/refugee) 19–21, 33n4,
116, 155
decline, of empire 65
dehumanization 45–6
democracy, and citizenship 99–102
deportation 45, 137–8
detention centres 49–50, 118
difference, cultural category of 132
Dikeç, M. 100
Dimoula, Kiki 130–1
disaffection 4
discrimination 31, 148; and prejudice 2
disillusionment 41
disinvestments, and vulnerable
populations 3
diversity, pedagogy of 158

Dog Whistle Politics (López) 15
Dublin Convention (1990) 52n1
Duggan, Mark 22, 76, 80–1
Dureghello, Ruth 39

economic inequalities 77, 79
Elias, Ruth 47
EMA (Education Maintenance Allowance)
78, 88n1
emancipation 94
"Empire 2.0" 59
empire 58, 63–4
England: race and nation in 63; working
class, and racism 68–9
Englishness 58; British imperial project
63–4; decline 65; racializing capacities
of 64; vision of 63–6
Enlightenment 156
equality at work, against racialization of
labour 117–20
Eritrea 37
Eurocentrism 28
"Euro-Islam", establishing 136
Europe: Black Lives Matter in 19–34, 69,
87; crises in 1–17; financial crisis in
(2007–2008) 3–4, 41, 84; genealogies
of racism in 43–4
European Network of People of African
Descent (Berlin) 22
Europeanness 31–3
Euroscepticism 65
exploitative racism 95

Fanon, Frantz 46
Farage, Nigel 58, 60, 62, 66, 68
fascism: bordering on 92; spectres of
50–1
Ferguson Is Everywhere campaign 22,
34n8
Fidesz (political party) 6
Field, Frank 58
financial crisis: in Europe (2007–2008)
3–4, 41, 84
5 Star Movement 7
foreign criminals 10
foreignness (allochthony) 129, 136
Foucault, M. 150
Fox, Liam 58, 59
Frankl, M. 53n4
Fraser, Nancy 93
freedom of movement 115–16

Gedye, George 51–2
Gefangene Herero (GH) 46
genealogies of racism, in Europe 40, 43–4

For Product Safety Concerns and Information please contact our EU
representative GPSR@taylorandfrancis.com Taylor & Francis Verlag GmbH,
Kaufingerstraße 24, 80331 München, Germany

Printed and bound by CPI Group (UK) Ltd, Croydon, CR0 4YY
08/06/2025
01896991-0015